KT-422-361

DENNIS POTTER

Pennies from Heaven

with an introduction
by Kenith Trodd

ff

faber and faber

LONDON · BOSTON

First published in 1996 by Faber and Faber Limited
3 Queen Square London WC1N 3AU

Photoset by Parker Typesetting Service, Leicester
Printed in England by Clays Ltd, St Ives plc

All rights reserved

© 1978 PFH (Overseas) Limited
Dennis Potter

© Introduction, Kenith Trodd, 1996

Dennis Potter is hereby identified as author of this work in accordance with
Section 77 of the Copyright, Designs and Patents Act 1988

*This book is sold subject to the condition that it shall not, by way of trade
or otherwise, be lent, resold, hired out or otherwise circulated without the
publisher's prior consent in any form of binding or cover other than that
in which it is published and without a similar condition including
this condition being imposed on the subsequent purchaser.*

A CIP record for this book
is available from the British Library
ISBN 0–571–17821–9

2 4 6 8 10 9 7 5 3 1

Dennis Potter is Britain's most acclaimed television dramatist. His plays for TV include *Blue Remembered Hills* (1979), *Brimstone and Treacle* (commissioned in 1975 but banned until 1987), the series *Pennies from Heaven* (1978), *The Singing Detective* (1986), *Blackeyes* (1989) and *Lipstick on Your Collar* (1993). He also wrote novels, stage plays and screenplays. He died in June 1994. *Seeing the Blossom*, his final television interview, was published in 1994.

by the same author

fiction

BLACKEYES
HIDE AND SEEK
TICKET TO RIDE
PENNIES FROM HEAVEN

television plays

THE SINGING DETECTIVE
CHRISTABEL
BLUE REMEMBERED HILLS AND OTHER PLAYS
(also includes JOE'S ARK and CREAM IN MY COFFEE)
LIPSTICK ON YOUR COLLAR
KARAOKE and COLD LAZARUS

plays

SUFFICIENT CARBOHYDRATE
BRIMSTONE AND TREACLE

other writings

SEEING THE BLOSSOM

also available

POTTER ON POTTER

CONTENTS

INTRODUCTION

As a making experience *Pennies from Heaven* was the sunniest and most gratifying of all the works by Dennis that I've been associated with. It started well and it got better and then the world told us we'd been involved in delivering one of the best. The process of film-making, even in luscious-seeming places, is at best mainly a grim and dedicated professional chore for nearly all concerned. With *Pennies*, although we were mostly in Shepherd's Bush and nowhere more glamorous than Newbury in the winter, more than a handful of that crew felt that in being part of it they were at the peak of their working lives. There was a highly unusual zest about which came not from someone telling them they had luckily signed on for some predestined hit but from a general happiness coming at us from the scripts themselves.

1976 should have been one of the best in Dennis Potter's career, and for me too, because I had produced the three varied and challenging BBC plays of his due for transmission that spring: *Double Dare, Where Adam Stood* and *Brimstone and Treacle*. But with *Brimstone* things started to go wrong. Despite being made openly and entirely within the system it was banned shortly before transmission. This more or less coincided (probably not by chance) with the BBC lapsing into one of its fits of paranoid confusion and trying to get rid of me as a contract producer because a brainstormer in Intelligence Liaison told them I was part of an international Trotskyist threat. Though this was quickly shown to be a ludicrous piece of mistaken identity (I had employed someone who was indeed a proud and public member of a revolutionary party), the combination of the veto on *Brimstone* and the personal cloud over me, meant that the *annus mirabilis* was looking to be a year to forget. Colleagues rallied with petitions and offers to march on Alasdair Milne, but, not for the first time, I listened instead to the quieter and cannier advice of Dennis Potter himself. Lying low was better than heroic high-profile he said, so I finished the film I was making in Ireland and took a temporary job at the

National Film School; teaching script – though conspiracy was more the subject on my mind.

Rather quickly Dennis's tactic turned out to be right. The BBC never admitted a mistake about my politics nor for more than a decade did they recant on *Brimstone*, but without either making the apology or giving the explanation they did very soon tell me that they would like Dennis and me to think of some more work for them. They were probably thinking in terms of an olive branch commission for a seventy-five-minute play, but Dennis, never one to believe that forgiveness should come cheap, asked for the space to write a 'novel for television', about eight or nine hours' worth. In one of those institutional ironies that aren't very funny at the time, the BBC pushed the decision back at me. Just reinstated as producer of *Play for Today*, I was told that Dennis could have his big spread only if I agreed to give up six productions by other writers. I agonized for them but not for long. Dennis didn't know what he would write about, most of the others did, but the big crazed risk was obviously the one to take and his was the talent in the ascendant. So we were suddenly committed to delivering quite quickly the biggest instalment of original dramatic television ever to come from one writer, and were off into a wonderful period of freedom with everything to lose. The BBC didn't want to hear from us at all until we had something to budget and even then I wouldn't be meeting any 'real' accountants. In those dreadful days, 'development' was only for dark rooms and 'executive' went with suites; 'treatment' belonged to doctors and 'committees' were kept in town halls. Appallingly, we were left to our own desperate creative devices, and I wonder how much worse the show was for lacking all the welfare support systems of today's drama departments? In the dozen or so years up to *Pennies from Heaven* Dennis had twenty-three original plays produced for television, mostly for the BBC. There were also the six hours of *Casanova* and two or three hefty adaptations. Even though Dennis was the kind of prodigy who might have forced much of himself through, even under the creatively hostile conditions of today's 'market', the chance of even half so generous an apprenticeship will never again be available to a writer in this medium.

I think we quickly settled that this big, unknown, frightening thing might well be set in the 1930s and include some popular music. This was an interest Dennis and I shared, though from different perspectives. Since childhood I'd had a fixation, for which eccentric is too normal a term, on the band leader Lew Stone. At Oxford Dennis had written an undergraduate profile of me in which he said that in the hierarchy of people I admired, Lew Stone stood much higher than any politician (I think I was chairman of the university Labour Club at the time). In *Isis*, under Dennis's editorship, I wrote a piece called *Smoke Gets in Your Eyes*, which tried to argue some status for popular music: 'Despite the mixture of gold dust and synthetic treacle, many pop songs communicate genuine emotion and capture the atmosphere of their period to a degree which seems to contradict the shoddiness of their raw materials.' The pitch for *Pennies from Heaven* was already in early draft.

I went on to write a book about Lew Stone but before that and coincidentally just after Lew's death in 1969, came the first of Dennis's plays that I actually produced: *Moonlight on the Highway*. The storyline has some blushing parallels with what I've been admitting about my take on this music. The leading character is a young psychic wreck whose only inner consolation comes from listening to records by Lew Stone and Al Bowlly. All the music in the play is by Stone and Bowlly, and David Peters, that main character whose name sounds like a half-focused recall of Dennis Potter, actually lip-synchs to one of them in a mirror for a moment. While the music is clearly endorsed as the only emotional support system to offer Peters relief or aspiration, because Peters is such a tortured figure and because the play itself has such an itchy, uneasy atmosphere, its power in 1969, when many of Dennis's contemporaries were into Hendrix, R. D. Laing, early Loach and lateish Godard, is that of a storm that the world wasn't really taken by. The music and its associations are offered as an ambiguous, tentative route for a sad no-hoper, not something from which general delight can be generated. And this bleak pushiness went back to Dennis's own orientation at the time – fighting hard but through pain and dislocation, not *joie de vivre*.

Over the next few plays and years the music hung around his

writing as peripheral grit or textural prop, never quite going away. The titles of *Angels Are So Few, Only Make Believe, Double Dare, Lay Down Your Arms* and *Paper Roses* are all songs and there's scarcely one of those pieces, certainly not the ones with which I was involved, where the music isn't somewhere used in more than illustrative or ambient fashion. Sometimes, as in the use of Louis Prima's wild pasta version of 'That Old Black Magic' in *Brimstone*, the song asserts and tracks the very genre pivot, when, now or never, the audience has to accept, or not, that Martin is the devil. Or in *Paper Roses* where the use of some of Noël Coward's clinically bitchiest words from a song called 'The Younger Generation' invites us at once to belittle and patronize and accept with something like love a main character who has another act to go but who isn't going to survive in a world transforming about him. Of course, there is always another way to achieve any dramatic moment, but it's fair to say that Dennis became creatively dependent on the old song repertoire. Speaking not only from beyond *Pennies* but also *The Singing Detective* and *Lipstick on Your Collar* as well, he admitted: 'The songs are genuine artefacts I'm picking up but it's not serendipity. You're picking them up in order to use them, so it's part of the drama, as though you'd written the tune yourself. You reclaim it in order to remake it so it takes on the reverberation of all that's around it and then those little lyrics start having added ironies.' Until *Pennies from Heaven*, 'added ironies' is a good enough summary of how he used that material.

For Dennis the time taken physically to write the scripts was very often the fastest bit of the process. Gestation was usually longer, more intensive and I was much more involved in the gestation of *Pennies* than in anything else of his. Dennis never enjoyed the idea that he needed to collaborate for a moment with anyone on anything but in that early stage I don't know what else we were doing. For a while both the genre and subject matter were completely up in the air, as was the main character. Al Bowlly himself, or a fictional version, was for a time the model, but the trainspotting possessors of the Al Bowlly ark and archive would have noisily distracted too much attention (they loathed *Moonlight on the Highway*), and to write nine hours set in 1930s show business would have meant taking on bio-pic conventions and defining the fictional world too heavily in terms of posh night-club London. Also, as producer, I certainly didn't want our characters to be musicians because I'd just done Colin Welland's *The Wild West Show* about Rugby Union where the task of finding actors who could handle a ball next to prop forwards who could speak a line or two was pretty terminal.

The music stopped for a bit as we talked about doing a story around a perfect murder, and it was here that something very essential to the underpinning theme of *Pennies* and its strong narrative spine began to emerge. I came across a not very famous, not very perfect thirties murder in which a commercial traveller – with a prissy wife he didn't get on with, sexual complication as he roved the country and financial trouble in spades – tried to incinerate a look-alike and assume his identity. Suddenly the ingredients of small-time salesman, personal chaos, aspirations that could only be pursued at the fringe of pathological territory and an ordinariness that couldn't but burst its bounds were all there. And something else both transcending and specializing the squalor was present as well – the idea of the double, the person who may be mistaken for you, who may take the blame for you or for whom you may be obliged to take the blame. I think once Dennis had got to that point, he knew the character and was able to graft on to that lone murderer a Bonnie and Clyde motif where the idea of an exciting sexually charged murder upped the thrillerish ante and also stretched the narrative. So the *Pennies* universe was forming, but for every cutting or trial transcript I was sending him I would probably send ten songs. We both clearly knew that the music or what the music did was still crucial to how these eight hours were going to come to life.

Then Dennis found his breakthrough, ringing me early one day to ask what I thought of an opening scene in an unenviable Wembley Park bedroom (I think the site of his own first marital home) in which a dejected husband is suddenly cheering himself up by miming to a woman's voice singing a not very classy 1932 'ballad'. I think I said, 'Keep going' – he'd probably already written most of Episode 1 – and was then seized by a panic that didn't recede fully for months. The essence of Dennis's way with the songs was to dislocate us firmly from the entrenched naturalism of television drama. He had been at war with these conventions ever since he had Nigel Barton making a direct address to the camera and had reconstructed his school days by putting him in a class of adult ten-year-olds. That had worked but would an audience, then as now addicted most of all to the literalism of *Coronation Street*, accept transitions from straightforward if tip-top dialogue to our hero looking absurd as his voice suddenly becomes that of dance-band singer on a very surfacey seventy-eight? I think my own anxiety at the early pre-production stage was guilt as much as professional funk because being required to make *Pennies* work was like undeservedly being given tricky keys to paradise.

I dissipated my terror by quickly appointing Piers Haggard as director. He brought a more appropriate track and personal record than any producer or writer has a right to. He'd recently directed the Chester Mystery plays which had maximized the potential of using a TV studio not to photograph boring flat-lit facial reality but as a fulcrum for (then) state-of-the-art excitement. He'd also directed musicals on television and he had tremendous stamina which I knew this enterprise would die without an excess of. And he was an optimist on an almost military scale, taking over my fright and Dennis's uncertainties, assuring us in a way you didn't argue with that it was going to work, and wonderfully. For me his over-riding achievement was in yanking, converting and homogenizing the maddeningly technical and logistical dog's dinner that TV drama was in those days. Interior scenes were thoroughly worked on in rehearsal for two or three weeks, then made against the clock (and the union) in the studio with multi-camera video tape where the lighting traditions were prosaic and uninspiring. However, the outside scenes were done on film using the best that the burgeoning 16mm colour stock and style could offer – then it all had to be converted back to video and the editing technology was razor-blade basic. What Piers did was to make it all look one superb appropriate thing, and beyond that make an emotional unity of the everyday down-beat world the characters moved around in and the yearning aspirational dimension coming in and out of the songs. Piers realized the material triumphantly, gave it its own integrity of style and kept it well away from the threat of camp.

If Piers was in-waiting for the job of director, the casting process was more hazardous and tricky. Dennis, at least 60 per cent seriously, suggested Roy Hudd and Spike Milligan for the male leads. My own first fancy was for Nicol Williamson but he turned us down (and now has a unique record for he also spurned the leads in both *The Singing Detective* and *Karaoke*). A more conventional search for the right Arthur Parker led us through Alan Bates, Hywel Bennett and Michael Elphick (all of whom did great things in later Potter works). Then, through a hunch which first seemed cranky but has turned out to be sublime, we came to Bob Hoskins with whom I'd already worked. Then . . . but to go on like this would be to embark on a roll-call of tedious self-satisfaction because it's true that on *Pennies* almost everything went well. Much of that really led back to the difference in Dennis himself from the time of making *Moonlight on the Highway* to when he wrote *Pennies*.

1977 was for Dennis a virtual cocoon of personal satisfaction, comfort and happiness which I doubt he enjoyed before or since in his entire life. It's slightly banal to have to credit for that change a drug called Razoxin which he experimented with at this period, but everyone who knew him then testifies to an extraordinary transformation in the man. From a slightly embittered and reclusive cripple frequently having to endure lengthy periods living under a Cellophane eiderdown, he became for a blissful while a running, jumping and loving adorable human being. In that euphoria he wrote *Pennies*. Someone said that *Pennies* is almost the only one of Dennis's pieces of work where he seems unequivocally to like and recommend his principal characters. It's a strange thing to say of a work where the hero is a liar, cheat and coward whose only achievement in life is to go to the gallows for a murder he didn't happen to commit, whose wife is a repressed *petite bourgeoise* who can't love or be loved, and whose girlfriend is someone who abandons her needy family to go on the game in London, murders an innocent old man and gets away with it. The fourth principal is a stuttering pathological derelict. Could the life get lower? But what you actually experience through this quartet are people who are certainly beneath the angels but somehow by not very much, and although, with or without the songs, they are in a fantasy world, it is also a world of great, moving reality where the way people talk and the often mad interplay of their actions never ceases to have the ring of its own truth, even when it involves resurrections of the body on Hammersmith Bridge and coincidences which shouldn't pass, but do, the test of our own belief.

As a hero Arthur is notably different from some of Dennis's other main characters, particularly Philip Marlow in *The Singing Detective*. Arthur is always perceived externally, you make your own judgement on what he says, you take him at face value, you don't go into his past or his interior life and on the rare occasions he tells us something about his past, it's better not to believe it. Where we glimpse his internal life is through the dreams and pieties of the lyrics. Pro forma shallow though they mostly are, the songs actually do much more than illustrate the azure, sunny side of the world and contradict it with the cheap reality of life. The idea we once had in production of putting the narrative in black and white and the songs in colour would have been disastrous because there is no such total dichotomy between the two worlds. The songs aren't just the expressions of Arthur's fantasy. Quite often they express someone else's emotional ambition, particularly and wonderfully comically in the famous 'You Rascal You' sequence (Episode 1) where Joan and her girlfriends 'say' what they would really like to do to their men. And as Eileen sings 'In the Middle of a Kiss' (Episode 6) when they are on the run, she's allowed to imply a tragic depth and insight about her feelings which isn't eloquent elsewhere. The sentimental raw material has indeed been 'reclaimed' and then mined out of banality into a golden context.

However, this book is a version of *Pennies* in which you don't hear the songs. It therefore puts a great demand on the narrative, dialogue and sheer construction, and also on what you might call Dennis's philosophy, because without hearing the songs or even reading the lyrics, the message or religious position or philosophy they represent is still very vibrant in his text. In key places like the boarding house scene (Episode 2) Arthur annihilates the bit-of-skirt cynicism his fellow salesmen display about Eileen into the *Pennies from Heaven* 'shining' ethic which comes entirely from the sentiments of the lyrics. More tellingly later when they are on the run and the drama comes towards its grimiest, Eileen is there with a surprising maturity of judgement to tell Arthur that life can't be like the songs. Incidentally, if anything major of Dennis himself is in these characters, it is surely less in Arthur, the feckless essentially uncreative salesman with his bag of song-sheets, than in Eileen, the *ingénue* from the Forest of Dean. First she is seduced by someone who represents a glamorous London. Then once she is 'up there' herself it isn't long before she's showing wisdom and insight well beyond those of her mentor. The trajectory is that of Dennis's own early career – from being a virgin in the pastoral sticks to becoming a desirable and successful metropolitan icon almost overnight.

I have always felt that as a story *Pennies* is one of Dennis's strongest, largely because it turns on one simple piece of ruthless and naturalistically unacceptable sleight of hand. You have to accept that Arthur and the Accordion Man are parts of each other, that they fall haplessly into each other's clutches and that it's the tramp who escapes into his own death leaving Arthur inevitably to pay for his crimes. Everything turns on that and turns well. The discursive bits – Eileen with the Pimp (Episode 4) and with the MP (Episode 5) – are necessary digressions and very funny in a piece built on such a scale.

For me, the authenticity litmus test for *Pennies* and its hero is similar to that met by Philip Marlow. Both characters resonate passionately inside the individual psyches of their audiences. People relate to Arthur and Philip because of their empathic *unlikeness* to themselves. They say that through Arthur or Philip, Dennis knows what *I* think, how *I* feel. I used to get this wrong and ask enthusiasts of this kind: Did you leave your wife? Were you abandoned by your lover? Are you keen on the songs? Have you been in hospital? Almost always not, but through the very bizarreness and desperation of his characters a very common humanity and general rapport is forged between the strange fictions and the Everyman in the audiences. I don't feel in touch with all of the criteria for recognizing great literature, but I'm sure that in this respect Dennis Potter measures up well to one of them.

Kenith Trodd

The first episode of *Pennies from Heaven* was broadcast on BBC I on 7 March 1978. The cast was as follows:

ARTHUR PARKER	Bob Hoskins
JOAN PARKER	Gemma Craven
HIKER	Kenneth Colley
EILEEN EVERSON	Cheryl Campbell
BARRETT	Arnold Peters
PIANIST	Sam Avent
IRENE	Jenny Logan
HEADMASTER	Freddie Jones
MAURICE	Spencer Banks
DAD	Michael Bilten
DAVE	Philip Jackson
ALF	Bill Dean
MRS CORDER	Bella Emberg
POLICE INSPECTOR	Dave King

Episode 1: 'Down Sunnyside Lane' only:

CONRAD BAKER	Nigel Havers
MARJORIE	Rosemary Martin
JUMBO	Robert Putt
WILL	Keith Marsh
BETTY	Tessa Dunne
CARTER	Wally Thomas

Episode 2: 'The Sweetest Thing' only:

BANK MANAGER	Peter Cellier
CUSTOMER	Cyril Cross
TED	Roger Sloman

Episode 3: 'Hand in Hand' only:

MINER	Frederick Bradley

WOMAN PATIENT	Maryann Turner
BLIND GIRL	Yolande Palfrey
POLICE CONSTABLE	Roger Forbes
DETECTIVE INSPECTOR	John Malcolm

Episode 4: 'Better Think Twice' only:

CAFÉ PROPRIETOR	Tony Caunter
CAFÉ CUSTOMER	Tudor Davies
TOM	Hywel Bennett

Episode 5: 'Tiptoe Through the Tulips' only:

TRAMP	Paddy Joyce
MICHAEL	Nigel Rathbone
MAJOR ARCHIBALD PAXVILLE	Ronald Fraser
MAN IN QUEUE	Reg Lever
BUSKER	Ronnie Ross
WAITER	Alan Foss
MAN ON BRIDGE	Chris Gannon
SECOND INSPECTOR	Laurence Harrington
SHOP MANAGER	David Webb
CUSTOMER	Robin Meredith

Episode 6: 'Says My Heart' only:

PEDESTRIAN	Steve Ubels
FARMER	Philip Locke
SERGEANT	John Ringham
CONSTABLE	Tim Swinton
JUDGE	Carleton Hobbs
PROSECUTING COUNSEL	Peter Bowles
CLERK OF THE COURT	Stanley Fleet

Producer	Kenith Trodd
Director	Piers Haggard
Designers	Tim Harvey, Bruce Macadie
Film editor	David Martin
Film photography	Ken Westbury

1 'DOWN SUNNYSIDE LANE'

CAPTIONS
*Detailed, slightly idyllic paintings of leafy suburban street
(Metroland), early 1930s.*
*It is night, but a crescent moon shines above the semi-detached villas,
silvering everything.*
*A man with a trilby hat is walking his dog. A young man and his
girl kiss goodnight by a lamp-post.*
*Parked car. Hedges. Wooden gates. Doorways with leaded glass.
Bay window lit and unlit.*
*All as evocative as a song-sheet from the period, yet also as detailed
as archetypical, as a Norman Rockwell Saturday* Evening Post
painting.
*Camera moves from general scene to particular details; panning,
cutting, mixing to the bounce of the music, and eventually narrowing
down to one particular upstairs window, shown lit, then unlit.*
*Music: from opening of 'Down Sunnyside Lane', as recorded by Jack
Payne and BBC Dance Orchestra, September 1931, with vocal by
Billy Scott-Coomber.*

INT. A DARKENED BEDROOM IN ONE OF THE VILLAS. NIGHT/
DAWN
*Out of the darkness, and as final transition from the caption, bring
up the luminous hands of a huge alarm clock (the type with an
outside bell): twenty-past six. Music ('Down Sunnyside Lane')
continues. Move across to the double bed, where a husband and wife
are asleep.*
*Opening title comes on screen exactly as and in pace with the singer
who releases exactly the same words.*
*Moving into close-up of the husband, who has suddenly, and rather
startlingly, popped open his eyes. There is a strange, dead, blank look
in them, as though he has been sleeping in the land of the dead.*
He is ARTHUR PARKER, *mid-thirties – he was about eighteen in
1916 – a 'commercial traveller' in sheet music, gramophone records,
etc.*
He swivels his eyes and stares at the alarm clock, waiting for it to

1

clang, then, picking up the words of the song, with an intense, whispered venom –

ARTHUR: (*Hiss*) Some day if luck is kind. S-s-some day!
(*Immediately, the alarm bell rings, urgent and noisy.* ARTHUR *looks at it sardonically, making no attempt to silence it. Then his hand suddenly plunges down on the clock, like a bird of prey, and chokes it into silence.*)
Hey-ho!
(*He turns to look at* JOAN, *his wife, a woman of about thirty. It becomes a speculative stare – and then, as she does not stir, a hungry one.*)
(*Softly*) Joan . . . ?
(*She does not move. But we sense that she is now awake.*)
Joanie. Joanie, my pet? Are you awake? Eh? C'mon, sugar.
(*He puts his arm around her, and pulls her into himself.*)

JOAN: (*Reluctant*) Mmmwa . . . wha . . . ?

ARTHUR: (*Urgent*) C'mon Joanie – sugar – wake up, my pigeon . . .
(*She tries to wriggle from his grasp, pushing his hands from her breasts.*)

JOAN: No – Arthur – don't –

ARTHUR: Oh, now – Joan – Joanie –

JOAN: (*Mock sleepy*) Too early – I'm not awake – there isn't time –

ARTHUR: There's always time for this.
(*She has to push his hands away again.*)
(*Becoming too urgent*) Come on, Joan. Be a sport. Come on, old girl! Joan!

JOAN: Arthur! Stop it! No, Arthur – you'll be – *Arthur*, no, I said. No.

ARTHUR: (*Anguished*) Why not? Why?
(*Abruptly, she pulls the cord dangling above them. The light comes on, very bright.*)

JOAN: You said you wanted to get away early. That's what you said.
(*The sharpness in her voice makes him stop grappling.*)

ARTHUR: (*Sullen*) You never want to nowadays, do you? Never.

JOAN: Never?

ARTHUR: Not what *I* call want to. Not really *want* to, I mean.

2

JOAN: (*Brisk*) That's a very silly thing to say, Arthur dear. And I'm not even properly awake yet.
ARTHUR: (*Hopeful*) But it's best like that – nicer – when you're a bit sleepy and – Joan? Joanie – eh? Please?
(*Fractional pause.*)
JOAN: Make us a nice cup of tea, will you, lovey?
ARTHUR: (*Savagely*) Bloody tea!
JOAN: (*Shocked*) Language!
(*He stares at her, then swallows.*)
ARTHUR: Look here, Joan. I'm going to be away from home for the next four days and nights, and –
JOAN: There's no need to swear, though.
ARTHUR: No, but you ain't being very –
JOAN: (*Cutting in*) There isn't. Is there, Arthur?
ARTHUR: I was – whatdysay? – exasperated – and it wasn't much of a cuss –
JOAN: (*Again cutting in*) Well, *I* don't think it's very nice. Not in the house.
ARTHUR: (*Savagely*) Not anywhere! (*He swings angrily out of bed.*)
JOAN: (*Sweetly*) But especially not in your own home, Arthur.
(*He looks down at her with a steady, baleful expression.*
She takes his look, smiles and tilts her head, consciously pert, in a manner copied from the cinema.
At which point, start music: 'The Clouds Will Soon Roll By', recorded by Ambrose & his Orchestra, July 1932. The intro by the band – before the vocal begins – oozes quietly under dialogue.)
ARTHUR: (*Changing tone*) Cup of char is it then, old gel?
JOAN: Ar-thur.
ARTHUR: (*Grin*) Common, am I? (*His moods are very volatile.*)
JOAN: I knew that from the start. My Mummy warned me about *that*.
ARTHUR: (*Proudly*) Common as muck!
JOAN: You make a very nice cup of tea, though.
(*Music slightly louder.*)
ARTHUR: She said hopefully. (*He leers at her.*)
JOAN: Oh – but you *will*, won't you – ?
ARTHUR: I will if *you* will.

3

JOAN: Make the tea – oh but – ?

ARTHUR: No. The other.

JOAN: (*Harsher*) What?

ARTHUR: The other. A bit of the other.

JOAN: (*Quietly*) You filthy beast.

(*They look at each other. Her face is hard. He drops his eyes. Then, suddenly, he appears to sing – he mimes to the voice of Elsie Carlisle as the vocal of 'The Clouds Will Soon Roll By' begins. He does it wholly in the conventions of a musical – totally in earnest. For a moment,* ARTHUR *and* JOAN *are in a film musical.*)

(*Music out, abruptly. Fractional pause. They seem frozen in position. Then:*)

What did you say?

ARTHUR: (*Mumble*) Nothing. I'll make the tea.

JOAN: (*Crisp*) Thank you, Arthur.

(*He passes across the foot of the bed, face dead. He pads, in pyjamas, out of the room, like a zombie.*

A moment's pause.

She considers, then calls out:)

You're all right, Arthur! You're one of the best!

(*She smiles sweetly to herself, then lays back on the pillows with a contented sigh, pouting rosebud lips.*

Wipe screen from left to right.)

INT. THE KITCHEN. DAY

Begin on the kitchen cabinet, with its flap down, revealing a now almost museum-like collection of tins and packets (Bisto, Oxo, etc.) vintage 1934–5.

Pull back to show ARTHUR *and* JOAN *at the table, a large Shredded Wheat packet between them – 'Britons make it – It makes Britons'.*

JOAN: (*Concerned*) Are you sure you won't have something? Not even a boiled egg. A lightly boiled egg, mmm?

ARTHUR: (*Remote*) No. Nothing.

JOAN: (*She tries to speak 'trippingly'*) You've got an awfully long way to go, Arthur. *Gloucester.* It's a long time to be motoring.

ARTHUR: (*Sniff*) Way out west. Towards the sunset. Tum-ti-tum.

(*She sips her Camp coffee, watching him carefully.*)

JOAN: I wouldn't want to go to the back of beyond without a

4

cooked breakfast. You *need* something inside you to motor as far as *Gloucester*.

(ARTHUR *looks at her, challengingly.*)

ARTHUR: I'm used to feeling empty.

JOAN: What do you mean?

ARTHUR: I *like* feeling empty.

(*She sighs, crooking her little finger on her cup.*)

JOAN: (*Smiles*) Now you know you don't! What funny things you say when you're in one of your *moods*.

ARTHUR: (*Flat*) One of my moods?

JOAN: You know what I mean, Arthur. Don't be ob-tuse.

ARTHUR: Say what you like, Joanie, I feel –

JOAN: (*Pert*) I always do.

ARTHUR: (*Doggedly*) Say what you like, I feel empty.

JOAN: (*Laughs*) Well, if you don't eat, *dear!*

ARTHUR: Empty. There's nothing inside me. Nothing. Nothing at all.

(JOAN *looks at* ARTHUR, *frowns, then decides to laugh.*)

JOAN: You've got all your or-gans and things, dear.

ARTHUR: That's as maybe. But I *me* – I'm empty – blank – I've got nothing (*taps his heart, melodramatically*) *here.* Nothing at all!

JOAN: What? Not even a song?

ARTHUR: (*Blinks*) What?

JOAN: A song in your heart. Not even an inky-dinky little tune?

(*Again,* ARTHUR*'s mood changes. He reaches down to the bulging briefcase, packed ready on the linoleum.*)

ARTHUR: I keep those in my bag. Not in my heart.

JOAN: And in your head.

ARTHUR: *And* in my head. Quite right. (*He hugs his bag into his chest.*) I don't suppose there's a chap in all England who knows more about the songs that sell than I do. Not one.

JOAN: But *do* they sell, Arthur? Enough, I mean.

(*He looks at her, gloomily, pursing his lips.*)

ARTHUR: It's the shopkeepers, ennit? Ignorant little bleeders.

JOAN: (*Genuinely shocked*) Arthur!

ARTHUR: (*Quickly*) Sorry, old girl. Sorry.

JOAN: You may have talked like that in your *parents'* home, but I'd –

5

ARTHUR: (*Vigorously*) It *is* the shopkeepers, though! And they *are* ignorant. No, listen a minute, Joan, hold on! I know what I'm talking about. Never you mind about my dad being a bricklayer – this is something I *know* about, see?

JOAN: (*Snootily*) *I'm* not arguing.

(*He opens his bulging briefcase, and takes out a copy of 'Roll Along Prairie Moon'. The way he talks now shows that this is, indeed, something he knows and cares about.*)

ARTHUR: Now *this* one, see. 'Roll Along Prairie Moon'. Jack Jackson's band is playing it almost every night for the nobs at the Dorchester. It's on the wireless three, four times a day. A *marvellous* song. He's just made a gramophone record of it. *Marvellous* record – a month from now every butcher's boy and every postman will be whistling it. (*Starts to hum.*) Da-di-dah-dah-dah. (*Face changes.*) But how many actual orders will *I* take for this over the next three, four days? These shopkeepers – ach, they've got hair in the nostrils and wax in their ears! Do they ever listen to the wireless? Do they ever dream any sort of dream – or look at the moon? No. Can't do. Can't do! Do they know what sort of world we're living in? A month from now, I'm telling you, a month, and they'll be ringing up the wholesaler, oh yes, cutting me right out of it. Joe Soap. They'll have to, see, because first one customer and then another and then a whole busload will come in to the shop and say, Have you got that thing about the Prairie Moon? (*Sucks in his breath, imitating shopkeeper.*) Prairie Moon? Prairie Moon? they'll say. Don't you mean Harvest Moon or . . . Prairie Moon? No, no, never heard of it – are you sure you've got the title correct?

JOAN: Correctly.

(*He looks at her with distaste.*)

ARTHUR: I'm a *shopkeeper* now, enn I? This is the shopkeeper speaking.

JOAN: I see.

ARTHUR: (*With a glint*) They don't know grammar, see. And there's some of them as swears a lot. Effing and blinding. Oh, yes. Your shopkeeper cusses, your shopkeeper does.

JOAN: My father doesn't.

6

ARTHUR: Ah, yes. But he's a Methodist, ennhe? More a
Methodist than what you'd call a shopkeeper.
(*She goes to speak, then doesn't.*)
Prairie Moon? They'll say. These effing and blinding
shopkeepers. No – never effing heard of it.

JOAN: Arthur.

ARTHUR: (*Quickly*) They won't even remember how I *told* them
it'd happen. Oh, no. Prairie Moon? They'll say to me,
tomorrow or the next day – Prairie Moon? No call for that
sort of stuff round here.
(*Fractional pause.*)

JOAN: There isn't a prairie at Gloucester, is there?
(*He glares at her.*)

ARTHUR: No – a desert!
(*She laughs, then, reluctantly, he does too.*)

JOAN: Don't you think you'd better start to make tracks? I
thought you said you wanted to get away early.
(*He looks at her.*)

ARTHUR: You see – there *was* time. Plenty of time.

JOAN: Oh well, never mind.
(*He still stares at her, eyes melancholy.*)

ARTHUR: After all, I'm my own boss. The clock is not my
master.

JOAN: Ah, but if you work for yourself, you have to work even
harder to make a go of things.
(*His expression has not changed.*)

ARTHUR: Joanie?

JOAN: Oh, Arthur. Don't you ever leave go?

ARTHUR: It'd be nice down here. Eh?

JOAN: Here?

ARTHUR: (*Eagerly*) In the lounge. On the – on the settee? Shut
the curtains?
(*The eagerness suddenly dies as he sees her expression.*)
No. Well. It was just a thought.

JOAN: A very peculiar thought an' all.

ARTHUR: Peculiar? Peculiar? Ach! –
(*He puts song back in case.*)
Don't you ever listen to the words? In the songs. In these
songs.

7

JOAN: Ah. But that's not real life.

ARTHUR: Real life? You tell me what real life is, then!
(He rises to go.)

JOAN: You'll be back Thursday, then?

ARTHUR: Back to real life. Yes. About tea-time on Thursday.

JOAN: *(Smiles)* Tea for two.
(He pecks her on the cheek, ready to go.)

ARTHUR: More than tea, I hope, love. There's a new moon on
Thursday.

JOAN: *(Smiles)* Same old moon, really. Take care, dear. Drive
very, very carefully. Moon or no moon.
(Wipe from right to left.)

CAPTIONS

*As before, detailed paintings of Arthur's car (vintage 1930) on the
road west from London.*

Pan along the road, settling on sign: OXFORD 40, GLOUCESTER 98,
and on the old, triangular warning signs, such as STEEP HILL *or*
MAJOR ROAD AHEAD. *Some traffic, too, in either direction.*

*Moving to the car itself, and then to pictures (paintings) of Arthur at
the wheel and into big close-up – at the same time, music.*

*Music: 'Roll Along Prairie Moon' as recorded by Jack Jackson and
his band at the Dorchester. August 1935. The 'vocal' is Fred Latham.*

Mix swiftly from caption Arthur to real ARTHUR, *as he mimes just
the opening words of the song.*

Cut in:

INT. A MUSIC SHOP. DAY

In tight: a SHOPKEEPER *shakes his head, emphatically.*

Cut back:

INT./EXT. IN THE CAR. DAY

ARTHUR *does not mime, but holds a brooding silence, eyes fixed on
the road ahead, as the singer, the song, the prairie moon, rolls on.*

Mix:

INT. ANOTHER MUSIC SHOP. DAY

Again in close, another SHOPKEEPER *smiles and, alas, declines.*

Mix:

8

INT./EXT. IN THE CAR, AND ON THE LONDON–GLOUCESTER
ROAD. DAY
The song ends, abruptly. ARTHUR*'s hands clench on the wheel.*
ARTHUR: (*Hiss*) Bastards! Cloth-eared-nits!
(*Up ahead, a man of about Arthur's age and height is waiting
in the long grass at roadside, thumb out, hoping for a lift.*
A glint comes into ARTHUR*'s eyes. He slows a little.*
*The man on the verge flaps his arm eagerly. As he lowers his
arm, grinning, sure now of a lift,* ARTHUR *suddenly accelerates
and cackles to himself. But his window is open, and a single
word shouted by the* HITCH-HIKER *is just about heard.*)
HIKER: (*Off, shout*) – ugger!
(ARTHUR *brakes suddenly and waits. A moment – then sound
of footsteps on the road. Hesitantly, the* HIKER *leans in.*)
I – ah –
ARTHUR: (*Sternly*) *What* did you shout?
(*A flash of genuine fear in* HIKER*'s eyes.*)
HIKER: Shout? I didn't shout nothing, sir.
ARTHUR: Anyfing.
HIKER: What?
ARTHUR: I didn't shout *anyfing.*
HIKER: No. Nor me neither, sir. Nothing.
ARTHUR: (*Amused*) Ignorant sod, entcha?
HIKER: (*Stiffening*) Hold on. Hold on. I got my dignity, y'know.
ARTHUR: You haven't got a motor car, though, have you?
(*The* HIKER *seems to consider.*)
HIKER: Not at the moment. No, sir.
ARTHUR: Do you want a lift? Is that it?
(*The* HIKER *looks at him dubiously, and again seems to
consider the matter.*)
HIKER: How far are you going, sir?
ARTHUR: (*Half amused*) How far do you want to go?
HIKER: Gloucester. (*And then aggressively.*) Are you going *that
far* sir?
ARTHUR: I'm a free man. I might. I might not. I'm unpredictable.
(*The* HIKER *stares at him.*)
HIKER: I'll get in then?
ARTHUR: By all means. (*Catches sight of his case.*) And your case
too, I suppose. No extra charge.

9

HIKER: (*Stupidly*) Oh, thank you. Thank you very much, sir.
(*He goes round the car to get in on the other side, a peculiarly jerky, rather odd individual.*

ARTHUR *looks at him with rather scornful amusement and starts the car.*

The HIKER *hunches into himself, in almost a foetal position, staring at the ribbon of road ahead in something like fear or anxiety.*)

ARTHUR: (*Puzzled, irritated*) Too fast for you?

HIKER: (*Tight*) Nice – um – nice cars, these ve-hic-les.

ARTHUR: Not bad. Not a bad old girl at all.

HIKER: W-wish – (*He stops, abruptly.*)

ARTHUR: What?

HIKER: (*Gulp*) W-wish I had one.

(ARTHUR *looks across at him with a glint of amusement.*)

ARTHUR: These ent for the likes of you, these ent.

HIKER: No. (*Pause.*) But all the, all the same . . . (*He falls into an abrupt silence.*)

ARTHUR: (*Eventually*) What you got there?

HIKER: A squeeze-box.

ARTHUR: Really? (*Pleased*) A piano accordion? You play it? – Properly, I mean?

HIKER: (*Simply*) It's my living, sir.

(ARTHUR *looks across, rather incredulous.*)

ARTHUR: You a musician? In a band, I mean.

HIKER: In a band?

(*Again, he falls silent, staring at road.*)

ARTHUR: Well – are you?

(*The* HIKER *repeats it as though awestruck.*)

HIKER: In a band?

ARTHUR: For Christ's sake!

HIKER: (*Gulp*) W-well – no – not actually *in* a band, actually a band, no, sir, no. I'm more – um – I'm more what we in the business call a – (*seems almost to shudder*) – a – sol-so-lo-ist. Sir.

(ARTHUR *again looks across, unsure what to believe.*)

ARTHUR: (*Half scornful*) But you don't give *concerts* and that, do you?

HIKER: I give concerts.

ARTHUR: Where?
  (HIKER's *eyes flick from one side of road to other.*)
HIKER: Oh, here and there. One place and another.
  (*And then, disconcertingly, he starts to shake with an almost silent laughter.*)
ARTHUR: (*Sourly*) You're a funny kind of bloke!
HIKER: (*Gurgle*) One place and another.
ARTHUR: (*Angry*) Like where? The Albert bleed'n 'All?
HIKER: (*Suddenly solemn, as if quoting*) Wherever two or three or p-preferably four busy streets – (*gasp*) – intersect.
  (*A moment's silence. Then they both roar with laughter.*
  Iris-out into next scene, with diminuendo on accordion.)

INT. ARTHUR'S HOUSE. KITCHEN. DAY

Begin (at centre of iris) on Camp Coffee Essence bottle ('ready aye, ready') as JOAN *tips a black, sticky spoonful into a cup.*
She lifts up already boiling kettle, with dreamy, preoccupied air, a magazine perilously tucked under her arm, and slops boiling water into the cup.
As we follow all this (milk, sugar etc.), an incredibly smooth, suave, almost comically class-conscious masculine voice insinuates itself out of vision. And by her expression, it is a voice, thought, in her head.
SMOOTHIE: (*Out of vision*) I wish you knew Gertie Lawrence. She is my ideal of a capable, beautiful and desirable feminine thing – the embodiment of personality and feminine charm.

INT. LOUNGE. DAY

SMOOTHIE: (*Out of vision*) Go and see her, and you will detect, even across the footlights, that magic femininity and conscious attractiveness which – as I maintain – is within your power to acquire. Study it and *learn* from it.
  (*During which* JOAN *takes her coffee and a biscuit into her 'lounge' and sinks with a contented sigh into armchair, opening up magazine.*)
JOAN: Study it and learn from it.
  (*Close-up magazine pages.*)
SMOOTHIE: (*Out of vision*) Then one of the first to gain from my attempt to make lovely woman lovelier still will be you.

JOAN: Will be me.
> (*She sips her coffee reflectively. Mix into caption sequence.*)

CAPTIONS
In loving pastiche of 1930s women's magazine. Fiction illustration, a girl, who is clearly the actress playing JOAN, *is being wooed and won by various smooth young men in evening clothes, dinner jackets etc. The music (without words) is 'Red Sails in the Sunset'. Lantern-jawed heroes, cocktails, dance floor, sports car, ski-slope etc. Mix back into:*

INT. LOUNGE. DAY
Enraptured JOAN *enmeshed in her dreams, magazine open on her knees, coffee cup in her hands. And back into:*

ROMANTIC, LAVISH CAPTION SEQUENCE
Sharp cut to:

INT. THE LOUNGE. DAY
Dreamlike, JOAN *puts down her coffee, rises, raises her arms, and, exactly on cue, mimes to Al Bowlly singing 'Blue Moon'. Abrupt stop as heavy rat-a-tat sounds off, on the front door. Startled, transfixed almost, she takes a moment to lower her arms and change her stance. Straight cut:*

EXT. THE FRONT DOOR. DAY
A suave young man with a pencil moustache stands at the door, a small case in his hand. In contrast with his appearance, though, he is whistling crudely between his teeth. He quickly stops doing it as he hears the door start to open. As JOAN, *a little cautiously, opens the door, he flashes her a gleaming smile, and gives the subtlest suggestion of a little bow. He is called* CONRAD BAKER.
CONRAD: Good morning, madam. Is your (*conscious hesitation*)
> mother in by any chance?
>> (*It's the voice of the earlier* SMOOTHIE.
>>> *Wipe from left to right.*)

INT. AN INN, ON THE LONDON–GLOUCESTER ROAD. DAY
ARTHUR *and the* HIKER *have fresh pints, they sit at a small round
table with wrought iron legs shaped like a lion's head at the top. Beer
pumps (from the wood) behind them at bar.*

HIKER: (*Blowing top of beer*) This is – this is very kind of you,
    sir. Very very kind indeed.

ARTHUR: (*Smirk*) That's what we're here for, ennit? To help
    one another along (*drinks*) life's (*drinks*) road. Ahhh, that's
    good.

HIKER: Oh. Oh. (*Stops. Starts again.*) Christian.

ARTHUR: Yes. I suppose it is, really. Cheers, anyhow!

HIKER: Cheers, sir.
    (ARTHUR *wipes his mouth.*)

ARTHUR: Now, then. How much do you reckon you can pick
    up in a day's busking?
    (HIKER *looks all around, like an accountant.*)

HIKER: Depends.

ARTHUR: On the weather, I suppose. Yes. But – a day like
    today, say?

HIKER: (*Ponders*) Oh – between five and seven bob, sir.
    (ARTHUR, *impressed, whistles.*)

ARTHUR: As much as that, eh?

HIKER: S-sometimes.

ARTHUR: Next pint on you then, pal.
    (*He says it with a grin, but the* HIKER *jerks to his feet like a
    frightened animal.*)

HIKER: (*Almost shouting*) No – I can't – haven't –

ARTHUR: (*Amused*) Hey, now. You're a funny old lad, you are.
    Sit down and stop bellowing.

HIKER: (*Quivering*) But I haven't got any – any –

ARTHUR: Come on, now. I'm only pulling your leg.
    (*The other repeats the phrase as though it has a literal
    meaning.*)

HIKER: Pulling – my – leg?

ARTHUR: Money's not the only fing in this life, you know.
    (*The* HIKER *stares down at him, calmer now.*)

HIKER: No, sir. Quite so-o, sir.
    (*One more glance at* ARTHUR *to make sure, then he sits down
    again, clenching both hands round his pint.*

ARTHUR *looks across at him, a bit amused, a bit puzzled, and perhaps even a little alarmed.*)

ARTHUR: How do you live, then? I mean, where do you sleep – ?

HIKER: Places. Different places.

ARTHUR: You got no family, then? Not married or anything – ?

HIKER: (*Smirk*) I don't belong to anyone and nobody belongs to me.

ARTHUR: There's a lot to be said for that. If you can manage it.

HIKER: (*Pleased*) I'm a – whatdyacallit – a – gentleman of the r-road!

(*They both drink, eyeing each other.*)

ARTHUR: (*Eventually*) What sort of tunes do you play on that accordion of yours?

HIKER: (*Stiff, half-whispering*) Hymns.

ARTHUR: (*Anxious*) What did you say?

HIKER: Hymns, sir. (*He sucks in his breath, weirdly.*) S-sacred songs and s-solos.

(ARTHUR*'s look at him now is full of comic horror and indignation.*)

ARTHUR: That – Gawdluvaduck – what a waste of a squeeze-box!

(*The* HIKER *sits in stiff, morose silence, then sips gingerly at his beer. Then he leans in, conspiratorial.*)

HIKER: The old r-rugged cross, sir.

ARTHUR: (*Hostile*) What about it?

(*The* HIKER*'s eyes flick from side to side, then he leans in again, as if imparting a profound secret.*)

HIKER: Rock of Ages, sir.

ARTHUR: Hymns, yes. I know they're bleed'n hymns, don't I!

HIKER: There is a green hill far away.

ARTHUR: (*Very irritated*) Without a city wall.

(*Silence. They both look away from each other.*)

Yes, well . . .

(*He goes to finish his drink.*)

HIKER: (*Suddenly*) That's all I can play, you see. I don't know any other tunes, sir.

Sharp cut:

INT. ARTHUR'S AND JOAN'S LOUNGE. DAY

CONRAD, *the salesman, has got his case open on the settee.* JOAN, *a little uncertain, stands watching, alert.*

CONRAD: Believe me, *Miss* –

JOAN: Mrs.

CONRAD: Really? Well – I wouldn't have . . . *(oily smile)* Believe me, *madam*, I wouldn't have accepted my present – ah – post if I did not have absolute and total faith in this particular product –

JOAN: *(Interrupting)* Yes, but you *would* say that anyway, wouldn't you?

(He looks at her with sad eyes.)

CONRAD: Ah, miss – madam – I know with what truth it is possible to make such an accusation against the vast majority of the members of our – ah – fraternity – but I assure . . .

JOAN: Of which my husband is one.

(CONRAD blinks, stops, momentarily nonplussed.)

CONRAD: Oh. Is he? A – oh. I see.

JOAN: A commercial – um – well, some people say 'commercial traveller' but I don't care for the phrase myself –

CONRAD: No indeed not! He's – um – in . . . ?

JOAN: Music – sheet music. Songs, you know. On commission.

CONRAD: Songs. How very nice.

(He seems momentarily at a loss.)

JOAN: A different line of business, of course.

CONRAD: *(Brightening)* Very different. Poles apart, in fact. Songs deal in dreams – correct me if I am wrong – yes, dreams and make-believe – my goodness me, we can't live without them – but . . .

JOAN: My husband can't. That's for sure.

(He looks at her, and a light comes into his eye.)

CONRAD: But I don't deal in dreams, you see – no matter how pleasant they might be. Well – at least not now. Not at this particular moment I don't, though there have been . . .

JOAN: What do you mean?

CONRAD: Well now, you are either an attractive woman or you aren't. In the last – um – resort you can't really hide the difference.

(*They look at each other. She tenses a little.*)

JOAN: That's very much a man's way of looking at things.

CONRAD: Ah. But why do the ladies use lipstick and face powder, madam?

JOAN: Because it makes them feel nice, I suppose.

CONRAD: But mostly it makes the gentlemen feel that they are even nicer. Am I right?

JOAN: Possibly.

CONRAD: Put powder and rouge on a – pardon me – on a face like the back of a bus, however – and it makes no difference. Not to the gentlemen. I can assure you of that. It's still a face like the back of a bus.

JOAN: I think that's rather cruel.

CONRAD: (*Sigh*) Very cruel. But the songs don't deal with that kind of truth, I'm afraid, madam.

JOAN: Thank goodness.

CONRAD: Thank goodness, indeed. Though, if I may say so, it's not a problem that affects you personally.

JOAN: (*Simper*) I don't know what you mean.

CONRAD: I am speaking – ah – professionally, of course.

JOAN: Of course.

CONRAD: And it is my experience madam, that over-attractive young ladies such as, pardon me, yourself, should not scorn the occasional beauty aid. It is not a question of *gilding* the lily, madam, but of – shall we say? – seeing the lily in the morning dew, at its present and prettiest.

JOAN: That's – that's very nicely put, Mr – ah –

CONRAD: Baker, Conrad Baker.

JOAN: But I don't like buying anything that I . . .

CONRAD: (*Cutting in rapidly*) Quite right. Quite right too!

JOAN: What is the principle of this thing? I mean – how does it work?

(*The 'thing' has been in his hands since 'gilding the lily': it is a bogus skin and beauty aid, once common at this time. It is a circular suction pad on a gilt handle, which is supposed to be patted on the face and neck.*)

CONRAD: The pitter-patter, as we call it – may I explain? (*She half nods*) – is to put it very simply, a scientifically designed suction pad which creates a small vacuum when in use –

that is, when patted gently, up and down, all over the
lady's face and neck . . .

JOAN: Oh, yes I've seen one advertised.

CONRAD: Not this one, madam. If I may correct you for a
moment. *This* model is mathematically balanced to provide
the *exact* amount of suction. I think it's no secret if I say
that the model you are thinking of gives only a crude
approximation of the suction needed. Very much a hit-
and-miss affair altogether.

JOAN: Oh I see. (*She doesn't. It's all lies anyway.*)

CONRAD: But why – you are asking – why use suction pads at
all? I can't pull the wool over *your* eyes, can I?
(*He laughs, and then she does too.*
     And then, without any interruption in what they are doing,
they 'sing' 'Smoke Gets In Your Eyes' by Bing Crosby, 1935.
Abrupt stop. Music stops.)
I can't pull the wool over your eyes, can I?

JOAN: But what *is* the point of these – what do you call them? –
suction things?

CONRAD: I'm glad you asked that. Some ladies don't, believe it
or not. (*Smile*) Ask, I mean.

JOAN: How foolish!

CONRAD: (*Rolling his eyes*) Some people.

JOAN: Quite!
(*They look at each other, half speculatively.*)

CONRAD: The suction – the vacuum created by the pad, this
pad – when pulled firmly but gently away from the face
creates the gentlest possible – *pressure* –

JOAN: Pressure.
(*Something is going on.*)

CONRAD: (*Smiles*) Exactly. You have it, precisely. And you will
understand that this *pressure* stimulates the tiny blood
vessels which lie beneath the skin, bringing new softness
and a fresher bloom to the face. The skin, so to speak, is
re-vit-al-ized.

JOAN: Really? I mean – truly.

CONRAD: Truly. Hand on my heart, Mrs – ah –
(*He puts his hand on his heart.*)

JOAN: Mrs Parker.

CONRAD: Cross my heart, and hope to die – but it does *more* than revitalize. The pressure, when used daily – daily, mind you – *pats* away, pitter-pat pitter-pat pitter-pats away, any slightest suggestion of excess fat round the line of the chin, slo-o-wly obliterates the very first faint *hint* of crow's feet round the eyes and – moreover –

JOAN: (*Half ironic laugh*) Goodness.

CONRAD: Yes – *moreover* (*Laugh*) – You can use it – you should use it – to apply any lotion or face cream – vanishing cream, that sort of thing.

JOAN: Really?

CONRAD: Because, you see – (*Almost lifts up on his toes*) – because the vacuum, the suction pad, is so designed, Mrs – ah – Parker – that it *propels* the lotion or the ointment deep into the *pores* where it can *properly* do what the chemists designed it to do.

(*'Propels', 'properly', 'pores', said with conscious alliteration, as in the bad reading of a poem.*)

JOAN: Quite a little miracle worker, isn't it?

(*He darts a sharp look at her to see if there is any irony in her tone: there isn't.*)

CONRAD: You have a fine way of expressing yourself, madam.

JOAN: Well it's so important, really isn't it? Proper speech seems – well, nobody appears to bother very much any more, do they?

CONRAD: (*As though admiringly*) How right you are!

(*Iris-out, in a star shape.*
Sheet music covers, 1930s.)

SWIFT CAPTION MONTAGE
Sheet music covers, 1930s.
Music: 'There is a Green Hill', played on gutsy piano-accordion.

EXT. STREET. GLOUCESTER. LATE DAY
The HIKER, *morose looking, but with his eyes shut, his thoughts mastering a near impossible task, finishes playing 'There Is a Green Hill'.*
A moment then:

HIKER: (*Loud, but flat*) Thank you very, very much, sir. Thank

you very, very much, madam.
(*But the few people who are passing take absolutely no notice at all.*)
(*Same tone*) Thank you very, very much, sir. Thank you very, very much, madam.
(*Still they pass, taking no notice.*
   Pan up street. Mix:)

INT. A MUSIC SHOP. SAME STREET. LATE DAY
ARTHUR *at work, notepad in hand, song sheets spread out.*
ARTHUR: (*Sniff*) I don't think you're being altogether fair to yourself, that's all I mean, Mr Barrett.
BARRETT: I think I know what my customers want, you know, Mr Parker.
ARTHUR: 'Course you do, 'course you do. (*Looks at him.*) I expect you listen to the wireless a lot – eh?
BARRETT: Not much time for that. No. Not a lot.
ARTHUR: So you didn't hear the Lew Stone band last night, then?
BARRETT: A bit of it.
ARTHUR: (*Triumphantly*) Well – he played 'Prairie Moon' – and Jack Jackson's just made a recording. They'll be in and out of that door there asking for the sheet music.
BARRETT: No, no. They're not so quick off the mark as that round these parts. (*He seems impatient.*) And in any case – if you don't mind me saying so –
ARTHUR: (*Mock bright*) Go ahead. Go ahead.
BARRETT: Well, if there *is* a call for it, or anything else, I just have to give the wholesaler a tinkle.
ARTHUR: And wait about a week. Whereas –
   (*Ting! From bell on door.*)
   Whereas, if you order, say, a dozen now, then you're ready for –
   (*He stops as shopkeeper sucks in his breath sharply and shakes his head vigorously, then:*)
BARRETT: Excuse me – Can I help you madam?
   (*A woman in her mid-thirties, not especially beautiful, with something hesitant in her manner. She is* EILEEN EVERSON, *an infant school teacher in nearby Forest of Dean.*)

EILEEN: I wonder if – you see, what I'm looking for is . . .
   (*Zoom to* ARTHUR, *staring at her.*
   While BARRETT *and* EILEEN *transact their business,*
   ARTHUR *'sings' 'Seeing is Believing' by Lew Stone in the*
   traditional cinema musical mode.
      The woman and the shopkeeper do not notice this.)
BARRETT: And I'll certainly do my best to get it for you.
EILEEN: Thank you. Thank you very much.
ARTHUR: Is it anything I can help with, Mr Barrett?
BARRETT: (*Shortly*) No.
EILEEN: Shall I pay for it now, or –
BARRETT: Oh, no, when it comes in will do. Give it say – oh,
   ten days. Or a fortnight. Yes, call in a fortnight today, Mrs
   – ah –
EILEEN: (*Embarrassed*) Miss. It's Miss Everson, care of Joyfill
   Junior School, Berry Slope.
BARRETT: Coleford, is that – Miss?
EILEEN: (*Shy*) Near Coleford, yes. Thank you. I'll be – in then,
   in a fortnight.
BARRETT: Very good, Miss. We'll see what we can do.
   (*She goes out of the shop like one who does not know how to*
   make an exit.
      ARTHUR *watches her go with now hungry eyes, then quickly*
   jabs the order book at BARRETT.)
ARTHUR: Right you are, then, Mr Barrett – if you'll just sign for
   what you *have* ordered.
BARRETT: I'm sorry I can't take more, but – (*He shrugs.*)
ARTHUR: (*Urgent*) Hurry up, old man, if you don't mind.
   (BARRETT *looks at him and signs.*
      ARTHUR *gathers up his stuff hastily, looking at the door, tips*
   his hat and scurries out.)
BARRETT: (*As door shuts*) Ride him, cowboy.
   (*Derisively. Fast wipe.*)

EXT. RAIN STARTING. STREET. GLOUCESTER. LATE DAY OR
DUSK
ARTHUR *bobs quickly along, trying to see* EILEEN *up ahead, a*
determined, intent look on his face.
Move on ahead of him to pick out EILEEN. *She comes to the*

HIKER, *who is now playing 'Rock of Ages' on his accordion.*
EILEEN, *hesitatingly stops to listen. But it is starting to rain.*
HIKER: (*Monotonously, flat*) Thank you very, very much, sir.
Thank you very, very much, madam.
(*Closer shot of* EILEEN's *face. She seems curiously moved, and
stands absolutely still.*
ARTHUR, *following, also stops, sufficiently at a distance to
observe both the* HIKER *and* EILEEN. *But his eyes settle on*
EILEEN.
Fast fade.)

INT. JOAN'S AND ARTHUR'S LOUNGE. DAY
Close in on JOAN, *her whole face smothered in a white cream, like a
minstrel mask. She sits, rather tense, bolt upright on a wooden chair,*
CONRAD *leaning in attentively, with a potentially lascivious smile.*
CONRAD: (*Gently*) All on, Mrs Parker?
JOAN: (*Rather timidly*) Yes.
(*He looks closely at her, then seems to catch himself.*)
What's the matter?
CONRAD: Your face – (*turns away*) I beg your pardon, Mrs
Parker –
JOAN: (*Tense*) But what is it? What's wrong?
(CONRAD *looks back at her, frank.*)
CONRAD: Nothing. There's nothing, just nothing *wrong* with
your face at all. It –
(*A calculated pause.*)
JOAN: (*Rigidly tense*) Yes?
CONRAD: It is simply that – I *am* sorry – but, yes, it is a very
beautiful face.
JOAN: *I* don't think you should say that.
CONRAD: Of course not! I was – trapped – for a moment – I'm
very sorry – but you see, day by day, I see face after face,
ladies' faces, you understand – professionally, I mean –
and so I look, I suppose, for a certain *standard* to hold up
as the anatomical ideal.
(*He is leaning in, close.*)
JOAN: (*Almost a whisper*) You think I am beautiful?
(*Fractional pause.*)
CONRAD: (*Evenly*) Yes, yes, I do.

21

(*Pause.*)

JOAN: (*A quiet statement*) You think I am beautiful.
    (*Pause.*)

CONRAD: (*Urgent*) What is your name? Your christian name?
    (*She looks at him, eyes widening in a creamy white face.*)

JOAN: Joan. Joan Parker.

CONRAD: (*Half whisper*) Joan. My name is Conrad. Conrad
    Baker.

JOAN: (*Trembling*) H-hello.

CONRAD: (*Nervously*) What I would like – what I very much
    want to do . . .
    (*He trails off.*
      *She is silent. He runs his tongue over his dry lips, and starts
    again.*)
    Would you mind if I gave you a kiss?

JOAN: (*As though willing*) You want to give me a kiss?
    (*He leans in to do so.*)

CONRAD: With all my heart, Joan.
    (*As their lips touch, she suddenly – with a shriek – slaps him
    hard, once, round the face, with such force, and such surprise,
    that he is knocked right over, falling on to his backside, face
    shocked, mouth open.*)

JOAN: (*Evenly*) You filthy beast!
    (*Fast fade.*)

EXT. STREET, GLOUCESTER. DUSK

The HIKER *finishing 'Rock of Ages' on accordion.*

A moment, and EILEEN, *rather hesitant, steps forward, fumbling in
her purse, and puts two pennies in the hat.*

Pull out – ARTHUR *watching, enraptured.*

HIKER: Thank you very, very much, sir. Thank you very, very
    much, madam.

EILEEN: (*Awkwardly*) It was very nice.

HIKER: (*Startled*) Pardon, lady?

EILEEN: (*Embarrassed*) It was nice – a nice hymn.
    (*The* HIKER *glows.*)

HIKER: (*Too ecstatic*) Sh-shall I play you another one, lady?
    (*She starts to retreat.*)

EILEEN: I – ah –

HIKER: (*Almost shouting*) 'The Old Rugged Cross'! I'll play 'The Old Rugged Cross'!
EILEEN: (*Retreating fast*) No – it's all right – thank you.
(*He starts the sonorous chords.*

    ARTHUR *starts after her, then decides it is hopeless. His shoulders droop, he stares wistfully.*

    He turns back to the accordion player, who is thumping out the hymn.)
ARTHUR: (*Angrily*) Shut up, for gawd's sake! Half wit!!
(*The accordion stops with a strange wail. The* HIKER *looks at* ARTHUR, *blinking, bewildered.*

    The two men hold the look, virtually toe-to-toe.

    Then, strangely, in a sudden spurt of emotion, and without knowing why, ARTHUR *embraces the* HIKER, *who starts to cry.*)

INT. JOAN'S AND ARTHUR'S BEDROOM. DUSK
JOAN *sits at the dressing table looking into the long tilt mirror. She stares and stares at her face. Her finger traces the line of her jaw and cheek bones. Then, in a sudden decisive action, she starts to rub cold cream all over her face, making a sticky white mask.*
Iris-out.

INT. A CHEAP CAFÉ. GLOUCESTER. NIGHT
ARTHUR *watches with puzzled interest, even fascination, as the* HIKER *wolfs down a plate of sausages and chips.*
ARTHUR: How long is it since you had a proper meal, then?
(*The* HIKER *carefully empties every bit of food from his mouth before answering.*)
HIKER: I eat here and there, you know, sir.
ARTHUR: Now and again, more like.
(*More food plunges into the other's mouth.*

    ARTHUR *pushes his plate away, almost untouched.*

    The HIKER'*s mouth, full of food, comically stops chewing, and he stares incredulously at Arthur's plate. Then:*)
HIKER: Aren't you hungry, sir?
ARTHUR: Oh, I'm hungry all right.
HIKER: D-don't you like it . . . ?
(ARTHUR *lights a cigarette, and blows out smoke.*)

23

ARTHUR: (*Not really addressing the other*) When you think about
things – before you go to sleep at night, when your head is
still, and . . . No, I don't want it, you can have it. And
good luck to you, mate.
(*The* HIKER *beams, empties his mouth and 'sings' 'Pennies
from Heaven'.*

*After a few lines he comes to an abrupt stop, he eats some
more sausage, then, bang, starts 'singing' again.* ARTHUR *joins
in.*

Pause. One eats, the other watches.)
Where you going to sleep, then?
(*The* HIKER *pretends not to hear, lowering his head over his
plate.*)
(*Irritated*) Did you hear what I said?
HIKER: Alley.
ARTHUR: What?
HIKER: Where I was playing. There w-was an alley.
ARTHUR: It's coming down cats and dogs! You can't do that!
(*Seemingly unconcerned, the* HIKER *empties his plate.*)
HIKER: Bit of rain never hurt me, sir.
ARTHUR: And stops calling me sir.
(*The* HIKER *nods, looks at Arthur's plate.*)
Here y'are then. Greedy sod.
HIKER: (*Delighted*) Th-thank you, sir.
ARTHUR: Stop it!
HIKER: I've always liked me a sausage. Ever since I don't know
how long.
ARTHUR: (*Irritated*) You don't chew your food proper. Bolting
it like that. (*Looks at him again*) What do you do when –
(*He stops, slightly embarrassed. Then he starts again, almost
talking to himself.*) There was a girl, wasn't there, who gave
you some coppers just before we came in here.
HIKER: Yes.
(*Silence.*)
ARTHUR: She was beautiful. (*Silence.*) She was the sort to make
a bloke feel –
(*He looks at the* HIKER, *who has cleared the second plate.*)
HIKER: She gave me tuppence.
ARTHUR: That's the one. Beautiful, beautiful. You know, the

24

way she held her head and that. The way she walked. S'funny how it can – what are you grinning about, you fool?

HIKER: She gave me tuppence!

ARTHUR: Is that all you got? Didn't anybody else drop a penny in the hat?

HIKER: I didn't do very well. No.

ARTHUR: (*Snort*) You can't live on tuppence. You're doing even worse than I am.

(*The* HIKER *stares at* ARTHUR, *then drops his head – lower and lower.*

ARTHUR, *embarrassed, fumbles in his pockets, and puts a shilling on the table.*)

Here's a bob. Go on – take it. Feel rich!

(*Instead of picking up the coin, the* HIKER *makes a sudden grab for* ARTHUR*'s hand. Much to* ARTHUR*'s embarrassed consternation he tries to kiss it. It is too excessive and slobbery.*)

HIKER: God bless you . . . b-b-bless you.

ARTHUR: Hey! Hey! Stop it, you silly – no! Christ – (*He wrestles his hand back.*) What are you? A nancy boy or something?

(ARTHUR *has got up to go.*)

HIKER: Sorry. Sorry, sir. Sir?

ARTHUR: (*Going*) Sleep on the bleed'n pavement for all I care.

(*And out he goes.*

Stay with HIKER, *forlorn, eyes swelling. Then he picks up one of the plates and licks it clean.*

Pull out to show proprietor of café looking at him in distance, and about to come across and remonstrate.*)

CAPTIONS

Moon over Gloucester.

Pan down to cathedral, silvered in the light mix into streets – 1930s cars, people walking, pub signs, fish and chip shop etc.

Music (without words) is 'Prairie Moon' on piano.

Mix into:

INT. HOTEL PUB BAR. NIGHT

Somebody playing on piano ('Prairie Moon') in big crowded bar, with great panache. Drinks all along the top of the piano, shaking with the vibration. The pub pianist sweeps on, unbroken, from 'Roll Along Prairie Moon' into 'Blue Moon' and then a 'moon' medley. He has a cigarette in his mouth, of course.

Pull out. Eventually picking up a magpie-eyed ARTHUR, *enjoying the piano, looking at the scatter of accompanied women in the bar. He drifts towards the pianist, and leans on piano.*

ARTHUR: Very nice. Very nice.

PIANIST: What? (*Doesn't change expression.*)

ARTHUR: A good medley, this. Very nice.

PIANIST: Umph.

ARTHUR: But heavy on the left hand. That's my only criticism, old pal.

PIANIST: Bugger off. (*Said dispassionately, his hands still thumping the keys.*)

ARTHUR: (*Shrug, moving off*) That's the trouble with you amachewers – too heavy on the left hand.

(ARTHUR, *moving away, sees a blowsy, false-blonde woman standing at the bar, drinking gin and orange, laughing and talking with two middle-aged, working-class Gloucestrians.*

Zoom in on Arthur's eyeline to her painted nails, red lips, overblown voluptuousness.

Back with ARTHUR, *who actually wets his lips, we go with him as he sidles towards the trio, his glass in his hand. As he approaches, their conversation becomes distinct: all delivered in ripe Gloucester accents.*)

JUMBO: Oo, no – we spent the best part of the day down on the sands Ay – and had plenty to yut [*plenty to eat*] an' all.

WILL: We had these gurt bag of doughnuts, see.

MARJORIE: (*Boozy laugh*) Doughnuts!
(*She becomes aware of* ARTHUR.)

WILL: Lovely 'uns, mind. Fresh, real fresh. Straight out of the ovens.

JUMBO: Don't talk to Marj about buns in the oven, for God's sake.
(*They splutter and laugh.* MARJORIE *hooting, gives* ARTHUR *the eye.*)

MARJORIE: No fear there, boys!

WILL: No, but they had more jam in 'em these here doughnuts than any I've sid afore now.

JUMBO: That's right, mind. Quite right. Near nigh half a pound of stro'berry jam packed in the middle of 'um. No word of a lie.

WILL: (*Chipping in*) Anyway – old Alan, thou knows him was off fram there paddling a bit –

MARJORIE: (*Gurgle*) Paddling! Washing his fit, more like!
(*They laugh, and so does* ARTHUR, *calculatedly. He edges forward still more until he is virtually part of the group, though still not really noticed by the two men.*)

JUMBO: One thing's for sure – him didn't need to roll his trousers up. Thoy be already half a yard above his boots, byun um?

MARJORIE: Nice ankles a' got, though.
(*More laughter. Piano still thumping away in the background.*)

WILL: Thou's only got one thing in your yud, Marjorie.

MARJORIE: (*Looking at* ARTHUR) Nice though, yunnit?
(ARTHUR, *grinning nervously, goes to speak.*)

WILL: (*Insistent*) Anyway – him had his doughnut at last, old Alan did. Squatting down on the sand, thick big hanky knotted round his yud to keep the sun off. (*They laugh again.*) 'Mind the pips under thee tith, Alan,' we said. 'Them doughnuts is fill of stro'berry jam.' *Anyway* – him eventually bit into these here doughnut, *snap*, like a bloody old crocodile – and him chewed a bit, chewed a bit – (*mimics horrified expression*) Here! – a' said – *There yunt no bloody jam in mine!*
(JUMBO *is laughing in anticipation.*)

JUMBO: That's what a' said – you should have seen his face!

WILL: Tee! hee! Then – tee! hee! – then Doris shouted at'n – 'No!' her said, 'it's all down your shirt, you dirty bugger!'
(*But though* WILL *and* JUMBO *are laughing at the memory,* MARJORIE, *distracted by* ARTHUR, *does not laugh.* JUMBO *looks at her, puzzled.*)

JUMBO: See, him had bit'n so hard, the jam had squished out in a great sticky lump all down his shirt – and Doris was thinking of her Monday marnin' wash tub.

MARJORIE: (*Half-attending*) Very funny.
(*The two men look at each other. And, comically, at the same time notice by-play between* MARJORIE *and* ARTHUR.)

WILL: Hello, hello.

27

JUMBO: Seen summat, hast Marj?

MARJORIE: *Was* there jam in his doughnut?

> (WILL *and* JUMBO *howl with derisive laughter.*)

JUMBO: Who's thou got thee eye on, Marj?

> (ARTHUR*'s grin is stretched tight with sick embarrassment.*
> MARJORIE *shows momentary embarrassment.*)

MARJORIE: Shut th' up, Jumbo.

> (WILL *and* JUMBO *wink and nudge at each other.*)

WILL: Just say if we be in the woy.

> (*They titter again.*)

MARJORIE: (*Amused, now*) You's always in the woy, Will. That's what we're bin trying to tell tha'.

ARTHUR: (*Hot*) Would you – can I get the drinks in?

WILL: Aye!

JUMBO: Can you? Well – nobody'll say no, d'wit.

ARTHUR: (*Hot*) What'll it be? Same again? (*He looks at their pints of mild.*)

JUMBO: (*Quickly*) I'll have a drop of shart, sir. Whisky.

WILL: And I ool. Whisky. Thanks very much.

> (ARTHUR*'s face registers irritation, quickly controlled.*)

ARTHUR: Right, then. Two whiskies – And you – ah –

MARJORIE: (*Simper*) Marjorie. Gin and orange, love. As per usual.

ARTHUR: My pleasure, lady.

WILL: (*Cackle*) Only doosn't expect anything in . . .

> (MARJORIE *turns on* WILL, *face suddenly hard and vicious.*)

MARJORIE: Kip quiet, Will!

> (*As* WILL *gapes,* JUMBO *laughs, and* ARTHUR *gets the drinks at the bar.*
>
> MARJORIE *suddenly turns and 'sings' 'Zing! Went the Strings of My Heart' by Lew Stone.*
>
> ARTHUR *hands her the gin and orange with a leer and takes up the song.*
>
> She swigs the gin, in a vulgar fashion, then continues 'singing'.
>
> ARTHUR *has edged up to her ear.*)

ARTHUR: (*Urgent whisper*) Have you got a place of your own, duckie?

MARJORIE: Not really, no. My old man's there.

ARTHUR: I've got a car, you know.

MARJORIE: (*Eyes widening*) You got a *car*? Honest?

JUMBO: (*Intruding*) Now! Now! What's going on here? (*With a laugh.*)

MARJORIE: Birds and bees. (*Cackle.*)

ARTHUR: (*Embarrassed*) I dunno about that. My mum and dad never told me.

WILL: You're not from round these parts.

ARTHUR: No, London.

JUMBO: Cosn't see the smoke coming out of 'n?

WILL: What do you do? For a living, I mean.

(ARTHUR *looks at him, a bit offended by such brazenly direct questioning. Then his eyes shift.*)

ARTHUR: I'm in the music business.

WILL: (*Impressed*) Bist?

JUMBO: Brass band instruments – is it? Plenty of bands round here, and in the forest.

ARTHUR: The forest?

JUMBO: Forest of Dean. Just over the bridge a bit.

ARTHUR: Oh. No – not brass bands. (*Straightens, proudly lying.*) I'm a songwriter, actually. (*This is what he most wants to be in the world.*)

MARJORIE: (*Delighted*) You write songs?

ARTHUR: Yes, I – well, yes.

JUMBO: (*Half-suspiciously*) What sart of zongs, ol' un?

(ARTHUR *takes a quick drink.*)

ARTHUR: You know, for dancing and that.

(*He takes another quick drink.*)

MARJORIE: I d'like a good song, mind.

JUMBO: Tell us one.

ARTHUR: What?

JUMBO: One what thee's wrote. Tell us one.

ARTHUR: Oh, well – I –

JUMBO: (*To* WILL) Him ant wrote nern, Will.

WILL: No-o. Unless it's 'Roll Me Over In the Clover'.

(JUMBO *and* WILL, *a little tipsy, roar with laughter.*

MARJORIE *is staring at* ARTHUR *with bright, beady calculation.*)

ARTHUR: That's what *all* the songs are about.

JUMBO: Get away!

ARTHUR: (*Earnestly*) Yes, yes, they are. Thank God!

MARJORIE: They wouldn't put them on the wireless if they was about – you know.

JUMBO: Shagging.

(WILL *and* MARJORIE, *rather shocked, shush him up.*)

(*Sniggering*) 'Lay Me Down And Do It Again'.

MARJORIE: You'll be chucked out, Jumbo.

(*She indicates sign behind bar:* NO SPITTING. NO BAD LANGUAGE. NO GAMBLING.)

ARTHUR: (*Suddenly morose*) They'd stamp it out if they could.

WILL: Who would? Wha's thou on about?

ARTHUR: The people in charge. Them that runs the bloody place.

MARJORIE: They'll never do that! (*Her high, rising, gurgle of a laugh.*)

ARTHUR: No, no – I'm serious. I mean it. They don't want us to think it is very nice. Dirty, they call it.

JUMBO: (*Cackle*) Ay – and I do!

MARJORIE: Never did *me* any harm, boys.

(*Laughter.*)

ARTHUR: (*Doggedly*) I'm serious. It's the truth.

MARJORIE: Oh, we know you're serious, all right. (*Leans in, mock conspiratorial.*) Where's your car, then?

ARTHUR: Outside the cathedral.

(*Roars of laughter. During which, by the door at the far side of the bar,* EILEEN, *looking very nervous, quickly comes half in, looks all about with swift darting glances, and hurriedly withdraws.*

Pick up ARTHUR *as he glimpses her. He quickly puts his beer down on the bar, and abruptly moves after her.*)

(*Muttering*) Excuse me.

MARJORIE: Hey! Hold on a minute –

(*But he has gone and we go with him.*)

CAPTIONS

Outside pub, at night, drawing of ARTHUR *and of* EILEEN, *and streets of 1930s Gloucester. These are rather idealized pictures as on a magazine cover.*

ARTHUR *gets closer to* EILEEN.
Music: 'I've Got a Date with an Angel', without singer.
Mix into real ARTHUR:

EXT. NARROW SIDE STREET. NIGHT
ARTHUR *reaches* EILEEN.
ARTHUR: (*Gulp*) Excuse me, Miss –
    (*She stops, startled, turning to him.*)
EILEEN: (*Frightened*) What is it . . . ?
ARTHUR: Begging your pardon – but I couldn't help noticing
    that –
    (*He stares at her, so enraptured that his words trail away.*)
EILEEN: (*More frightened*) What do you want?
ARTHUR: Oh. I'm sorry. I – well, you went into that pub up the
    road – and I thought something might be wrong and so
    I . . .
EILEEN: (*Rising tone*) If you don't leave me alone –
ARTHUR: (*Quickly*) No! No – you don't understand! I was
    wondering if you needed any help – if I could do anything
    or –
EILEEN: No thank you. I don't need anything. No.
    (*She turns on her heel and walks quickly away.*
       ARTHUR *watches her go, a forlorn expression on his face. He*
    watches her out of sight, sighs. Turns to go back.)

CAPTION
At the moment of turning, ARTHUR *becomes the face of a cowboy*
below the moon on a romantically drawn songsheet, 'Roll Along
Prairie Moon'.
Begin music: Al Bowlly singing 'Roll Along Prairie Moon'.
Mix through to notes forming on staves. Retaining staves mix
through to:

EXT. ARTHUR'S CAR PARKED IN WASTE GROUND. NIGHT
Music: Al Bowlly singing 'Roll Along Prairie Moon'. Moving slowly
closer and closer to the car, music continues. During closing stages
mix to the ungainly, ill-lit grapple on the back seat of the car between
ARTHUR *and* MARJORIE.
Silence – prolonged.

31

ARTHUR *suppresses a sob in his throat.*

MARJORIE: Are you all right, love?

ARTHUR: (*Crying*) Yes. Em – yes – I'm all right. It's just –

MARJORIE: Come on, now. It was worth ten bob, wasn't it?
(*Move close in on* ARTHUR.)

ARTHUR: (*Tight*) Yes.

MARJORIE: Drive us home, then, duckie.

ARTHUR: Get out and walk.

MARJORIE: I'm not bloody walking, mate!

ARTHUR: And I'm not bloody driving!

MARJORIE: Oh, you're a right one, you are. Eyes too big for
your belly, were um?

ARTHUR: Look –

MARJORIE: (*Screech*) Now *you* look, bastard . . . !

ARTHUR: (*Alarmed*) All right. All right. I'll drive. Just hold your
noise.

MARJORIE: I should think so an' all.
(*As they begin to clamber to the front:*)

CAPTION
Front of Arthur's house, sunny and clean.

INT. JOAN'S AND ARTHUR'S LOUNGE. DAY
JOAN *and a couple of women friends are having morning coffee.*
They are called BETTY *and* IRENE, *two women in their thirties, one
with pearl nails, the other with crimson. 'Posh' voices.*

BETTY: And I sometimes say to him, Joan – I really do, I say I
wish *you* went away now and again, like Joan's Arthur
does.

IRENE: What does he say?

BETTY: Oh, he just laughs, the lazy lump. (*She laughs.*)

JOAN: Yes. But at least you know what he's up to, Betty. Not
that Arthur –
(*Fractional pause.*)

IRENE: (*Quickly*) Oh no. Not Arthur. You can be certain of that.
(*She looks at* BETTY, *who looks at her.*)

JOAN: (*Smile, unaware of crossed look*) You can never be *quite*
sure of anything, actually. But Arthur's a good old stick, I
suppose.

32

BETTY: Yes. I like Arthur, in one of his gay moods, especially.
(*Chink of cups on mouths.* BETTY *and* IRENE *exchange quick glances.*)
JOAN: You wouldn't say that if you heard him singing in the bath.
(*They laugh.*)
IRENE: John is the one for that. I think he's trying to crack the mirror or something.
(*They smile, and drink.*)
BETTY: Are you getting any Jubilee mugs or beakers, Joan?
JOAN: Well, the ones *I've* seen have been terribly ugly.
IRENE: It's nice, though. To have something.
JOAN: He's a good old sort.
BETTY: Arthur – ?
JOAN: No, silly. The King.
(*They all laugh.*)
IRENE: They say his father was an awful one for the ladies. Edward the Seventh.
BETTY: Times have changed.
IRENE: Mmm. I wonder.
(*They all look at each other. A faint shadow falls.*)
JOAN: (*Eventually*) There's a lot of silly stuff and nonsense taught to young girls about marriage nowadays. In the magazines, and things.
BETTY: They haven't invented anything better, though.
IRENE: No – and I don't suppose they ever will.
(*A pensive silence.*)
JOAN: Have you ever tried one of those vacuum pad things? You know, for the face.
BETTY: Ab-solutely useless.
IRENE: So I've heard.
BETTY: It just leaves faint red marks on the skin. Stands to reason, really.
JOAN: Where did you buy it from, Betty? A man at the door?
BETTY: Crikey, no. I wouldn't do that!
IRENE: You can't trust that sort of person.
BETTY: I got it at the chemist's. Why do you ask?
JOAN: (*Shiftily*) Only there was a chap up and down here yesterday –

IRENE: You *didn't* fall for it, did you?

JOAN: (*Severely*) No, Irene, I didn't. What do you think I am – a fool?

IRENE: Some of them can be pretty sm-o-o-th, dear.

JOAN: He was quite nice looking, I suppose.

BETTY: I wish he'd call on *me*, then.

(JOAN *and* BETTY *laugh, but they also look at each other, a little shocked.*)

IRENE: Want a change do you, Bet?

BETTY: (*Snort*) Get off. The less of *that*, the better.

IRENE: Oh, I don't know, it's quite nice on a Sunday morning.
(*They simper.*)

JOAN: I think I'd rather have a cup of tea, though.
(*The simper becomes a hoot.*)

BETTY: Do you ever dream of –
(*She stops.*)

IRENE: Listen to the gel. Dream of *who* or *what*, Betty?
(*Two faces fixed on her.*)

BETTY: The Prince of Wales. (*And she claps her hand to her mouth in mock – and yet real – embarrassment.*)

IRENE: Trouble is, I've heard it said he's a bit of a bolshie on the quiet.

JOAN: Oh, everything's going to pot if you ask me. I wouldn't be a *bit* surprised.
(*Fractional pause.*)

IRENE: (*To* BETTY) You don't actually dream that you and he – um – *you know*.

BETTY: (*Embarrassed*) Not *that*, no. But I did dream that we were dancing a foxtrot and – oh, now you'll *tell* everybody!
(*They gurgle with laughter.* JOAN *falls silent first.*)

JOAN: I still think the magazines print a lot of bunk about marriages.
(*The other two stop smiling.*
  Silence.
  A real awful silence.)

BETTY: Yes, well . . .
(*Silence. Slowly bring up music as the three wives look at each other, eye to eye, as though to a pre-arranged signal.*
  In turn, and in chorus, and in difficulty, they 'sing' the

bouncy 'You Rascal, You' as sung by the Blue Lyres at the
Dorchester, March 1932.

In between the verses there are some very lively stretches from
the band: during this – and the effect will be extremely comical –
the three wives sit absolutely stone-cold still looking impassively
at each other. Then Irene 'sings' while the other two act like a
backing group. Another impassive silence during the
instrumental, but then, in unison, they start to rock gently in
their easy chairs in time to the music. Betty's turn to 'sing', then
again, for the final surge of the band after the 'vocal' they revert
to static impassivity. Fade with music fade.)

EXT. COUNTRY ROAD. DAY
*A quiet, sunny stretch between high hedges. Birdsong. A moment of
sweet calm after the aggressive song. Then the drone of a motor car –
and Arthur's vehicle comes into view. A sudden bang! from the
exhaust pipe, and birds fly up from the trees and hedges.
Mix into:*

INT./EXT. INSIDE CAR
ARTHUR *at the steering wheel, his face tight, strained. But as we
watch it brightens. His eyes take light. He smiles.
Traditional wavery dissolve into:*

INT. CORNER OF DANCE FLOOR. NIGHT
*Band, off, playing 'Dancing Cheek to Cheek' (Heaven, I'm in
heaven, etc.)* ARTHUR *and* EILEEN, *in evening clothes, swirl into
full shot. There is an ecstatic, adoring look on her face. They
suddenly stop dancing (while music continues) as though
overwhelmed by emotion, and kiss – gently, then lingeringly, then
with passion. She breaks, with difficulty.*
EILEEN: *(Moved)* Oh, Arthur. Arthur – I love you so. I love you
  so!
ARTHUR: Shh. Don't talk. Don't say anything.
  (*And they come together again to dance.*
    Traditional wavery dissolve into:)

INT./EXT. INSIDE CAR
ARTHUR *coming up in close-up, out of the waves. His eyes, still*

35

*smiling, narrow as he concentrates on the road up ahead. Then he
expels his breath in a low hiss.*
ARTHUR: My Christ. The loony.
 (*Up ahead, through the windscreen, standing forlornly at a
 bend in the road, is the* HIKER.)

EXT. THE OPEN ROAD. DAY
*In mid-shot, Arthur's car approaches and slows and then speeds up
again and passes the watchful, then hopeful, then disappointed*
HIKER.
*Long shot: the last widening stretch between the disappearing car and
the lonely figure at the roadside.*
Move in very slowly to the HIKER, *a single figure in landscape.
Silence. Then sudden warning trill of a blackbird. Silence. His face is
empty now – vacant even. Big close-up. His eyeballs seem unstable.
They suddenly roll upwards, out of control.*
Pull out fast – in a jerk, so to speak – and it is clear that the HIKER
is starting an epileptic fit.
The HIKER *collapses. His heels drum on the tarmac road. His head
thrashes in the long grass and thorn of the verge.*
*Crash in organ, church organ. Then a mighty congregation singing
'Rock of Ages'. Observe the fit, dispassionately. The hymn rolls on.
Move slowly back into close shot of the suffering* HIKER.
*The hymn suddenly dips down, as though to let in a chunk of
another sound. Heels drumming, body thrashing. And, off screen, in
a small space during the hymn it seems, the sudden, surging, German
rant of the Chancellor of the new Reich, Adolf Hitler. Hitler's voice
submerged by the hymn. A mere suggestion.*
The body starts to thrash less as the hymn dies away.
*A car passes then a delivery van with the Bisto Kids poster on the
side. The drivers do not see.*
'Ah! Bisto!' – go with the poster.
Wipe right to left into:

INT. JOAN'S AND ARTHUR'S KITCHEN. DAY
Taking up from the Bisto poster, JOAN *is stirring and tasting a stew
in a big pot on the 1930s electric stove. She decides to add more salt.
Off, the sounds of a car arriving, parking, its doors slamming.
Wooden spoon in her hand. She cocks her head to listen. Sound of*

*key turning in latch of front door. She stands, with a little smile, still
holding the spoon.*

ARTHUR: (*Calls, off, from hall*) Coo-ee!

JOAN: Coo-ee!

> (*She puts the spoon down, wipes her hands on frilly, flowered
> apron, turns – and* ARTHUR *is in the kitchen.*)

ARTHUR: (*Spreading arms*) Home again, pigeon.

> (*She moves to him.*)

JOAN: Safe and sound, darling.

> (*They embrace. Rather mannered, and a bit guilty,* ARTHUR
> *puts her back to arm's length so that he can, smiling, take a
> good look at her, his head slightly cocked.*)

ARTHUR: And how's the most beautiful girl in the world?

> (*She laughs.*)

JOAN: Oh, Arthur.

ARTHUR: I've missed you every minute of the time and every
second of every minute.

JOAN: That's nice.

ARTHUR: And what's my lovey-dovey been doing?

> (*She breaks away.*)

JOAN: Cooking a stew for her big brute of a hubby.

ARTHUR: M-m-m. I can smell it. De-lic-ious! Come on, give us
a kiss.

> (*She is a little irritated.*)

JOAN: Oh, Arthur.

> (*Some of the glow goes out of him.*)

ARTHUR: It wasn't a bad little trip.

JOAN: Did you do well?

ARTHUR: Not bad, not bad. It's pretty open territory, you
know.

JOAN: (*Laugh*) What? The Prairie?

ARTHUR: (*Laugh*) It felt like it, a bit. I needed a lasso, anyway.
Shopkeepers!

> (*She frowns slightly.*)

JOAN: Didn't they want to buy?

> (*His body shows unease as he moves about the kitchen. She is
> watching him through slightly narrowed eyes. There is tension,
> now, between them.*)

ARTHUR: Oh, yes. The usual sort of thing, you know.

(She laces her hands.)

JOAN: Not very well, you mean.

(He shuffles about the kitchen, as though looking for something to distract her attention.)

ARTHUR: Oh, as well as I expected. Next time'll be a lot easier –

(He lifts the lid of the pot on the electric stove.)

Oh, this looks nice, Joanie. My favourite! Mmmm!

(Her expression has not changed.)

JOAN: Only we don't want to draw out *any more* from Daddy's money. Do we?

(He puts the lid back.)

ARTHUR: *Your* money.

JOAN: Yes – but money Daddy worked hard all his life long to save. Very very hard indeed.

(He stares moodily out of the kitchen window.)

ARTHUR: Yes, well –

JOAN: But we don't, do we, Arthur?

ARTHUR: I suppose I could always add another line just so long as it's not door-to-door stuff.

(He turns and looks at her at this point. Her expression changes.)

JOAN: No, Arthur. I don't think I'd like you to do that.

(Encouraged, he smiles.)

ARTHUR: Things'll work out, pigeon. You'll see.

JOAN: I hope so.

ARTHUR: *(Declaims)* 'Every day in every way I am getting better and better.'

(And he beats his chest. She laughs.

Iris-out swiftly to:)

EXT. THE ROADSIDE. DAY

The HIKER, *eyes open, lies calm and still in the grass. He spits out some blood, from where he had bitten his tongue. Gingerly, he feels round his mouth and jaws. Then he puts out a hand and clasps, or touches, the case which carries his piano accordion. And smiles.*

Clip-clop further down the road of a horse and cart.

The HIKER *quickly gets to his feet, brushing himself down. Horse and cart draws up to him. Tentatively, the* HIKER *puts out a thumb, almost pleading. The old man on the cart looks down at him with a smile.*

CARTER: I bent going far, mind!

HIKER: (*Excited*) Anywhere, sir – anywhere!

CARTER: (*To horse*) Whoa there, girl. Whoa, my beauty. (*To* HIKER) Get th'on up, then. And welcome.

(*Grinning with delight, the* HIKER *clambers up alongside the* CARTER.)

HIKER: Very, very kind of you, sir. Very, very kind, sir.

CARTER: Holt on wi' thee zur, laddie. Gee up gee!

(*Clip-clop. The cart rolls on. Move in to* HIKER, *grinning, twisting head from side to side to look over the hedges and fields.*)

HIKER: N-nice. Nice, very nice!

CARTER: Eh?

HIKER: The world, sir. Isn't it a b-beautiful world!

CARTER: (*With conviction*) 'Tis that!

(*Longer shot. Long shot horse and cart and two heads from behind.*

Mixing into – on piano accordion music:)

CAPTIONS
Idyllic: horse and cart and two heads, from behind, clopping towards sunset, music – on accordion, without words – a few bars of 'Roll Along Prairie Moon'. Hold chord, which becomes dissonant. Wipe at same time to same or similar captions as at opening.

CAPTIONS
Detailed, slightly idyllic paintings of leafy suburban street (Metroland) 1930s. A moon silvers the neat villas.
Camera moving from general to particular, ending on one particular window.
No music.
Mix through to:

INT. JOAN'S AND ARTHUR'S BEDROOM. NIGHT
On the mix, ARTHUR, *panting, falls back, love-making finished.* JOAN *lies absolutely still, and quiet.*

ARTHUR: (*Gasp*) Thank you – thank you. (*Pause. He recovers.*

Sadly.) You don't – you don't like it very much, do you?

JOAN: I didn't say anything.

ARTHUR: No – you didn't. Not a word. Not a bleed'n word!

(*She turns over, angrily, facing away from him. He half props himself up on an elbow, and looks down at her.*)

It – Joan? – listen, my love – it isn't meant to be a-a-well, a duty or anything like that and –

JOAN: Let's get some sleep, shall we?

(*Silence. He holds his position. The alarm ticks noisily.*)

ARTHUR: (*Choked*) It – it's supposed – Joan. Joanie? Angel? It's – *paradise*. It's supposed to – like in the songs and, and . . .

(*His words trail off. Is she already asleep?*

Start music, quietly.

Move slowly in to big close-up of ARTHUR. *Right on cue, he starts to 'sing' 'Down Sunnyside Lane' as before.*

When ARTHUR *has completed mime to the first verse, his face goes dead. His lips stop moving. For the first time in the play, the mime 'dries'. The song continues.* ARTHUR's *face slowly relaxes; a glisten of tears. Relentless close-up of* ARTHUR, *crying.*

Music out with a bounce. Sound of ARTHUR's *restrained, wretched tears only.*

And then ARTHUR *stops. The clock ticks fast and loud.*

Slowly pull out. Before camera movement is completed, go to: 'Blue Moon', or similar in 30s song-sheet mode.

Fade out.)

2 'THE SWEETEST THING'

CAPTIONS
Small boys and girls, 1934–5 vintage, on their way through high-hedged lanes and road to the village junior school in the Forest of Dean. A tight, chattering, even sometimes cartwheeling throng. Two eight-year-olds having a conker fight etc. Hopscotch etc.
Coming to the school itself, an old high-windowed, drab building next to a squat church and a graveyard and some fine old oak trees. Before the end of these deliberately 'nostalgic' graphics, bring in sound of (Forest of Dean) children singing 'All Things Bright and Beautiful'.
CHILDREN: (*Singing, exuberantly*)
    All things bright and beautiful,
    All creatures great and small,
    All things wise and wonderful,
    The Lord God made them all –
    etc., etc.
    (*Slow mix during this:*)

INT. VILLAGE SCHOOL. FOREST OF DEAN. DAY
Into actual classroom – the one big one in the school, where about a hundred plus seven- to ten-year-olds are standing at desks and at the front.
Move along faces of the four teachers: the HEADMASTER, *small and fierce and old, a fat woman, an ancient wisp of a woman, and, finally,* EILEEN *from 'Down Sunnyside Lane'. They sing half-heartedly, except for the* HEADMASTER, *but their eyes continually flick-flick over the pupils, except for* EILEEN, *who seems pensive or pre-occupied.*
CHILDREN: (*Singing*)
    The rich man in his castle
    The poor man at his gate –
    He made them high and lowly
    And order'd their estate
    etc.
    (*Huge clatter-clatter as those standing at their desks sit and the*

rest sit on the floor. They dutifully fold their arms behind their backs, and sit bolt upright, eyes front.)

HEADMASTER: Not a word. Not a sound. (*Pause.*) Good.
(*Pause. Opens Bible.*) 'And when he was entered into a ship, his disciples followed him. And, behold, there arose a great tempest in the sea, insomuch that the ship was – '
(*Abruptly, he breaks off and plunges into the body of the class, holds one smirking boy by the ear and slaps his face, strides back and resumes without comment.*)
'Insomuch that the ship was covered with waves: but he was asleep. And his disciples came to him, and awoke him, saying, Lord, save us: we perish.' *One sound! One more sound, that's all*! 'And he saith unto them, why are ye fearful, O ye of little faith? Then he arose, and rebuked the winds and the sea; and there was a great calm. But the men marvelled, saying, what manner of man is this, that even the winds and the sea obey him?'
(*He closes the book. Boredom creeping on to all the young faces.*)
What manner of man is this? What manner indeed! Silence in class!
(*Pause. Backs stiffen, faces stiffen as his eyes rake along the ranks.*)
I have something very important to say.
(*Pause. Suggestion of a sigh on* EILEEN's *face. The* HEADMASTER, *when speaking, goes up and down, up and down, on the balls of his feet.*)
It has come to my attention that some of you boys have been singing 'God Save Our Old Tom Cat', to the tune of the National Anthem.
(*Horrified silence.* EILEEN *barely suppresses a smile.*)
Now, then. I will say this once, and once only. This sort of thing will not do. It will not do at all! And if I see or hear of any nasty little guttersnipe who does it again – (*looks all about*) I shall cane every boy in the school. Every single one of you. Is that clear? Mmm? Is – that– clear?
CHILDREN: Yessir!
HEADMASTER: To make fun of the National Anthem in this way, and to compare His Majesty King George the Fifth to

an old tom cat – and in Jubilee Year too! – well – you ought to be ashamed, thoroughly ashamed. (*Silence as he looks all around, slowly, deliberately.*) You live in the greatest country in the world, bar none. In the greatest Empire the world has yet seen. Bar none. (*Silence.*) Miss Everson will now read to you from Psalm Thirty-five. Listen carefully. Listen ve-ry carefully, or –

(*The 'or' hangs menacingly as, a little flustered,* EILEEN *steps to the big desk and the open Bible.*

All eyes switch to their favourite.

Pan around faces as thirties music starts – intro. to 'You've Got Me Crying Again', recorded by Ambrose.

Back to EILEEN *as she smooths down the page and clears her throat.*

Band music, soft, continuing.)

EILEEN: Psalm Thirty-five. A Psalm of David.

(*Slight pause, music continuing. Closer in to* EILEEN. *She looks up from the Bible, and starts to 'sing' to Elsie Carlisle's vocal of the same recording.*

A pause – band continues – as she looks at the CHILDREN.)

And my tongue shall speak of thy righteousness and of thy praise all the day long. (*She shuts the Bible, and the music stops dead.*)

HEADMASTER: Thank you, Miss Everson. Boys and girls, you will now disperse in a quiet and orderly fashion to your own classrooms. Standard Four will stay where they are at their desks. And no talking!

(*As the* CHILDREN *get to their feet, with much deliberate scraping and bumping, wipe left to right.*)

EXT. A WOODLAND PATH, FOREST OF DEAN. DAY
A smiling and chattering crocodile of seven-year-old boys and girls (Standard One) being taken on 'a nature walk' by their class teacher, MISS EVERSON.

EILEEN: Keep together now, Standard One. Join up at the back, there. I don't want to lose any of you, do I?

(*They like her, and so they laugh. The stragglers close up.*)

Ah, now! Here's a nice little clearing. Isn't this a nice little spot?

CHILDREN: Yes Miss. Lovely, Miss. Ooo yes.

EILEEN: Yes, I think so too! Let's all gather round this nice tree stump. It's like a seat, isn't it?

BOY: Or a teacher's desk, Miss.
(*Laughter.*)

EILEEN: Yes, very like! Shall it be *my* desk?
(*Sounds of delighted assent.*)
All right, then. This is my desk. I'm going to sit here, and this will be my desk.

GIRL: But where be ours, Miss?

EILEEN: Oh, but you've each got a teeny little desk too. Every one of you!

CHILDREN: (*Variously*) Where, Miss? We ant, Miss? Was mean, Miss?
(*She claps her hands.*)

EILEEN: Shh! Shh! Quiet, children, please!
(*They fall silent.*)
Now I want you all to close your eyes.
(*A babble.*)
Close them tight. Very very tight. So that no light gets through. Close the doors. That's right. Have you all got your eyes shut tightly? Have you?

CHILDREN: Yes, Miss. Yes, Miss Everson!

EILEEN: And nobody is peeping? Nobody at all?

CHILDREN: (*Together*) No-o-o, Miss!

EILEEN: (*Smiles*) Then all you have to do now – without opening your eyes, mind! – is to stand *on one leg*!
(*Laughter and shouts.*)
No – no falling down – no laughing – just stand on one leg, doesn't matter which leg – stand on one leg with your eyes locked and bolted shut. Are you doing it?

CHILDREN: Yes, Miss Everson!

EILEEN: Good. Now when I have counted to ten, and only when I have finished counting, you will open your eyes and you will see on the grass a little desk for each one of you.

CHILDREN: Oooh, Miss!

EILEEN: Nobody else will see your own special little desk except *you*. So don't let anybody say you haven't got one, because *they* won't be able to see it. Will they?

CHILDREN: No-o-o, Miss.
(*They have played this game before.*)
EILEEN: I'll start to count. The magic count. Are you ready?
Are you all ready?
CHILDREN: Re-e-eady, Miss!
EILEEN: One – two – *three – four* –
(*Take up the count, so to speak, in rapid dissolve to:*)

INT. BANK MANAGER'S OFFICE. DAY
The MANAGER, *in pin-stripes etc., looking severely across an expanse
of walnut at a nervously morose* ARTHUR PARKER.
MANAGER: *Five* hundred pounds is no small amount of money,
Mr – ah – Mr Parker.
ARTHUR: No. I – no, it isn't. But I thought that in –
MANAGER: (*Cutting in sniffily*) And with all such *large* sums, of
course, the question of adequate collateral cannot, alas, be
evaded.
ARTHUR: (*Blank*) Pardon?
(*Deliberately stylized, the* BANK MANAGER *puts the tips of his
fingers together and smiles icily.*)
MANAGER: Security, my dear sir. *That* is the absolutely crucial
factor in these affairs.
ARTHUR: (*Hopelessly*) Well, you know how I am placed, sir. You
can see what's what and how-do-you-do, eh?
MANAGER: (*Sigh*) Yes, indeed. But you have to understand that
The Bank cannot simply . . .
ARTHUR: I *know* it'll be safe. I'm not frightened of a bit of hard
work. I'm an honest bloke all right.
MANAGER: You see, your wife has a deposit account with this
branch, and if she or you could –
ARTHUR: (*Quickly*) That's hers, that is. Something quite
separate. Her dad willed her that, so –
MANAGER: Yes. But if that could be put up as –
ARTHUR: Don't you bleed'n well understand?
(*The* MANAGER *blinks at him, shocked.*)
MANAGER: Really, Mr Parker. That sort of language will not
help one little bit.
ARTHUR: (*Aggressively*) What *will* help, then? You tell me!
MANAGER: That's what I have been trying to do.

45

ARTHUR: Without dragging in my wife's cash.

MANAGER: Which represents your best – indeed, only – chance of getting an overdraft of the size you are proposing.

(ARTHUR *stares at him, bitterly.*)

ARTHUR: So it's no, then.

MANAGER: (*Spreading hands*) It's nothing personal, needless to say – but as far as The Bank is concerned, you have very few tangible assets.

(ARTHUR *taps his skull, hard.*)

ARTHUR: What abaht this, then? (*When angry or moved, his London accent comes through heavily.*)

MANAGER: Oh, I don't doubt your capacities to –

ARTHUR: (*Cutting in*) *This* (taps head again, *too vigorously*) is what you sell things wiv, mate. It's what's in 'ere that matters. And I know what I'm on about . . .

MANAGER: (*Sigh*) Mr Parker . . .

ARTHUR: (*Sweeping on*) I know the kind of songs that sell, I do. Got an instinct for it. And I get thirty *per cent* of every songsheet I push to the retailer. Nearly.

MANAGER: But *nearly* thirty per cent of sixpence –

ARTHUR: Oh, they're not all a tanner, you know. There's some sheets as – ach, what's the use. What's the good of setting up on your own in the England of today!

MANAGER: The times are difficult, I agree.

ARTHUR: And why? Because of dry rot, that's why. It was salesmanship that made this country great, and it'll be salesmanship that'll *keep* us great. Dry rot. That's what's doing the damage. Dry rot. The stuff you got between your bleed'n ears, old pal.

(*The* MANAGER *gives a comical double-take, then lurches to his feet.*)

MANAGER: Yes, well – I think we've concluded the useful part of our business, Mr Parker.

(*But* ARTHUR *stays firmly seated.*)

ARTHUR: I'll take my account somewhere else.

MANAGER: That is your privilege, of course, sir.

ARTHUR: I expect they'll drag you over the coals, your head office will. When they find out.

(*The* MANAGER *looks at his watch ostentatiously.*)

MANAGER: Ah, well. We all make mistakes, Mr Parker. But now, if you will excuse me, I'm afraid I have another –
ARTHUR: 'Course. I'd settle for a hundred.
(*The* MANAGER, *still standing, purses his lips and shakes his head, mournfully.*)
MANAGER: I'm sorry to have to say that the same difficulties would stand in the way of virtually any amount, sir.
(*As* ARTHUR *stands, indignant, start music.*)
ARTHUR: You mean you'd bring a man down – (*clicks fingers*) just like that? You mean bugger.
MANAGER: (*Cold*) Good day to you, Parker.
(*Music: Roy Fox Band: 'Without That Certain Thing', vocal by Peggy Dell.*
ARTHUR *leans in to him as the song bubbles up into his mouth. The* MANAGER *has more or less ushered the 'singing'* ARTHUR *to the door.* ARTHUR *shakes his arm free, on the verge of violence. The* MANAGER *raises a warning finger and takes up the song. Then:*)
ARTHUR: All right, King Kong. All right. I know my own way out. No need to push!
(*The picture 'turns over' to:*)

EXT. PATH IN WOODS. FOREST OF DEAN. DAY
Emerging out of what seems a thicket – because of a spiral in the narrow path – come three black-faced, booted, weary-tread coalminers, carrying 'bread' satchels and (unlit) carbine lamps. They tramp on together, not talking: a father and two sons – Eileen's FATHER *and* BROTHERS. *Eventually one of them –* MAURICE, *the youngest – speaks:*
MAURICE: Dist thou see thik butterfly?
(*The other two cannot be bothered to answer. In a moment, up ahead, the chatter of approaching* CHILDREN.)
DAD: Hark.
MAURICE: Kids. A yup of kids.
DAVE: They should be in school.
DAD: Ay.
MAURICE: It's what our Eileen'd call a Nature Walk.
DAD: Squit!
DAVE: Thou bist right, Dad!

47

MAURICE: Oh, I dunno. Do um good. Bit of fresh ayer.

DAD: Should be learning their tables, Maurice.

DAVE: Ay. Chunt the sart of schooling *we* had, is it Dad?

DAD: (*Sardonic*) Ay – and look where it got the both on ya!

(*They come face to face with the happy crocodile of seven-year-olds, and* EILEEN.

Many – most – of the CHILDREN *immediately babble 'how be, Mr Everson' and 'hello, Dave', 'how bist, Maurice'.*)

DAD/DAVE/MAURICE: (*Variously*) How be. How bist, o'butty. Well done, little 'un. etc.

(EILEEN *looks a little embarrassed.*)

BOY: (*Smirk*) It's your Dad, Miss!

GIRL: And thy brothers, Miss!

EILEEN: Hello, Dad. Maurice. Dave. Finished early?

DAVE: Sent whum [home], our Eileen.

DAD: Shart working agyun. Bloody disgrace.

EILEEN: Dad!

MAURICE: Not in front of the little 'uns, Dad!

(*The* CHILDREN *fall silent.*)

DAD: (*Embarrassed*) Thoy won't come to no harm if thoy don't hear wuss than that in their lives.

EILEEN: (*Angry*) Come along now, children. Don't dawdle. Keep walking please. Keep in your line.

(*The three* MINERS *stand back to let the* CHILDREN *through.*)

DAVE: (*Jeeringly*) Kip 'em in order, Eileen! Clip their earholes far 'um, o'butty!

MAURICE: (*Embarrassed*) Highsht up, mind, Dave. That chunt fair on her, look.

EILEEN: Quiet children! Don't dawdle!

(*She flashes a scalding look at* DAVE *as they pass.*)

DAVE: (*Calling*) Hurry up on whum, our Eileen. We d'want our tea!

(EILEEN *tilts her nose, on ahead now.*

The three MINERS *are alone again. They resume their tramp.*

MAURICE *looks at* DAVE, *a little nervously.*)

MAURICE: Thou doosn't want to show her up like that, Dave.

DAVE: Her d'want bringing down a peg, our Eileen.

MAURICE: Not in front of her class, her don't. That wasn't very nice, our Dave.

DAVE: Shut thee mouth.

DAD: Hey, hey. None o' that!

DAVE: Dad – him do nag at I wuss than a bloody 'oman!

MAURICE: All I said was –

DAVE: (*Cutting in*) I d'know what thou's said! I don't mean her any harm, now do I? Doesn't be so soft!

(*They plod on in silence. But* MAURICE, *more sensitive, keeps glancing at his brother.*
  Iris-out into:)

EXT. ARTHUR'S CAR ON LONDON–GLOUCESTER ROAD. DAY
Music: bright version (non-vocal) of 'Roll Along Prairie Moon'.
A signpost zooms by – GLOUCESTER 37M.

INT./EXT. INSIDE THE CAR. DAY
ARTHUR, *at the wheel, alone, is whistling angrily, and a bit flat, the same tune as the music fades. There is a bleak expression in his eyes. He stops whistling.*
Pause.

ARTHUR: Bitch. Stuck-up tightarsed *bitch*!

(*Into his angry face, eyes, dissolve.*)

INT. LOUNGE. JOAN'S AND ARTHUR'S HOUSE. DAY
JOAN, *his wife, arms folded, is putting* ARTHUR *down.*

JOAN: No! No, Arthur, no, no, absolutely no. I'm not going to let you waste another penny of that money!

ARTHUR: Joan – listen a minute – just *listen* to me . . .

JOAN: There's nothing new you can say. No, Arthur. You'll have to get a different job or do better at the one you've got.

ARTHUR: With my worldly goods I thee endow!

JOAN: Oh, crikey! Listen to it!

ARTHUR: And vice versa! Vice versa! What's yours ought to be shared and what's mine –

(*Her mocking laugh makes him stop. He advances on her with raised fist. She shrieks and backs away.*)

JOAN: Arthur! Don't you dare! Ar-thur!

(*Rapid dissolve.*)

49

INT./EXT. INSIDE CAR

ARTHUR's *face reliving the scene, hands so tight on steering wheel that his knuckles whiten.*

JOAN: (*Out of vision. Rising scream*) No-o!
    (*Sound of single smack on flesh, off. Gasps, off.*)

ARTHUR: (*Off, choked*) Joan – I didn't – Joan! – I'm sorry – please –

JOAN: (*Off, sobbing*) Get away from me! You cad. You rotten cad, Arthur!

ARTHUR: (*Off*) Don't, Joan. Don't. Oh, don't. Can't you see how low I am –

JOAN: (*Off, snarling*) I can see how *low* you are, all right!
    (*Sharp cut from* ARTHUR's *pained eyes to:*)

INT. LOUNGE. DAY

JOAN *has backed up against the flowered wallpaper, hissing at* ARTHUR.

JOAN: Low. Low. Low. Dis-gust-ingly low.
    (ARTHUR *looks at her, suddenly flat.*)

ARTHUR: (*Quietly*) Please don't say that.

JOAN: (*Articulating deliberately*) Low. L-o-w.
    (*Pause. They look at each other.*)

ARTHUR: Joanie?
    (*Very gently, he puts both his hands on her breasts. She just looks at him. Then, with contempt on her face, she grips both of his wrists and slowly, deliberately, lifts his hands away. They stand, a foot apart, eyes locked.*)

GRAPHIC

Slowly shrink picture so that it is set within the borders of what eventually turns out to be a mock-up songsheet cover.
Within this graphic, ARTHUR *replaces the palms of his hands flat on her breasts.* JOAN *goes rigid then seems to yield.*
Music: Lew Stone Band: 'Isn't It Heavenly'. Al Bowlly sings out of vision. And then in a surge, as the picture narrows even further within its decorative frame of bluebirds and cotton clouds, ARTHUR *rips away at Joan's dress or blouse. Together, pulling at each other, they slide down the wall until they are tangled upon the floor.*
As they make love, the picture diminishes until it is the merest dot set

50

in the lushly romantic song cover of 'Isn't It Heavenly'.
Song comes to an end.

GRAPHIC
As Bowlly's singing finishes, the 'dot' widens on the song sheet very
rapidly until it fills the screen again.

INT. LOUNGE. DAY
No border now.
With contempt on her face, JOAN *grips both of* ARTHUR*'s wrists and*
slowly, deliberately, lifts his hands away. They stand, a foot apart,
eyes locked.
Then ARTHUR *replaces his hands on her body.*
Fractional pause.
Wham! She cracks him round the mouth.
Cut on slow to:

INT./EXT. IN ARTHUR'S CAR ON GLOUCESTER–LONDON ROAD.
DAY
So sharp is the cut that ARTHUR, *at the wheel, seems to blink back*
the force of the blow. His eyes go blank. Then they come alive again
as, through windscreen, he sees GLOUCESTER, 18.

EXT. THE CAR RECEDING, PAST SIGNPOST. DAY
A few chords of 'Prairie Moon'.
Iris-out to:

INT. STANDARD ONE AT THE VILLAGE SCHOOL. DAY
EILEEN *is telling a story to rapt seven-year-olds.*
EILEEN: And so he stepped out from behind the trees and
    looked up at the little window at the top of the tall, tall, tall
    tower that had no door. 'Rapunzel! Rapunzel!' he called,
    softly, just as the wicked old witch had called, 'Rapunzel!
    Let down your hair!' Hearing the Prince's voice, and
    thinking it was the old witch, Rapunzel let down her long,
    shining, golden hair – all the way down, down, down to the
    bottom of the tower. And – (*she looks about*) and –
CHILDREN: (*Eager*) The Prince climbed up!
EILEEN: Yes. Just as he had seen the witch do. He climbed up

to the window on her tresses of hair.

LITTLE GIRL: (*Anxious*) Oodn't it hurt her, Miss?

EILEEN: Oh, no. I don't think so. It was so long and so strong, you see.

LITTLE BOY: (*Impatient*) Go on, Miss. Tell us.
(*Babble of assent.*)

EILEEN: No noise, now, else I won't go on. (*Silence.*) The Prince climbed up, and when he came to the window, Rapunzel stepped back in fear. Oh, she was frightened! She had never seen *a man* before, you see!
(*All the* BOYS *laugh and snigger.*)
Yes – some of you boys do well to laugh. She cried out in fear because she had never seen a man. But his face was so nice, his eyes were so kind, his voice was so gentle, and his hands were so soft that very soon she stopped being afraid. As for the Prince, well – what do you think he felt, Angela?

ANGELA: Him liked her, Miss.

EILEEN: Even more than that.
(*A hand up.*) Yes, Audrey.

AUDREY: Him fell in love, Miss. Rapunzel was his sweetheart.
(*All the* BOYS *laugh and snigger.*)

EILEEN: Yes, Audrey. He fell in love with her, and he asked Rapunzel to marry him. (*Silence. Her face changes.*)
(*Quietly*) It sometimes happens like that, you know. He looked at her, and looked at her, and decided that no one else in the whole kingdom, no one else in the whole world, would be good enough and sweet enough to be by his side when he one day became the King.
(*Fractional pause. Wipe right to left.*)

INT. MUSIC SHOP. GLOUCESTER. DAY

MR BARRETT, *the owner (from before) shakes his head, slowly.*

ARTHUR: You don't remember her? Oh, but surely you do! The last time I was here – fortnight ago –

BARRETT: No. Doesn't ring a bell. Sorry, old man.

ARTHUR: (*Frustrated*) The day you wouldn't order a couple of dozen copies of 'Prairie Moon'.

BARRETT: Of what?

ARTHUR: 'Roll Along Prairie Moon'.

BARRETT: And just as well, too.

(ARTHUR *looks at him, incredulous.*)

ARTHUR: What do you mean? Everybody's whistling that tune now – like I said they would.

BARRETT: They might be whistling it, old man. But nobody's asked me for it. (*Sniff.*) Just like I said.

(*'Ting' as shop door opens.*)

ARTHUR: (*Tartly*) Perhaps they go where they know they can get it, Mr Barrett.

(BARRETT, *turning to* CUSTOMER, *throws remark over shoulder.*)

BARRETT: People who whistle in the streets are not the sort to come in *here*, Mr Parker. (*To* CUSTOMER) Can I help you, sir.

CUSTOMER: Sheet music, please. For the piano.

BARRETT: (*Patiently*) Yes, sir, of course. Was there any particular piece . . . ?

CUSTOMER: Di-da-dum-dee-dee-dee.

(ARTHUR *stiffens.*)

BARRETT: Um. That's – what's the title, sir?

CUSTOMER: 'Roll Along Prairie Moon'.

(*Comical change of expression from* BARRETT.)

BARRETT: Oh, yes. Well –

(*He looks across at smirking* ARTHUR.)

You don't mean '*Blue* Moon'. '*Prairie* Moon'. Di-da-dum.

(ARTHUR *already undoing briefcase.*)

CUSTOMER: Different sart of song altogether. Bit of cowboy in it, see?

BARRETT: (*Flustered*) I'm – ah – I'm expecting some copies at any moment, sir, and if you'd like –

ARTHUR: They've already arrived, Mr Barrett!

(*He flourishes a copy, triumphantly.*)

CUSTOMER: I'll be blowed. That's a bit of luck, ennit?

(BARRETT *glares at* ARTHUR.)

BARRETT: Just the one copy then, Mr Parker. It'll help me out.

ARTHUR: It's not worth my while to deal in single copies, Mr B. . . . As you well know, old man. Dozens and half-dozens, if you don't mind.

CUSTOMER: (*Alarmed*) 'Ere, now – I only wanted the one. Just the one, mind.

BARRETT: Yes, sir. That's quite all right. We were talking about a business matter.

CUSTOMER: Only I don't want half a dozen, do I?

ARTHUR: One copy, sir. And good luck to you.

(*As he goes to hand over the copy,* BARRETT *intervenes re protocol.*)

BARRETT: Pardon me. You have to give it to *me* first, Mr Parker. We don't want to be in breach of the law.

ARTHUR: What law's that then, Mr B?

BARRETT: Please don't call me *Mr B*!

CUSTOMER: Busy Mr B. (*He cackles.*)

BARRETT: (*Sniff*) Any sale of goods in these premises *must* be transacted across *this* counter – (*Takes copy from* ARTHUR, *then gives it to* CUSTOMER.) – One shilling, sir.

CUSTOMER: A bob? Phew – bit steep, ennit?

BARRETT: (*Glaring at* ARTHUR) Too many middle men.

ARTHUR: And too many piddling little shops.

(CUSTOMER *puts down shilling.*)

CUSTOMER: I should have a good old scrap if I were you two. I'll be ref if tha's like.

(BARRETT *picks up coin, icily.*)

BARRETT: Thank you *very* much, sir. Good day to you.

(*Sniggering, the* CUSTOMER *waddles out.*)

CUSTOMER: Da di DAH dee dee DEEH.

(*'Ting'. Customer gone,* BARRETT *and* ARTHUR *look at each other with hostility. Then, by a common shift, and almost despite themselves, they both start to laugh.*)

BARRETT: All right. All right. I'll take half a dozen.

ARTHUR: Don't bankrupt yourself, old man.

(*And they both laugh again, warming to each other.*)

BARRETT: I suppose I could take a dozen. Just about.

ARTHUR: If you could jog your memory on that – ah – that *other matter* you can have them for nothing. With my compliments, old chap.

(BARRETT*'s smile dies.*)

BARRETT: It was my impression, Mr Parker, that you were a married man.

(*Fractional pause.*)

ARTHUR: (*Steadily*) No, sir. I am not married.

(*They look at each other.*)

BARRETT: I can't go giving you a young woman's name and address now, can I? Unless there's a very good reason, that is.

(*Fade.*)

EXT. COTTAGE. FOREST OF DEAN. EDGE OF WOODS. DAY
Approach, and dissolve –

INT. INSIDE. COTTAGE. DAY
Teatime – and DAD, DAVE, MAURICE *and* EILEEN *are seemingly crowded on top of each other in the stuffy little main room with Bible-sized windows.*
The three miners have washed and changed. They are all at a table with patterned table cloth, eating boiled eggs. EILEEN *obviously attending to them. She is pouring tea.* MAURICE *is taking the top off his egg.*

MAURICE: We'd wanna get some more grit for them hens, Dad. These shell is as soft as anything.

DAVE: (*Snigger*) As long as him yunt as soft as thou a'but!

(DAD, *with mouthful of egg, laughs, and has difficulty swallowing.*)

EILEEN: (*With distaste*) Oh, Dad. Not at the tea table. That's not very funny, Dave.

DAVE: 'Bout time we had a few jokes round here.

(MAURICE *is peering at his egg.*)

MAURICE: Holt on a minute! These here egg d'smell a bit off to me.

DAD: Get th'on. Him's as fresh as a daisy.

DAVE: (*Winking at* DAD) Give'n a sniff, our Maurice. Perhaps him bin under the bush a bit too long.

(*Gingerly,* MAURICE *bends to put his nose over the egg.*)

MAURICE: Him a' got a pong . . .

(*Abruptly,* DAVE *leans across and taps* MAURICE *hard and neatly on the back of the head.* MAURICE's *nose plunges down into the hot egg. Consternation! – it is extremely painful. The egg sticks to his nose. He grabs it away, howling 'hot! bloody hot!'*

DAVE *and* DAD *double up with laughter.*

Hands to his nose, which is dripping with hot yolk,
MAURICE *lurches to his feet and dances with pain. Tears stream
from his eyes.*

DAVE *is laughing so helplessly, and tilting his chair back so
far, that he overbalances.*)

DAD: Hoo, hoo, hoo. Funniest thing I a' sid in years!

DAVE: (*Howl*) Give'n a sniff, Maurice!

MAURICE: (*Shout*) You could a's scarred me for life, you great
soft bugger! Thik egg was *boiling*!

(*He plunges out to the back kitchen to wash his face, provoking*
DAVE *and* DAD *to fresh laughter.*

Fix on EILEEN*: she had half-smiled at first, then got angrier
and angrier, but held it down inside.*)

EILEEN: (*Evenly*) Thank God Mum didn't live to see *that*
exhibition.

(DAD *looks at her, almost guiltily.*)

DAVE: Leave our Mam out of it!

EILEEN: (*Evenly*) This house is getting more and more like a
pig-sty.

DAVE: Ay. Well, thou's want to clean it up a bit!

DAD: (*Guiltily*) Highsht up, our Dave. No call for that.

DAVE: Tell her to stop nagging I, then!

EILEEN: I'll tell you this, Dave. I'm not going to put up with
your lip much longer.

DAVE: (*Sullen*) Cont you take a joke, then?

EILEEN: Joke! Is that what you call it!

DAD: Now, now. We don't want no argyments at the table.
Let's have a bit of peace.

(DAVE, *trying to ingratiate himself with* EILEEN, *winks at her.*)

DAVE: Hark at Ramsay MacDonald there.

(*But she will not smile.*)

EILEEN: I'm not going to wash and cook and clean and do a
day's work if there aren't some changes in this house.

DAVE: A day's work! Is that what thou's call it – playing with a
yup of kids!

DAD: (*Warningly*) Dave!

(*Too late – something snaps in* EILEEN.)

EILEEN: (*Shout*) You ignorant sod! (*She rises inflamed.*)

56

DAD: Hey – language!

DAVE: Don't you speak to me like that.

EILEEN: Ignorant is what I said and ignorant is what I meant!

DAVE: Now look – !

EILEEN: No, *you* look. You come home half-cut whenever you've got a couple of bob in your pocket –

(MAURICE *comes back in, a red ring round his nose caused by the hot eggshell.*)

MAURICE: Look at what thou's done to my nose!

(*Which sets* DAVE *off again into hoots of laughter.* MAURICE, *angry, hits out at him.* DAVE*'s expression changes instantly. He puts his fists up, and looks venomous.*)

DAVE: (*Hiss*) If thou's want one, mind, our Maurice.

(MAURICE *backs away, nervously.*)

DAD: Not in the house! Not in the house!

EILEEN: (*Angrily*) Not anywhere – Dave! Stop it!

DAVE: Him yunt going to hit I!

MAURICE: Well, look at my nose, then. Look at'n!

(DAVE *still advancing.*)

EILEEN: (*Shout*) Dave! No!

EXT. OUTSIDE COTTAGE. DUSK. DAY

Pulling back swiftly. Inside, EILEEN *screams. At end of camera movement Arthur's car comes slowly up the lane, wheels crunching on earth and old ashes. The car stops, at a distance from, but with a view of, the cottage.*
Start music.

INT./EXT. INSIDE CAR. DUSK/DAY

ARTHUR *switches off the engine and stares, stares at the cottage through his windscreen.*
Move into close-up of ARTHUR, *music continuing: 'Dreaming a Dream' with the Ray Noble Orchestra and Al Bowlly vocal. As* ARTHUR *'sings' of love and devotion, dissolve – song continuing – to:*

INT. THE COTTAGE. DUSK

DAVE *and* MAURICE *exchanging punches – and it is obvious that* DAVE *is much rougher and much stronger.* EILEEN *is trying to stop them.*

Al Bowlly's words ironically contradict the scene before us.
Thump! Crack! And MAURICE *goes down, spitting blood.* EILEEN
scratches at DAVE's *face with her nails.*

INT./EXT. INSIDE CAR. DUSK
ARTHUR *still 'singing'. Music stops. Pause.*
Slam of door from house. Then EILEEN, *distressed, comes running
out into the lane.* ARTHUR *stiffens.*

EXT. OUTSIDE COTTAGE, AND THE LANE. DUSK
EILEEN *is too distraught, it seems, to pay any attention to the car.
She runs straight past it, and on down the lane or track that leads to
the woods.*
ARTHUR *gets out of the car, puzzled, unsure, and, still holding on to
the car door, looks at the cottage and then in* EILEEN's *direction.*
DAVE: (*Shout, from cottage door*) Eileen! Come th'on back – him
    yunt hurt! Eileen!
    (*A pause, a mutter. And the door shuts again.*
        Move in to ARTHUR. *He seems not to know what to do.
    Then he shuts car door, frowning, and walks down the lane in
    the direction* EILEEN *has just taken.*
        Fade.)

CAPTIONS – SUNNYSIDE LANE, AS BEFORE
Night in Metroland under a silvery moon.
Music: 'Down Sunnyside Lane' (without words).
At window of Arthur's house, dissolve:

INT. LOUNGE. JOAN'S AND ARTHUR'S HOUSE. NIGHT
Music slowly fades.
JOAN *is sitting alone, hands laced together, the curtains still open, in
near-darkness. Move slowly in so that her eyes gleam in near close-
up. Then, extraordinarily, she speaks the words of 'Prairie Moon'
with the quiet intensity of a prayer. She is under stress and her
emotion grows as she mimes the words.* JOAN *stops, then puts her
hands together in open prayer.*
JOAN: I need your tender light
    To make things right
    You know I'm so alone tonight

Far away shed your beams
On – on – (*She stops, then gets it out.*) On Arthur.
(*Pause as long as dare. Her foot starts to jig, angrily.*)
(*Eventually*) The silly bloody fool!
(*In a sudden angry twitch she gets up and shuts the curtains.
Which wipe screen to:*)

EXT. THE WOODS NEAR COTTAGE, FOREST OF DEAN. NIGHT
Trees – trees – trees, washed by moonlight.
Crunch, rustle, crunch of footsteps in undergrowth. ARTHUR *comes
into shot, looking a little furtive. He stops. His breathing stops.
Follow his eyeline – against a tree, and turned to face the tree rather
like a child playing hide and seek and counting to a hundred, is a
forlorn* EILEEN. *She has been crying.*
ARTHUR *watches, not daring to move.*
Mosaic-like dissolve to:

CAPTIONS
*Classic-style pen and ink drawings of the Brothers Grimm fairy tale,
Rapunzel, showing prince watching girl at window of tower in the
forest.*
EILEEN: (*Voice-over*) A handsome young Prince was out riding
    in the deepest part of the forest one day when he heard a
    young maiden singing at the window of a high tower that
    had no door.
    (*Mosaic-like dissolve to:*)

EXT. THE WOODS. NIGHT
Scarcely daring to breathe, ARTHUR *steps a little nearer and a little
nearer to* EILEEN – *very, very slowly, and with much tension.
During* ARTHUR'*s ultra-cautious approach, the gentle voice-over
narrative continues.*
EILEEN: (*Voice-over*) So sweet was the maiden's voice, and so
    enchanting was the glimpse of her pale face at the high
    window, that the Prince fell in love with her at once. He
    knew that he could not rest until he had won the maiden
    for his own.
    (*Silence. An owl hoots, long, low and thrilling.*
    A yard away from her now, ARTHUR *puts his slow foot down*

on a dry twig: snap!
      EILEEN, *frightened, whirls round to face him, hair awry,*
      face still wet with tears.)
EILEEN: (*Gasp*) Oh!
ARTHUR: (*Whispering*) Don't – don't be frightened . . . !
EILEEN: (*Frightened*) Who are you? What are you doing!
ARTHUR: Eileen.
EILEEN: What do you want! How do you know my name!
ARTHUR: (*Blindly*) Eileen.
EILEEN: (*Shrills*) Go away! Leave me alone!
ARTHUR: Don't. Please don't.
      (*Something in his voice calms her. She 'focuses' on him, and*
      lets go of the tree trunk.)
EILEEN: I've seen you somewhere before – ?
ARTHUR: (*Thick voiced*) Yes. In Gloucester. At the – in the
      music shop and in the – afterwards, in the street . . .
      (*Swallows.*) There's a song – Like in a song –
EILEEN: Pardon?
ARTHUR: They tell the truth, songs do. (*He steps forward.*)
EILEEN: (*Tense*) Stay where you are! Please!
      (*He stands rooted.*)
ARTHUR: I've been looking for you.
      (*She stares at him.*)
EILEEN: For me?
ARTHUR: I've been looking everywhere for you. Everywhere.
EILEEN: I d-don't underst–
ARTHUR: You've been in my head, Eileen. And in my heart. In
      my soul.
      (*Silence. She stares. He puts his hands up in a little gesture of*
      helplessness, then lowers them, pathetically. He whispers.)
      I want to talk to you. Please let me talk to you.
DAVE: (*Shouting, off*) Eileen! Ei-leen!
ARTHUR: (*Stiffens*) That's not your – your husb–?
EILEEN: (*Quickly*) My brother. It's my brother.
ARTHUR: (*Agitated*) But I've got to talk to you . . .
DAVE: (*Off*) Doosn't be so soft, Eileen! Come th'on back!
MAURICE: (*Off*) Ei-leen! Where bist!
EILEEN: I don't even know who you are, or nothing.
DAD: (*Off*) Dave – Maurice – stop shouting – she'll be back!

ARTHUR: (*Urgent*) Arthur. I'm Arthur. And I love you!
EILEEN: (*Embarrassed*) Don't be silly.
>   (*The three* MINERS *come into view. They stop, looking at*
>   ARTHUR, *at* EILEEN.)
DAVE: (*Crudely*) Hello, hello. What's this, then?
>   (ARTHUR *turns and looks at the three men.*)
ARTHUR: Good evening, gentlemen.
>   (*The three look at each other.*
>   *Start music. They sing.*)

THE WOODS, CHOREOGRAPHED
As they do, the woods change colour, being bathed in different lights,
theatrically.
Music: 'Couldn't Be Cuter', Lew Stone with vocal by Al Bowlly.
The THREE MINERS *'sing' 'Couldn't Be Cuter' and, to the bounce*
of the music, they approach. ARTHUR *looks at* EILEEN, *then smiles*
and takes up the song.
As the band takes over the THREE MINERS *give a little dance.*
EILEEN *steps clear of the tree as* ARTHUR *and the* THREE MINERS
reprise the chorus.
By the end all five are at their original positions.

EXT. THE WOODS. NIGHT
DAVE: (*Crudely*) Hello, hello. What's this, then?
>   (ARTHUR *turns and looks at the three men.*)
ARTHUR: Good evening, gentlemen.
>   (*The three look at each other, then*)
DAD:(*Suspiciously*) Everything all right, our Eileen?
>   (*She looks at* ARTHUR.)
EILEEN: Yes, Dad. This is – Arthur. He's –
ARTHUR: I'm a friend of Eileen's. That's my car back there in
>   the lane.
DAVE: (*Impressed*) Oh, I see. Got a car, have you – sir?
ARTHUR: I thought we'd all go for a little drive.
>   (DAD *looks down at his clothes.*)
DAD: Oh, now. I should wanna be togged up summat different
>   to this.
ARTHUR: (*Quickly*) That's all right. I'm not one for show.
DAVE: (*Wickedly*) No – but our Eileen is, mind!

(*They all laugh, tensely.*)

MAURICE: Well – what be we standing out here for?

DAD: (*Sotto voce*) Ask'm in for a cup of tay, Eileen.

DAVE: Ay. And a boiled egg!

(*The three men titter, like children.*)

EILEEN: (*Hesitant, to* ARTHUR)Would you like –

ARTHUR: (*Eagerly*) That's very nice! Yes – thanks awfully.

DAD: (*Worried*) Take us as you find us, mind.

ARTHUR: Oh, no ceremony. No ceremony at all.

(*Wipe left to right slowly.*)

INT. LOUNGE. JOAN'S AND ARTHUR'S HOUSE. NIGHT

JOAN *is shutting curtains. Turns into dark room then switches on the
standing lamp. She sits on settee, agitated. Lights a Craven A
cigarette, hand shaking. She blows out smoke.*

JOAN: (*To herself*) Come on, Arthur. Where are you?

(*Restless, she gets up and switches on the wireless. After warm-
up, Lew Stone's signature tune, 'Oh, Susannah' and the voice
of late Lew Stone introducing himself. She listens for a while,
then, very agitated, switches off.*)

INT. HALL. JOAN'S AND ARTHUR'S HOUSE

JOAN *goes out into hall. Looks at telephone, hesitates. Then dials.*

JOAN: (*Eventually*) Irene? Oh, I'm glad you're in. Yes – it's
Joan. No, I'm on my own, actually. Arthur is – (*slight
pause*) – one of his little trips, you know. At least – (*she
stops*) – no, no – nothing's wrong. Nothing's wrong
whatsoever. I was – well, I was just wondering if you were
– if you would like to pop round or – oh. No, no.
Nothing's wrong. What *could* be – Arthur? No – he's *fine*.
Ab-so-lutely top hole. Some other time, then. All right,
Irene. Enjoy yourselves. Yes. 'Byee.

(*She puts phone down, her face grim. Then she looks at herself
in the hall mirror. Gingerly, she touches her cheek bones, and
then the contours of her face.*)

Arthur. Don't go. Don't leave me.

(*Her eyes suddenly well with tears.*)

INT. STANDARD ONE. VILLAGE SCHOOL. DAY

EILEEN *orchestrating 7-times table at front of class.*

CHILDREN: Three-sev-ens-are – *twen*-ty-one. Four-sev-ens-are – twen-ty-eight. Five-sev-ens-are – thirty-five. Six-sev-ens-are – forty-two. Sev-en-sev-ens-are – forty-nine.

EILEEN: Seven sevens.

CHILDREN: Are forty-nine.

EILEEN: Seven sevens are forty-nine. That's a very good one. Seven times seven. We'll stop there and come back to it again. Seven-sev-ens-are – forty-nine. Just once more.

CHILDREN: Sev-en-sev-ens-are – fort-y-nine.

EILEEN: That's very good. Now, remember that. I shall ask one or two of you what seven sevens make during our story.
(*Rumble of noise.*)
Except that you won't get a story unless you sit ab-sol-ute-ly still and ab-sol-ute-ly quiet.
(*Automatically, they fold their arms behind their backs and sit bolt upright.*)
That's good children. Now – I want to hear a pin drop. I want to hear it drop half a mile away. Listen?
(*Silence. Her eyes, though, are sparkling.*)
Seven sevens are forty-nine. But what do seven dwarves make?

EXCITED VOICE: Snow White, Miss!

EILEEN: Quite right. Snow White and the Seven Dwarves. Quiet, now! Or we'll do some more of our tables.
(*An excited silence.*)
All right, then. That's good. That's very, very good. (*She opens the book on her desk.*) Once upon a time.
(*Sharp cut.*)

INT. HALL. JOAN'S AND ARTHUR'S HOUSE

JOAN *looks at herself in the hall mirror. Gingerly, she touches her cheek bones, and then the contours of her face.*

EILEEN: (*Voice-over*) Mirror, mirror on the wall, who is the fairest one of all?
(*Sharp cut.*)

INT. ROOM ABOVE PUB. GLOUCESTER. DAY

ARTHUR *shaving in small wash basin, half-lathered, peering into tiny mirror. And happy. Stretching his skin for the razor, he hums and dah-dees a few bars of 'Prairie Moon'. He finishes. Dabs at his face a bit. Then winks at himself.*

ARTHUR *sings a few lines from 'Couldn't Be Cuter' in his own voice, no music and utterly tuneless.*

Hammering knock on door.

OLD WOMAN'S VOICE: (*Off*) Hurry up, if you want any breakfast, Mr Parker! It's five to ten!

ARTHUR: Coming! (*Happily yodels*) On my wa-ay, Mrs A! (*Picture 'turns over'.*)

INT. DINING ROOM. THE PUB ('HOTEL'). GLOUCESTER. DAY

Four commercial travellers completing late breakfast. Three of them in a bleak mood.

TED: There's no reason to stay, but (*chew*) not when you work it out (*swallow*) when you really get down to brass tacks. (*Very gloomily spears some bacon.*)

BERT: (*Glum*) There's a lot of things about England I'd miss.

ALF: Like what, though? Not the bloody weather. Pardon my French.

BERT: Well . . . oh, I dunno. It's sentiment, really.

TED: Grumbling. That's what you'd miss. The sound of chaps grumbling and moaning. (*Grinning quietly to himself,* ARTHUR *wolfs down some slippery fried egg.*)

BERT: What we want is someone like that I-talian.

TED: Mussolini.

ALF: Anybody'do – so long as they rewarded a bit of hard work. (*Sniff.*) For the hours I put in, door to door, selling what is in fact a very good set of brushes – well, in any other country, in any other country in the world –

TED: (*Cutting in*) You'd be on a thousand a year. Or even more.

ALF: Exactly. But 'salesmanship' – it's a four-letter word in England.

TED: In America –

ALF: Ah, now you're talking!

TED: Over there, the self-same encyclopaedias I'm pushing are

the sort of – whatdtheycallit? – *franchise* that would allow
me to change my car every eighteen months if I felt like it.

ALF: They say Australia's wide open to.

BERT: But the pubs shut there at half-past seven in the evening.

ALF: That right?

BERT: Terrible, ennit! (*Snorts.*) But they don't slam the door in
your face like they do over here. They just don't want to
listen, do they! It's bloody heartbreaking.

ALF: Pardoning your French.

BERT: I mean – I go round shop after shop with this crockery –
very nice line – Jubilee design, spot on – oh, yes – but you
get some smarmy little creep in suede shoes turning up his
nose: 'Not our line, old chap,' you know the sort of balls.
Well, it's heartbreaking. That's the word *I* use. Heartbreaking!

LANDLADY: (*Approaching*) Everything all right, gents.

ALL: Very good. Thank you.

(*Beaming, she goes on through.*)

BERT: Bloody muck. Wouldn't give it to my old dog.

ALF: I like my bacon as thick as my thumb. This is more like an
ice cream wafer. Look at it!

(ARTHUR *still looking dreamily happy.*)

TED: When you work it out – taking all things into the
reckoning – we'd all be better off emigrating. This country
is going to the dogs. We picked the wrong side in the war,
if you ask me.

ALF: Your German is a very good soldier.

BERT: And a good chemist an' all.

TED: I mean, we've often met up in different towns and cities –
don't we, though? – and every . . .

ALF: Bristol last time. Wasn't it?

TED: Right. And it's always the same story. Always thumbs
bloody down, eh chaps? Thumbs bloody down. And today
won't be no different, you mark my words. What do you
think, Arthur?

(ARTHUR *has an inappropriately ecstatic look on his face, and
does not respond.*

*As the other three slowly realize this, comically, they one by
one stop eating to stare at him.*

ARTHUR *surfaces rather guiltily.*)

ARTHUR: What was that? What were you saying?

TED: I was saying we'd all do better for ourselves in some other country.

ARTHUR: What – leave England?

ALF: Blimey Arthur – where you been?

BERT: Don't suppose you're doing very well in your particular line are you, Arthur? So you was saying.

ARTHUR: Not doing very well?

TED: (*Snigger*) Wake up, old boy.

ARTHUR: I'm doing very well. Very very well indeed.
(*They are shocked. This is almost a breach of ethics.*)

ALF: (*Swallow*) Being sarkey, are you?
(ARTHUR *looks at him.*)

ARTHUR: Sarcastic? No – not me! I'll tell you something – (*very emphatic*) – everybody who has ever lived in the entire history of the world would want to be me if they could only know what I felt like inside. And that's the truth!
(*A shocked silence. The three others look at each other.*)

TED: Come on, Arthur. Pull the other one!

ARTHUR: That's the trouble with you lot. You walk around with grit and gravel in your eyes. You can't see what a beautiful world it is we live in. No – what are you gawping at – *beautiful* – and it *is*, it's shining, the whole place, *shining*. Can't you see?

BERT: Been drinking, Arthur?

ALF: Bit of skirt, more like.
(*They snigger.*)

ARTHUR: Go on, have a bleed'n snigger. Enjoy your acorns.

TED: Hey. Hey. No need to be offensive, old chap.

ARTHUR: Years and years, I've sat at tables like this with company like yours in places like this, and never once seen it for what it is –

ALF: Coo!

ARTHUR: I've had my ups and downs. We all have. I've – ah – well, I've sniffed around the ladies here, there and everywhere –

TED: You can say that again, old sport.

ARTHUR: I'm not denying it. But – all the time, without me knowing it – all the time there was this bleed'n cotton wool

between the inside of me and the outside of me. Know
what I mean?

BERT: Sounds like St John's Ambulance –
(*Titters.*)

ARTHUR: Ha bloody ha ha. *You* can't see, Bert, because you've
still got all that padding around you, packed around you.
And you, Ted. And you have, Alf.
(*The three look at each other, a little disturbed.*)

ALF: (*Hesitant*) What exactly are you on about? Sounds a lot of
mumbo-jumbo to me.

ARTHUR: Well, it would, wouldn't it?

ALF: (*Hostile*) Whatdyamean?

ARTHUR: Because – (*shrugs*) – because – well – you don't know
the young lady in question, do you?
(*The three are very relieved.*)

ALF TED BERT: A - ha!
(*Start bouncy music: 'Yes, Yes! My Baby Said Yes, Yes!', by
Ambrose, vocals by Sam Browne and backing singers.*)

ARTHUR: (*Sheepish*) It's impossible to explain. It's not the sort
of thing you can put into words.

ALF TED BERT: (*In unison*) Oh, yes it is!
(ARTHUR *looks at them, frowns, then opens his face in a big,
sunny grin. He 'sings' 'Yes, Yes! My Baby Said Yes, Yes!'
while the other three provide the 'Do-waa' backing.*
     *As the band bangs on, all four of them, in unison, push back
their breakfast plates, finished. A moment's silence – music
out.*)

TED: Did you get your hand up her skirt, Arth?
(ARTHUR *looks at him blankly.*)

BERT: Or a bit of the other in the back seat!
(ARTHUR *stares in horror.*)

ALF: Nice big tits, has she, mate?
(ARTHUR *lurches to his feet, struggling to speak.*)

ARTHUR: You filthy – you dirty little . . . I ought to have known
better! As if you – as if people *like you* ach! – You disgust
me!

TED: Hey – hey – no offence, now.

ALF: (*Nervously*) No animosity intended, old chap.
(ARTHUR *sways above table, trying to put words to a dream, or*

67

to an old ache.)

ARTHUR: (*Thickly*) Everything I've . . . everything I've ever
dreamed . . . everything I've ever hoped for – longed for –
(*hits his chest as though in pain*) – deep inside – right inside
me here, in my heart – Everything!
(*He has to stop, eyes rimming with hot tears. The other three try
to look every which way, horribly embarrassed.*)

BERT: (*Quietly*) We didn't know, Arthur. Now did we?
(ARTHUR *looks at him angrily, recovering.*)

ARTHUR: No! And you never will!
(TED *looks pointedly at his watch, and goes to get up.*)

TED: Ah, well. The grindstone beckons . . .
(*The others make assenting murmurs, but a surge of words
suddenly comes to* ARTHUR, *who holds them.*)

ARTHUR: Couldn't you hear yourselves, though? And can't you
look at the faces in the street, or on the doorstep? What's
wrong with them! Something is, something's wrong – must
be. We weren't put here for all this woe and belly-aching
and and . . . Dear God, I wish I was good with words!
(*Inspiration strikes. He lifts up his briefcase.*) It's all in here!
Of course it is! Months and months I been carrying this
stuff around – these songs – all these lovely songs – I've
always believed in 'em. Oh, yes. Faith in the goods. Well,
like you with your brushes, or your crockery or – yes,
you've got to believe in what you're selling, and me, I'm a
salesman, always wanted to be, never wanted to be
anything else.
(*They almost visibly straighten their shoulders, sharing the
creed.*)
But I didn't *really* know how it was or why it was that I
believe in (*slaps case*) what's in here. There's things that is
too big and too important and too bleed'n simple to put in
all that lah-di-dah, toffee-nosed poetry and stuff, books
and that – but everybody feels 'em. Or ought to. And they
know it, they bloody well know it when the chance comes
along!

TED: (*Incredulous*) What? Them songs?

ARTHUR: (*Ignoring him*) I'm not what you call a clever man, and
I've had a bit of Jerry shell in my bonce since I was sixteen

years old in the effing trenches – cor, that was a bloody
lark! – but we had something, we stuck it out, and it was
what we sang – oh, yes – worth more than a dry blanket,
they was . . . them songs. But that's not the half of it. It's
not just packing up your troubles in your mucking kit-bag,
no sir, no sir, no bloody fear, sir – arseholes to that! It's –
it's – (*He gropes for words like one gasping for air.*) Blimey, I
can almost taste it! It's looking for the blue, ennit, and the
gold. The patch of blue sky. The gold of the, of the bleed'n
dawn, or – the light in somebody's eyes – Pennies from
Heaven, that's what it is. And we can't see 'em, clinking
and clinking, all around, all over the place . . . just bend
down and pick 'em up!

TED: (*Snigger*) Pennies aren't much good to me.

ALF: Shh, Ted. Listen a minute.

(ARTHUR *undoes his briefcase and takes out bundle of
songsheets.*)

ARTHUR: Christ knows, we're not here for very long. I've seen
blokes – well, you wouldn't credit what I've seen. All their
pipes and tubes hanging out. Bloody hell, you say, bloody,
bloody *hell*, if there's a God, and if he allows this, then he's
a – a – well, I won't say it. I won't say the word. (*Almost
shudders.*) Except it's something *we've* made, or them that's
in charge, them that's always making a bleed'n mess.
Bastards. They'll lock a man up for flashing his ding-a-ling
on Barnes common and pin a medal on his chest if he
blows up a thahsand women and kids! Oh, I've seen it, I
have. (*Too distraught now.*) The things I've seen, the
terrible, 'orrible, ghaastly fings I've witnessed –
(*He sucks in his breath with a huge, juddering sob.*)

BERT: (*Concerned*) Steady old man. We know what you mean. I
was out there an' all.

TED: (*Savagely*) And it's nothing to what we're going to see!
(*Somehow, a big smile breaks through* ARTHUR*'s tears.*)

ARTHUR: Somewhere – see? – S-somewhere the sun is shining –
And do you know where? Inside yourself! Inside your own
head! That's what I found out last night!
(*The others give each other 'a-ah' looks.*)
As soon as I saw her – there's something – it's like as

though she was *hesitating* with her look and her walk, know what I mean? No. You don't. I shan't mention the lady's name. No fear. It's what she's sparked off inside *me*, you understand. Put the real meaning into them songs – I always knew they told the truth. And they do. They bloody well do! (*He looks at them, and is suddenly embarrassed.*) (*Mumbles*) Pardon me for speaking out of turn. (*Awkward little silence.*)

ALF: (*Puzzled*) But them songs – (*He stops.*)

TED: Half of 'em were dreamed up in a back office by a couple of Jew-boys with green eyeshades.

BERT: It's just a business, Arthur.

ARTHUR: (*Very angry*) You're ignorant! Ignorant!
(*He grabs up the songs and shoves them back into his bag.* TED *is half-amused, in a nasty sort of way.*)

TED: By the way, Arthur. How's the wife?
(ARTHUR *freezes, like one paralysed. Then:*)

ARTHUR: (*Evenly*) Why don't you get your false teeth seen to, Ted? They keep slipping when you talk, you know. That aeroplane glue must be wearing off.
(TED *looks a bit discomfited.* ARTHUR *strides away. Fractional pause.*)

ALF: (*In awe*) Cor – stone the crows.
(TED *makes a 'he's off his rocker' sign.*)

BERT: (*Laugh*) I think you're right there, Ted. He's well on his way round the bend.
(*But they feel uncomfortable, saddened, and obscurely envious.*)

TED: Poor sod. That's what I say.

ALF: (*Wistful*) Wonder what she's like, though?
(*They all look wistful.*
    Pause.)

BERT: Bit of all right by the sounds of it.
(TED *shakes off the mood.*)

TED: Ach! They're all the same in the dark, chaps.

BERT: (*Snigger*) No need to look at the mantelpiece when you're poking the fire.
(*Relieved, a spell or curse spoken, and, sniggering, they get up to go.*)

TED: Work, work. It's all work, ennit?

(Wipe right to left.)

CAPTIONS
*London street scenes, c.1935. Shop fronts, buses, trams, people
shopping etc.*
Music over (piano accordion): 'Pennies From Heaven'.
Narrowing to one busy street. Chords shift on accordion.
Dissolve into:

EXT. LONDON STREET. DAY
Closer shot of the HIKER *(from Episode I) making the shift into
'Rock of Ages', one of his three possible hymns. Still closer –*
HIKER: *(Monotonously)* Thank you very, very much, sir. Thank
   you very, very much, madam. Thank you very, very much,
   sir. Thank you very, very much, madam. Thank you very,
   very much sir . . .
   (In widening shot, nobody seems very responsive.
      Further along the pavement, two women approach. It is
   JOAN *and (from Episode I)* IRENE, *in splendid hats.)*
IRENE: No, I always go to this one when I'm this way – it's a
   nice teashop, and the éclairs are beautiful – spiffing!
JOAN: *(Laugh)* Oh, my poor figure.
   (But her expression suddenly changes. She lays her hand on
   IRENE*'s arm.)*
IRENE: Joan? What's the matter?
JOAN: *(Gasp)* I – oh, such a queer sensation!
IRENE: *(Concerned)* You look as though you've seen a ghost.
   *(*JOAN *pulls herself together, and laughs.)*
JOAN: The funniest thing – but see that busker –
IRENE: Oh, my Gawd. Listen to what he is play-ing!
JOAN: But for a minute, *(laughs, but a strained laugh)* I thought it
   was – Arthur!
IRENE: *(Gurgle of laughter)* Ar-thur!
JOAN: I know, silly isn't it? But something about him –
   (As she looks, zoom to her eye-line – to the HIKER.)
      *Superimpose: flash – and momentarily, almost subliminally,
   superimpose* ARTHUR *on and in same space as the* ACCORDION
   PLAYER, *and in same stance.*
      JOAN *blinks away the swift superimposition.)*

71

It was like someone walking over my grave. Do you know the feeling?

(JOAN *and* IRENE *are nearly up to the* HIKER.)

IRENE: Arthur wouldn't play *that* sort of tune.

(*They pass the* HIKER, *and both give him a curious glance.*)

JOAN: No! And Arthur wouldn't be seen dead in those sort of clothes! A proper ragamuffin.

HIKER: . . . very, very much madam. Thank you very, very much, sir. Thank you very, very much madam. Thank you very –

IRENE: (*Amused*) What a funny man! I wonder who darns his socks? Jesus, I suppose – Joan?

(*But* JOAN *has suddenly darted back to the* ACCORDION PLAYER *to give him a coin, almost as a gesture of propitiation.*)

HIKER: (*Mechanically*) . . . very, very much, sir. (*His tone changes remarkably.*) Oh, ta! Oh, thank you! Oh, very n-nice lady!

JOAN: (*Embarrassed*) That's all right.

(JOAN *gives the* HIKER *one quick, searching look and scurries back to* IRENE.)

IRENE: It only encourages them to be work-shy you know. I wouldn't give them a penny.

JOAN: (*Vaguely upset*) There was – something about him –

(IRENE *looks at her.*)

IRENE: Where *is* Arthur this time, by the way?

(JOAN *looks at her.*)

JOAN: He – I –

IRENE: Joan?

(JOAN *almost bursts into tears.*)

JOAN: I don't know!

(*Picture 'turns over'.*)

EXT. OUTSIDE VILLAGE SCHOOL. DAY
Huge burst of noise as scores and scores of small children explode out of the school, lessons over. They surge past Arthur's waiting car laughing and chattering.
ARTHUR, *beaming, window down, looks out at the school, waiting. He hands out Maltesers to some of the children, radiating bonhomie. A few moments, and, behind the other teachers,* EILEEN *appears,*

subtly 'hesitant'. ARTHUR *is able to watch her for a few seconds before she realizes he is there. Then she sees the car, and stops, shyly.* ARTHUR *gets out of the car and approaches. Then* ARTHUR, *too, stops. They stand a little apart, looking at each other, feeling awkward.*

ARTHUR: Hello.

EILEEN: Hello.

>   (*And again they look at each other. Start band intro.*)

ARTHUR: I hope you don't mind – (*his tongue feels thick in his mouth*) but I had to see you again. I – you don't mind . . . ?

>   (*She lowers her eyes.*)

EILEEN: (*Barely audible*) I don't mind.

ARTHUR: Only I can drive you home, you see. Or –

EILEEN: (*Not quite looking at him*) That's very nice.

>   (*He looks at her, swallows, and on the beat two–three 'sings' 'Just Let Me Look at You' by Lew Stone with Al Bowlly vocal.*
>
>   *They remain looking at each other as the music gently fades. Between them, in a heart shape, begin iris-out to:*)

41   INT. 1930S TEASHOP. DAY

JOAN *and* IRENE *at tea, in teashop complete with waitresses in little caps and frilly aprons.* JOAN *has obviously been weeping into her cup.*

IRENE: (*Reassuringly*) But he didn't *say* he was going for good, now did he?

JOAN: He didn't say anything at all. He just went.

IRENE: Was he due to go on one of his little trips, Joan?

JOAN: I – (*She looks at* IRENE, *forlorn.*) – I don't know, Irene. Perhaps that's half the trouble. I haven't been taking much of an interest –

IRENE: (*Snort*) No reason why you should.

JOAN: I don't know. I'm very worried.

>   (IRENE *sinks her teeth into an éclair.*)

IRENE: Mmm. Cream. It simply oo-zes out – (*Then, in an association she would certainly reject if it were conscious:*) Is everything else all right between you and Arthur, Joan. You know what I mean?

73

JOAN: (*Embarrassed*) You mean – ?
  (*Comically – but unaware, so to speak –* IRENE *wipes a little smear of cream from her rosebud lips with the tip of her little finger. She lowers her voice.*)
IRENE: Yes. In your bedroom, dear.
  (JOAN *drinks some tea.*)
JOAN: I – well, I don't really – *like* it very much . . .
  (*Fractional pause.*)
IRENE: I don't suppose any of us do, dear.
JOAN: Tarts do!
  (*They look about to see if anyone is listening.*)
IRENE: Or is it the money they like? I don't know.
JOAN: What a thing to be talking about.
IRENE: If you'd rather not . . .
JOAN: (*Quickly*) Some things are better said.
  (*They drink or eat, or play at it, awkward with each other.*)
IRENE: (*Cautiously*) And Arthur – he – well, he –
JOAN: (*Nod*) Wants it more often. Yes.
  (*Embarrassed silence.*)
IRENE: Still, that doesn't necessarily mean – you know – that he's looking for –
JOAN: Someone else. (*Her hand shakes on cup.*) Between you and me – and you won't breathe a word of this, will you?
IRENE: Of course not, Joan. What do you think I am?
JOAN: Well, I've sometimes had my suspicions. About another woman, I mean.
  (*A curious look comes into* IRENE*'s eyes. Hard, nasty even.*)
IRENE: Anyone in particular, Joan?
JOAN: (*Hesitant*) No. (*Then quickly*) This is absolutely between ourselves.
IRENE: Don't worry. You can trust me.
  (*Slightly suspicious glance from* JOAN.)
  Really – you can, Joan.
JOAN: I've sometimes thought – well – there's something about the way Arthur looks at – (*bites her lip*) – oh, I might as well say it! – The way he looks at Betty. Especially when she crosses those legs of hers.
  (*Excited gleam from* IRENE.)
IRENE: I didn't think you had noticed!

74

JOAN: You mean.

IRENE: Yes! Only I couldn't say anything, could I? I wouldn't dare.

JOAN: (*Upset*) What – has there been something going on behind my back then?

IRENE: I don't say anything has actually happened – not the whole way or – but I wouldn't put anything past Betty, not anything like that.

JOAN: I thought you and Betty were very close –

IRENE: We are. I like her. I like her a lot. But – well, she's practically a – what do they call it? – a nymphomaniac.

JOAN: (*Shocked*) Betty is! How do you know? I can't believe it!

IRENE: This is between us.

JOAN: It won't go further than this table, Irene.

IRENE: She told me herself that she had gone to bed with three men before she was married.

JOAN: No!

IRENE: Terrible, isn't it?

JOAN: What is it – a disease or a – or what?

IRENE: (*Bitchily*) Lust, dear.

JOAN: And she and – (*with difficulty*) – and Arthur, you think they – ?

(IRENE *calculatingly pauses to drink tea.*)

IRENE: (*Eventually*) I'm not saying that. What I *am* saying is that she gives him the eye. She can't help it, poor girl.

(JOAN *starts to cry again, quietly, held within.*)

Well – I couldn't tell you, Joan. Now could I? It's not the kind of thing you can bring up, just like that. Oh, don't be upset, dear. Please don't take it so hard. It's probably nothing – nothing at all.

JOAN: (*Thickly*) It's all my fault.

IRENE: Anyway, I'm sure he's not gone for long. Arthur knows where he's well off.

JOAN: This is the third day. And I haven't heard a word.

IRENE: Did he take any money or –

JOAN: No. Not much. Not that I know of. That's what the row was about – partly.

IRENE: That's what most rows are about.

JOAN: I'm frightened. I miss him more than – and if he goes

75

altogether, I – (*Her voice breaks.*)

(IRENE *reaches across the table and touches her arm, consolingly.*)

IRENE: Come on, now. Have some more tea.

JOAN: It'll make me choke!

IRENE: He'll be back. You see! Arthur's got too much sense, Arthur has.

(*Wipe left to right.*)

INT./EXT. IN ARTHUR'S CAR. WINDING FOREST OF DEAN ROAD. DAY

ARTHUR *at wheel,* EILEEN *beside him. Words are a bit difficult. He essays to speak several times – then, at last:*

ARTHUR: Lovely round here, ennit?

EILEEN: (*Proudly*) Oh, yes. The Forest of Dean is the most beautiful place in England.

ARTHUR: I think you're right. (*He looks across, almost furtive.*) Especially with you living in it.

EILEEN: (*Prim*) The landscape is nothing to do with people – not in *that* way.

ARTHUR: I think you're wrong, you know. You're wrong in my case. It's when I – when I look at you, the scales fall off of my eyes. Begging your pardon, Eileen.

(EILEEN *looks down at her hands folded in her lap.*)

I haven't given you any offence, have I?

EILEEN: I – no.

ARTHUR: Are you sure? Only I don't want to speak out of turn.

EILEEN: I'm not very – at ease. With people. (*Fractional pause.*) With men, I mean.

ARTHUR: That's all right, love. I've got enough cheek for both of us.

(*Pause. They are both, furtively, examining each other.*)

EILEEN: (*Simply*) You won't tell lies. Will you, Arthur.

(*A faint shadow.*)

ARTHUR: Not if I can help it.

(*Pause.*)

EILEEN: And you are not married. You promise.

ARTHUR: (*Harsh laugh*) Do I look like a married man?

(*But he changes gear, needlessly.*)

76

EXT. ROAD THROUGH FOREST. DAY
Arthur's car accelerating away. Silence – except for cacophony of birds.
Move slowly in to road surface, and there, squashed, is a dead bird.
Diminuendo chords of 'Pennies From Heaven' on a piano accordion.
Fade.

CAPTIONS
The Sunnyside Lane graphics – moon over Metroland – ending on Joan's window. Dissolve.

INT. JOAN'S BEDROOM. NIGHT
JOAN, *in bed, restless, reads, or looks at a magazine. Her attention is caught.*
SMOOTH VOICE-OVER (MALE): No matter how charming you may be or how fond of you your friends are. You cannot expect them to put up with halitosis –
ANOTHER, HARSHER VOICE-OVER: Unpleasant breath.
VOICE-OVER: – for ever. They may be nice to you – but it is an effort.
THE HARSHER VOICE-OVER: Don't fool yourself that you never have halitosis as do so many self-assured people who constantly offend this way.
VOICE-OVER: Read the facts in the lower right-hand corner and you will see that your chance of escape is slight.
(*Caption card: a caption, in the original print style, comes bombing out of the screen in a spiralling whirling movement:*
READ THE FACTS:
$^1/_3$ HAD HALITOSIS.
SIXTY-EIGHT HAIRDRESSERS STATE THAT ABOUT EVERY THIRD WOMAN, MANY OF THEM FROM THE WEALTHY CLASSES, IS HALITOXIC. WHO SHOULD KNOW BETTER THAN THEY?
Caption out.
JOAN *stares at the page, eyes widening in alarm.*)
JOAN: (*Voice-over*) 'Recognizing these truths, *nice people* end any chance of offending by systematically rinsing the mouth with Listerine. Every morning. Every night. And between times when necessary, especially before meeting others.'

(She stares at the page, fear on her face. Over her shoulder appears the picture in the ad, sadly sitting out on Palm Court dance floor while man and woman dance happily by.

Swift dissolve to:)

INT. PALM COURT HOTEL-STYLE DANCE FLOOR, A CORNER. NIGHT

As though animating the advertisement picture ARTHUR *and an anonymous woman dance past the isolated* JOAN, *who turns her head away in pain and then stares at the floor.*
The off-screen band is playing 'Isn't It Heavenly'.
Dissolve.

INT. JOAN'S BEDROOM. NIGHT

JOAN *in a mortal terror. She then, pathetically, breathes on the back of her hand, then smells her own breath. As she does, suspiciously, the telephone jangles in the hall downstairs. She says 'Arthur!' in a little choke and runs, literally runs, to get to the telephone.*
The magazine drops to the floor. Zoom in to the Listerine ad: 'Halitosis makes you unpopular.'

INT. THE HALLWAY. NIGHT

JOAN, *in a flurry, panting even, picks up the telephone receiver.*
JOAN: Arthur? (*But it isn't.*) What? Who – who is it, please? Yes, I was in bed, but – what am I wearing? My night – (*Then she realizes, and stops, with fascinated horror.*) Who is this? (*Stop – she listens. Then her face changes.*) I think you are evil, whoever you are. You should be locked up! (*And puts phone down. She stands, trembling, looking at the phone. And then at her own reflection in the hall mirror. A pause, then:*) Mirror, mirror on the wall –
(*She stops, then, almost without any introduction, she 'sings' the first 'mimed' song of Episode 1 –*
'The Clouds Will Soon Roll By', Ambrose, sung by Elsie Carlisle.
As the song nears its end, using the mirror, very slow dissolve so that JOAN's *'singing' face becomes a sort of haunting after-image, to:)*

78

INT. THE COTTAGE. FOREST OF DEAN. NIGHT

Song continuing through long dissolve, and into the scene – where
DAD *is clearly saying goodnight to stiff* ARTHUR, *stiff* EILEEN, DAVE
and MAURICE.

*As he does, and as the song finishes, he indicates with a quick jerk of
his head that* DAVE *and* MAURICE *should also say a tactful
goodnight.* MAURICE, *a little awkwardly, scraping his boots, gets up
almost at once.*

MAURICE: (*Shy*) Aye, well. Time for me to get up the 'ooden
     hill as well. Marnin' d'come too early for I. (*Hesitates.*)
     Goodnight, then. All.

ARTHUR: (*Eagerly*) Goodnight, Maurice.

EILEEN: Goodnight.

     (MAURICE *looks at* DAVE, *who seems to have been drinking.*)

MAURICE: Byun you coming on up, Dave. We be on earlies,
     mind.

DAVE: (*Obtusely*) Not ik, o'but. Thou go on. Shan't be long.

     (MAURICE *hesitates. Then goes.* ARTHUR *and* EILEEN *give
     each other the swiftest of glances. Laboriously almost,* DAVE
     completes the rolling of a cigarette.)

     'Sthou want one, Arth?

ARTHUR: Pardon?

DAVE: A fag.

EILEEN: No. He doesn't.

     (*Comically, both* DAVE *and* ARTHUR *look askance at*
     EILEEN.)

DAVE: (*Amused*) Your voice is higher than I thought, o'but.

EILEEN: Well, he doesn't.

DAVE: That's women for tha', Arth. They d'know what tha's
     want and what tha' doesn't want even afore you do!

ARTHUR: No – I don't want one, though.

DAVE: (*Snigger*) All the same if tha's did!

     (*Silence.* ARTHUR *and* EILEEN *look at each other again: when
     will Dave go? The silence lengthens.* DAVE *seems to settle.*)

     First time I have ever met a songwriter.

     (ARTHUR *shifts uncomfortably.*)

ARTHUR: Is it? (*But he has to clear his throat.*) Is it?

DAVE: Brass bands is more in my line. But I d'like a good zong,
     mind. Oh, aye.

79

ARTHUR: (*Lamely*) Yes.

    (EILEEN *is frowning at* DAVE.)

DAVE: Why doesn't tell us some of the ones as you'a made up, then?

ARTHUR: Well –

EILEEN: Not everybody wants to boast.

DAVE: That's all very well – but –

ARTHUR: (*Quickly*) It's not been my main job, see. I've been selling other people's songs while getting me own – um – *my* own collection together. I've got this small team going from music shop to music shop –

    (DAVE *looks at him, half in respect, half in suspicion.*)

DAVE: You got men working for tha', hast?

ARTHUR: (*Swallow*) Only a couple. It's a very small business. Getting bigger, though.

DAVE: And you got *an office* an' all?

    (ARTHUR *is feeling uncomfortable.*)

ARTHUR: The trouble is – overheads. Especially nowadays. So –

DAVE: What – ant you got nern *an office*, then?

    (*He says 'an office' as though it were immensely grand.*

    EILEEN *looks at* ARTHUR, *interested.*)

EILEEN: Haven't you, Arthur?

ARTHUR: Oh, yes. But – well, it's not very big or –

DAVE: (*Pleased*) Still. You a' got *an office.*

ARTHUR: – and – I'm hoping to get a better one. Things are getting better, you see. Every day in every way.

    (*Silence. They wait for Dave.*)

EILEEN: It's getting late, Dave. You've got to be up at half past five.

DAVE: Oh, doesn't thou worry about me, our Eileen. I be no trouble in the marnins – unlike some. (*sniff*) And you do want to be going if you be driving all the way to Gloucester, Arthur.

ARTHUR: Oh – it's only sixteen miles.

DAVE: It's an hour on the bus.

ARTHUR: I can do it in half that time.

DAVE: Speed man, be you? Like whatsisname. Campbell.

ARTHUR: Well, I don't believe in wasting time.

    (*He looks at* EILEEN, *who is twitching her foot in irritation.*)

DAVE: How many horse power is it thik car of thine –
EILEEN: (*Suddenly*) For God's sake!
  (DAVE, *startled, breaks off.*)
DAVE: What's the matter with thee – (*Then light dawns.*) Oh.
    Oh. Aye. Well – (*Suddenly very embarrassed,* DAVE *lurches
    awkwardly to his feet.*) I didn't realize how the clock was a-
    ticking on. I'll say goodnight then.
ARTHUR: (*Immensely relieved*) Goodnight, Dave.
DAVE: (*Awkwardly*) That's all right, o'but.
EILEEN: Goodnight.
  (DAVE *looks at her and is somehow too embarrassed to say
  anything. Comically, he half nods, half bows, and clumps to the
  door of the enclosed staircase which rises out of the room.*
    As he goes, ARTHUR *and* EILEEN *scarcely dare look at each
  other. But they do – in sidelong fashion. And immediately burst
  out laughing. Almost at once, the latch rises on the staircase
  door and* DAVE *puts his head round.*)
DAVE: (*Aggressive*) Doesn't thou laugh at me, mind!
  (*They choke back their amusement.*)
EILEEN: We weren't doing that, Dave.
DAVE: No? Well, you'd better not! (*And he closes the door.*)
  (ARTHUR *and* EILEEN *look at each other. She is no longer
  amused, not a bit.*)
EILEEN: Sometimes – !
ARTHUR: (*Moving closer*) What's the matter, love?
  (*She gives him a steady look.*)
EILEEN: I feel as though I'm – suffocating in this house. I don't
    think I can stick it out much longer.
ARTHUR: I see what you mean.
  (*But she immediately feels disloyal.*)
EILEEN: Oh, they're good, really, my family. But since Mum
    died – it's not the same any more. And we're all very
    different from each other.
ARTHUR: It's hard to believe you are Dave's sister.
EILEEN: Is it? In what way?
  (*This is a sort of invitation, which* ARTHUR *takes.*)
ARTHUR: There's something – sort of – hesitating about you,
    Eileen. No, not in that way. More like a – a lilt in a song. I
    don't know how to describe it. It's not any one thing, it's

81

everything, all together. Specially when you look sideways.

EILEEN: (*Shy*) Do I look sideways?

ARTHUR: Not so much sideways, no. Not exactly sideways. (*Nervous laugh.*) I mean, you ain't got a squint or anyfink.

EILEEN: You sound real London sometimes (*but she is pleased by that*).

ARTHUR: (*Bitterly*) Yes, and my wife –
(*He stops dead. She draws in her breath.* ARTHUR *lowers his head.*)

EILEEN: (*Faintly*) Arthur?
(ARTHUR *rocks gently in distress, almost hugging himself for comfort.*)

ARTHUR: (*Eventually*) God rest her soul.
(*Pause.*)

EILEEN: (*Tense*) Arthur?

ARTHUR: That's why I don't like motorbikes. I bloody hates 'em!

EILEEN: D-do you mean – ?
(*He nods vigorously, seemingly distressed.*)

ARTHUR: Three years ago now. But when I think abaht it – the waste – senseless waste – her broken young body . . .

EILEEN: (*Moved*) Oh, don't cry, my dear.

ARTHUR: (*Sob*) She was looking in a shop window. The butcher's, it was. She knew how I liked a lamb chop – (*sob*) this motorbike – out of control – (*He 'cannot' finish.*)

EILEEN: (*Distressed*) Do you, Arthur?

ARTHUR: What?

EILEEN: Like lamb chops?
(*He suddenly buries his face in her. She stiffens at first, virginal, alarmed, holds her hands back.*

But as ARTHUR *sobs, and determinedly nestles in,* EILEEN *cradles his head in her hands and bends down to him.*

But ARTHUR *is busy.*)
(*Gasp*) Oh. Arthur – I –
(*The buttons of her dress or blouse are being remorselessly undone.*)

ARTHUR: Oh, my darling (*sob*) my darling. This is the first time I've felt *anything* since that day . . .
(*She is unsure of what to do.*)

82

EILEEN: I've never – (*gasp*) – I don't – Oh, please. Arthur?

ARTHUR: (*Intensely*) Please, my love. Please, my sweet love. My angel.

EILEEN: Oh – I'm – I'm frightened –

ARTHUR: (*Sob*) Oh, dear God. Eileen! Please take the pain away!

EILEEN: I'll try – I'll try to take it away – poor Arthur – dear Arthur.

(*Deftly, he is getting her clothes off. They sink back, tangled together.*)

INT. THE COTTAGE, INLAID IN GRAPHICS

Gradually, as passion increases, the picture seems to shrink inside the borders of what will be a specially designed songsheet cover: 'Love is the Sweetest Thing', bordered with little cupids, hearts and flowers. Vocal over: Al Bowlly singing 'Love is the sweetest thing . . .', finishing 'I only hope fate will bring love's story to you!' during which the love-making is continued within a small oblong within the songsheet.

Without diminishing further, the oblong of activity goes totally blank. The song is continuing. The blank comes alive again.

SONGSHEET PLUS: INT. JOAN'S BEDROOM. NIGHT

Alive to close-up of JOAN *holding, even caressing, a large bottle of aspirin.*

Pull out, until picture occupies the whole screen again. JOAN *undoes the bottle, shakes some of the tablets out, shakingly holds a glass of water from the bedside table. A long pause. What is she going to do? The pause lengthens to what is just tolerable. Then, stricken-faced, she puts her tablets back, one at a time, into the bottle. Chink-chink-chink, they go, returning to the glass bottle. Neatly, tidily, she puts the bottle back on the bedside table, next to the glass of water.*

Pause.

JOAN: (*Deliberately*) Not over you. (*She lies back and stares at the ceiling. Deliberately*) You're not worth it, Arthur. You common little beast.

(*Pull slowly away, as if leaving the room. Dissolve on movement to:*)

CAPTIONS
'Sunnyside Lane' drawings, by moonlight.
Music 'Down Sunnyside Lane' through these detailed drawings. A different version of the song. By the end, a new figure has been drawn in: the HIKER, standing under a lamp-post, with his piano accordion.
Finish to the strains of 'Down Sunnyside Lane'.
    Fade out.

3 'HAND IN HAND'

INT. JOAN'S BEDROOM. THE HOUSE IN SUNNYSIDE LANE.
NIGHT.
This time, we do not begin with drawings.
It is dark, but a splash of moonlight sufficiently illuminates the room.
JOAN is asleep, her arm up on the pillow in a peculiarly defensive
posture. Hold. Silence. Then car headlights slide across the ceiling.
Outside, in a moment, sounds of car stopping, car door etc. Then,
from below, the sound of key in latch of front door, vaguely
menacing.
No music. Sound of slow footsteps on stair, menacing, and not at all
vaguely.
Pause.
Bedroom door opens, sending a broad shaft of half-light across the
room and on to the bed. A figure, a mere silhouette, creeps into the
room and stands quietly at the foot of the bed, looking down at the
sleeping woman. It is, we now see, ARTHUR.
He takes off his tie and knots it in his hand, like at least twenty
stranglers in the films. Close-shot, shadowy, ARTHUR, staring down
at his wife. His face goes to a snigger, then suddenly hardens.
Close-shot of JOAN, asleep. She stirs and wakes – and sits up with a
fearful start.
JOAN: (*Gasp*) Arthur?
    (*Fractional pause.*)
ARTHUR: No. It's King Kong, ennit?
JOAN: Arthur – what – ?
ARTHUR: You going to call for the police, then?
JOAN: (*Dry-throated*) W-what for?
    (*He steps forward into the moonlight coming through curtains.*)
ARTHUR: 'Cos I'm going to put this round your neck, you mean
    cow, and squeeze the bleed'n life out of you!
JOAN: (*Incredulous*) What?
ARTHUR: I don't mind swinging for you, you bitch!
    (*And ARTHUR lurches forward. But as he does she pulls on the*
    dangling cord of the light switch. They both blink at each other.
    He looks dishevelled.)

JOAN: Have you been drinking, Arthur?

ARTHUR: (*Mimics*) Have-you-been-drinking-Arthur?

(*They stop, and look at each other.*)

JOAN: (*Quietly*) I'm glad you've come back. Thank God you've come back.

(*This rather astonishes him.*)

ARTHUR: I like your bloody sarcasm. That's a good one, that is.

JOAN: No, Arthur. I mean it. I thought – I thought you'd left for good.

ARTHUR: I have! I've gorn, missis!

JOAN: And I – don't say that, Arthur. Please.

(*He revolves his head, somehow evasive.*)

ARTHUR: I mean, what do I want to stay *here* for? Why do I want to sleep in *that* bleed'n bed of nails!

JOAN: (*Almost brazenly*) Because I'm in it.

(*He stares at her.*)

ARTHUR: What do you mean – ?

JOAN: I can't bear the thought of being on my own.

(*He stays silent.*)

I can't Arthur. I know that now. I've even –

(*She stops, and there is something oddly shy in this that arouses him.*)

ARTHUR: (*Different tone*) You've even what?

(*She drags her eyes back on to* ARTHUR*'s face*)

JOAN: Put lipstick on.

(*He stares at her, ready to be belligerent.*)

ARTHUR: Whatdyamean? You always put bleedin' lipstick on!

(*She has to turn her face away again.*)

JOAN: No – on my – on – (*She gestures inconclusively at her own body.*)

ARTHUR: What? On your – (*Voice changes.*) On your nipples, Joanie? Have you?

(*She looks at him with an almost frightened smile, and nods quickly.*)

JOAN: (*Whisper*) You said you wanted me to.

(*He sits on the bed, excited.*)

ARTHUR: God, you are a gel, entcha!

JOAN: You said you wanted –

ARTHUR: But how did you know I was coming back tonight?

JOAN: I didn't.

ARTHUR: (*Pleased*) What? You bin putting it there *every* night, then? Just in case, like . . .

JOAN: I wanted you to come back.

(ARTHUR*'s eyes are glittering with excitement – and fear?*)

ARTHUR: Let's see!

(*But she instinctively puts up her hands. His disappointed contempt is immediate.*)

Oh, I see. Still the same, after all.

JOAN: (*Struggling*) No Arthur – not the same – but you're – I'm shy, Arthur.

ARTHUR: And I'm your hubby, enn I? (*As nasty as it sounds.*)

(*Slowly, excruciatingly, she exposes her breasts.* ARTHUR *stares in wonder – in awe, even.*)

(*Hoarse*) Blimey, Joan. God love a duck.

(*She is almost in tears.*)

JOAN: Do you – like it?

ARTHUR: Like it? I think it's – Gawd! It's bloody marvellous!

JOAN: Oh don't, Arthur. Please don't swear.

(*But he is staring at her lipstick-covered nipples in total, incredulous wonder.*)

ARTHUR: You *was* listening, then? All the time, you was listening to what I was – cor, Joan. Look at it! Proper little rosebud!

(*Like someone tentatively touching a fragile work of art, he touches her with one finger. Then, shyly, they look at each other.*)

JOAN: Where have you been?

ARTHUR: On one of my trips. (*Sniff.*) Business.

(*She looks down at her exposed breasts.*)

JOAN: Are they as nice as –

(*Fractional pause.*)

ARTHUR: (*Frown*) As nice as what?

JOAN: As nice as *hers*?

(ARTHUR *gets up, quickly.*)

ARTHUR: Now listen – !

JOAN: (*Quickly*) As nice as Betty's, for example?

(*Which stops him in mid-movement.*)

ARTHUR: Whose?

JOAN: Betty.

87

ARTHUR: What do you mean – ? What you on about?

JOAN: (*Swallow*) She –

ARTHUR: Come on! Say what you're trying to say! She what?

JOAN: She makes eyes at you. Well – doesn't she?

ARTHUR: (*Snort*) I should be so lucky!

(*Moment's pause.* JOAN *is hurt by this, and* ARTHUR *sees it. He tries to pull it back.*)

I wouldn't touch somebody like *her* with a barge-pole. Where – what on earth made you think a thing like that!

JOAN: It's – just something – I felt it, that's all –

ARTHUR: Well, you felt wrong!

JOAN: Arthur?

ARTHUR: (*Passionately*) Wrong, wrong! You're barking up the wrong tree altogether!

(*She is examining him, but nervously.*)

JOAN: But you have – slept with somebody else – Arthur? – you have, haven't you?

(*He looks down at her.*)

ARTHUR: Cross my heart and hope to die. I've never touched nobody since we was wed, Joan.

JOAN: Do you mean –

ARTHUR: (*Vigorously*) I mean what I say!

JOAN: But where have –

ARTHUR: Nobody! Do you hear! Nobody at all!

JOAN: (*Quietly*) I always felt – I used to – (*Changes.*) But you've wanted to, haven't you, Arthur? Please tell me the truth.

ARTHUR: I *am* telling you the truth! Almighty strike me dead on the spot! (*A slight quiver of recognition of what he has said.*)

JOAN: But you *have* wanted to?

ARTHUR: Wanting to is not the same as doing it. Is it?

JOAN: Would you like it if I – wanted to? With some other chap.

(*Slight pause.*)

ARTHUR: I – no. Not really. Not in – (*He sucks in his breath.*) No. I wouldn't mind –

JOAN: (*Deliberately*) Well, I don't want to.

ARTHUR: No, I don't suppose you do.

JOAN: But why do *you*, then?

ARTHUR: Because – because I'm – perhaps because I'm not as good as you are.

JOAN: It's not being good if you're not even tempted. It never, ever enters my head.
(*Pause.*
     ARTHUR *is looking puzzled, even hunted. He sits on bed again.*)
ARTHUR: Perhaps – men, they aren't the same. Perhaps? As the ladies, I mean. Do you think?
JOAN: But *most* men –
(*He interrupts angrily.*)
ARTHUR: Are dead inside! Yeh – and outside, an' all!
(*Pause.*)
JOAN: So I've been thinking about it.
ARTHUR: And?
JOAN: Perhaps it's my fault.
(ARTHUR *looks at her, then suddenly hangs his head.*)
ARTHUR: (*Heavily*) I sometimes think – (*He stops.*)
JOAN: (*Quietly*) Go on.
(*He works his face, then looks at her, venomously.*)
ARTHUR: I think that if I had the chance and it was a dark night, I'd fuck my own grandmother!
(JOAN *is horribly shocked, and instinctively covers up.*)
JOAN: (*Gasp*) Oh – Arthur! What a – (*gasp*) What a *foul* thing to – oh, dear God!
ARTHUR: (*Shout*) I don't mean it!
JOAN: (*Almost out of her mind*) To use that – that word – about your own –
ARTHUR: It's only a word!
JOAN: Arthur –
ARTHUR: Christ Almighty!
JOAN: Arthur! No!
(*Shaking inside, he looks down at his own hands, as though they were alien to him.*)
ARTHUR: I heard this story. A true story –
JOAN: (*Still distressed*) Like a navvy or – oh, Arthur – I never thought I'd hear . . .
ARTHUR: Shut up a minute! Listen!
(*She clamps her mouth, but looks at him with hatred.* ARTHUR *controls his voice, but his eyes slide away.*)
In the band, they are. Very well-known band, as a matter of fact. This man and this woman singer. They – well, at

the hotel where they were playing, see – (*He looks her full in the face.*) They gave the liftman a five-pound note to stop the lift between floors and turn his back.
(*Pause.*)

JOAN: (*Despite herself*) Why?
(*He starts to laugh.*)

ARTHUR: So that they could make love in the lift.

JOAN: (*Rising horror*) You mean – kiss and that – ?

ARTHUR: No – have a bit of the other! (*His laugh becomes a sudden, frightened half-sob.*)

JOAN: (*Eventually*) Then they are just animals, Arthur. And you know they are.
(ARTHUR *looks at* JOAN, *his eyes filling with tears.*)

ARTHUR: Are they, Joan? Are they?

JOAN: That's one of the most dis-gust-ing things I've ever heard.

ARTHUR: (*Voice thickening*) I wish – I wish –

JOAN: (*Freezing*) You wish what?
(*He makes a peculiar, distressed, hissing noise between his teeth, half way between a whimper and an accusation. Then he shakes his head.*)

ARTHUR: Nothing. (*Shakes his head again, and again.*) Nothing.
(*She is looking at him with horrified fascination.*)

JOAN: You wish *you* were that man, don't you!

ARTHUR: Joan, you don't –

JOAN: (*Rising tone*) You do! You do – yes, you do!
(*His face goes blank. Pause.*)

ARTHUR: (*Solemnly*) I wish I could play the piano.
(*She looks at him as though he is going mad.*)

JOAN: (*Rising tone*) What? Arthur?

ARTHUR: Or any instrument. Any one at all. Even a mouth organ.

JOAN: What are you talking like this for? You *have* been drinking, haven't you . . . ?

ARTHUR: Listen a minute.
(*Pause.*)

JOAN: (*Carefully*) I am listening, Arthur.
(*Pause.*

He sighs heavily, looks at his hands, then, he gets up, holding his hands carefully in front of him, and – as JOAN*'s mouth opens in incredulity – starts to conduct.*

On third beat, music: Thirties version of 'You and the Night and the Music'.)
Arthur!
(He puts his finger to his lips, and drops his arms from conducting position, and begins to 'sing'.

   After the song, he resumes his 'conducting' stance as the music continues. But gradually his arms slow and drop, and the music dips out.

   Pause.)
(Carefully) What are you doing, Arthur?

ARTHUR: Pretendin'.

JOAN: But what – and why?

ARTHUR: That I got me own band.
(They look at each other, then he puts his hands over his face, deeply upset. JOAN watches him for a moment with a frown. And then, since his distress does not abate, she gets out of bed and puts her hands on his wrists.)

JOAN: Why don't we have a nice cup of tea – eh?
(He puts down his hands.)

ARTHUR: What – at this time of night?

JOAN: Or Ovaltine, if you like.

ARTHUR: *(Upset)* All right, then. I'll make a cup of tea, shall I?

JOAN: No. I'll make it.

ARTHUR: *(Nearly crying)* Will you, Joanie? After I said *that word.*

JOAN: You won't say it again though, will you?

ARTHUR: No. Never. Never, never, never.

JOAN: Are you tired? You *look* tired.

ARTHUR: Yes. I am. I'm – whacked. Fagged out.

JOAN: You get undressed then, and *I'll* make the tea.
(He nods, but looks a bit furtive.)

ARTHUR: You – um – you won't wash it off, will you?

JOAN: Wash what off?

ARTHUR: *(Near-whisper)* The lipstick.
(She puts her hands to her bosom, protectively, then a strained smile.)

JOAN: No. I won't wash it off.

ARTHUR: You're a sport, Joan. A real sport. I gotta say it, gel.

JOAN: But first –

ARTHUR: Yes?

JOAN: We've got to talk. Haven't we?
ARTHUR: (*Glum*) Yes.
JOAN: We've got to talk about everything.
ARTHUR: (*Sighs*) Yes. Everythink.
JOAN: Don't say 'everythink', Arthur. (*Hesitates.*) Please, love.
ARTHUR: Everything. We'll talk about everything-g-g.
JOAN: Yes, (*as she goes*) we must. We will. Won't we?
ARTHUR: Only don't wash it off! Please don't wash it off.
JOAN: (*At door*) No.
    (*But she frowns as she goes out of the room.*
      Move slowly into ARTHUR. *His expression becomes pensive,*
    brooding.)
ARTHUR: (*Eventually*) Everything-g-g. (*Pause.*) G-g-g-g!
    (*Crash cut.*)

EXT. STREET. DAY
A powerful 1930s motorbike, at full throttle, roars at cameras. JOAN,
turning from butcher's shop window, mouth open in horror,
screams –
Crash cut.

INT. THE BEDROOM. SUNNYSIDE LANE. NIGHT
ARTHUR *surfaces out of his own imaginings. A violin starts, then, as*
ARTHUR *spreads his hands on an imaginary keyboard. The piano of*
'Roll Along Prairie Moon', the Al Bowlly version. Arthur 'sings'
softly.
Slow, romantic dissolve to:

EXT. THE SKY. NIGHT
A big yellow moon, scudded by wisps of cloud, as ARTHUR *continues*
to 'sing'.
Slow dissolve to:

EXT. OLD QUARRIES, FOREST OF DEAN. NIGHT
Wild, craggy, romantic scene, gleaming in night light. Picking up
EILEEN, *standing alone, pensive, her coat pulled around her, face*
tilting up to night sky.
Voiceover: ARTHUR *'singing' 'Prairie Moon'.*
    Iris-out.

92

Sweet music fading as JOAN *and* ARTHUR *sit up in bed, side by side, drinking tea from blue willow-pattern cups. Silence, except for chink-chink of cups. They both look sideways at each other, then quickly away again.*

ARTHUR: (*Eventually*) Shall we put the light out, then?

JOAN: When we've talked.

    (*Pause.*)

ARTHUR: What shall we talk about?

    (*Fractional pause.*)

JOAN: Why you went away like you did.

ARTHUR: Yes.

JOAN: And where you went.

    (*Fractional pause.*)

ARTHUR: (Sigh) Yes.

    (*But they do not talk they – chink, chink – finish their tea.*
      Pause.)

JOAN: I had tea in the Broadway the other day. With Irene.

ARTHUR: (*Tense*) Oh, yes.

JOAN: Funniest thing – (*She stops.*)

ARTHUR: What was?

JOAN: This man. Playing an accordion in the street. A layabout. They're all over the place, Arthur.

ARTHUR: An accordion. A piano accordion.

JOAN: And we were walking along, Irene and me – and – I had the strangest feeling – I thought it was *you* – playing this thing in the street –

ARTHUR: Me?

JOAN: Something about him – the way he . . .

ARTHUR: Did he look like me?

JOAN: Not a bit. Well, not really. But . . .

    (*He is interested.*)

ARTHUR: Then why did you think it was me?

JOAN: Something. Something you can't put into words. Like – it was like – a shadow, or – I don't know. It made me shiver. I felt quite giddy.

    (*Pause.*)

ARTHUR: What was he playing?

JOAN: A hymn. And not very well.

(*He looks at her, oddly.*)

ARTHUR: Funny sort of chap, was he?

JOAN: Very odd.

ARTHUR: But in what way?

JOAN: Oh, he kept on saying 'Thank you very, very much.'
Even when he wasn't getting anything. 'Thank you very,
very much, very, very much.' – What's the matter?

ARTHUR: Nothing.

JOAN: Do you know him or something?

ARTHUR: No. (*A hollow 'No'.*) How would I know a bloke like
that?

JOAN: (*Quietly*) Why did you go, Arthur?
(*Pause.*)

ARTHUR: Because I was fed up.

JOAN: With me? You were fed up with me, Arthur?

ARTHUR: You *belittle* me.
(*Pause.*)

JOAN: I'm only trying to – help you.

ARTHUR: I can't help the way I speak.

JOAN: (*Too quickly*) But you *can*, Arthur!

ARTHUR: See what I mean? Can you hear yourself?
(*Silence.*)
And then there's that money.

JOAN: Father's money.

ARTHUR: No – *your* money. It's yours. Every penny of it.
(*Silence.*)

JOAN: I'm frightened we shall have nothing for our old age.

ARTHUR: You won't have me, for a start.

JOAN: Don't, Arthur. Please don't say that.

ARTHUR: All I wanted was a bit of capital. That's not much
to ask. Not from your own wife. A little bit of capital
and a little bit of – (*looks at her, changes the word*) –
affection.

JOAN: I do – need you.

ARTHUR: (*Half-jeer*) Do you?

JOAN: Yes. I do. I don't want to be on my own.

ARTHUR: (*Still derisive*) But you don't like me on top of you, do
you?

JOAN: Do you have to put it that way . . . ?

94

ARTHUR: No. You can come on top of me, if you like. Make a
   change.
JOAN: Oh, Arthur.
   (*He mimes her distaste.*)
ARTHUR: Oh, Arthur!
JOAN: (*Passionately*) Does it matter that much? Does it really
   matter *quite* so much? All that, I mean.
ARTHUR: Of course it does! It's the main thing, ennit?
   (*Silence. But they are on the verge of shouting at each other.
   Then he turns to her, urgent, hard.*)
   Put the light out, eh?
JOAN: But we haven't said all the things we –
   (*Her voice trails off as, angrily, he pulls the light cord dangling
   above them. The room seems now to be almost completely dark.
        Out of the black screen, a perfectly crescent, silvery new moon
   forms itself. It slowly fills the screen.
        Music: Band intro to 'I Wished on the Moon', Maurice
   Winnick, singer: Judy Shirley.
        Dissolving slowly near end of musical intro to:*)

INT. DOCTOR'S WAITING-ROOM, FOREST OF DEAN. DAY
*A shabby, uncomfortable room with hard-backed wooden chairs, in
which half a dozen people sit, waiting, coughing, dull-eyed, shiftily
looking at each other.*
At end of musical intro, close shot of worried-looking EILEEN. *She is
'singing' 'I Wished on the Moon'. During the song one or two of the
patients go through the chocolate-brown door into the surgery.*
An old MINER *coughs, silicotic, the dust rattling like gravel in his
chest. The* MINER *catches* EILEEN's *eye, catches his breath, and
smiles at her.*
MINER: No school for you today then, Miss Everson.
EILEEN: (*Withdrawn*) No.
MINER: You're my grandson's favourite, you are, Miss Everson.
   (*She smiles a faint acknowledgement.
        A* WOMAN *comes out through the brown door, very upset,
   pushing a big handkerchief into her mouth to stop crying. She
   almost gets to the outer door to the street before an agonized cry
   bursts out of her.*)
WOMAN: What's the point? Where's the sense in it all?

(Everyone looks away. She goes on out.

Two of the patients lean in towards each other to whisper.

A small bell sounds, meaning 'next'. Hesitant, self-conscious, EILEEN *gets up, looks at the others, then goes to and through the door to the surgery.*

The two whisperers follow her with eager eyes, then lean in towards each other again.

Wipe left to right.)

INT. KITCHEN, ARTHUR'S HOUSE. DAY (BREAKFAST)

ARTHUR *scoffing down some bacon, ebullient.* JOAN *watching him, hands round her cup, something cold, or abused, in her eyes, but careful to disguise as much of it as possible from* ARTHUR.

ARTHUR: You see, I reckoned it out a long time ago. The days of sheet music is numbered, my love. What with the wireless and all – stands to reason, don't it? People don't make their own entertainment now, do they?

JOAN: It's a pity, though.

ARTHUR: In a way it is. But I'd rather listen to Lew Stone's band than hear some cloth-eared berk murdering the same tune on a pub piano.

JOAN: (*Not very interested*) I suppose so.

(*He takes too big a mouthful. Which, of course, she notices.*)

ARTHUR: (*Food in mouth*) That's right. 'Course it's so. So records –

JOAN: Arthur.

ARTHUR: What? Oh. (*Comically he empties his mouth.*) So it's gramophone records, ennit? That's where the money is, gel?

JOAN: But you don't know anything about them. (*Then, nervously*) Do you?

ARTHUR: Songs is songs. And I know *songs*, don't I?

JOAN: (*Half-reluctant*) Yes.

ARTHUR: Oh, I know my songs, all right. I can tell a hit from a dog.

JOAN: What's a dog?

ARTHUR: A song that don't sell. (*He sniggers.*) I can tell 'em a mile away.

JOAN: You haven't always known, though. Have you?

ARTHUR: Ah, well. That's the shopkeepers, ennit. They don't

96

know what people are whistling in the street. Half of them are stone deaf.

JOAN: And you want –

ARTHUR: Me own shop!

JOAN: (*Frightened*) But – it'll be risky – Arthur – wouldn't it be better to –

ARTHUR: (*Interrupting*) No risk whatsoever! None at all! All a chap needs is the capital, you see. That's what makes the difference, old girl.

(*Her anxiety is breaking through. She stares at him, biting her lip.*)

JOAN: But if you lose it all –

ARTHUR: Your dad's money be as safe as houses. So far.

JOAN: We've got nothing else to fall back on.

ARTHUR: Except our double bed eh? (*He laughs, then sees her face.*) You won't let me down, will you? You *said*.

JOAN: (*Dully*) No, Arthur, I've agreed.

(*He pushes his plate away and beams across the table.*)

ARTHUR: Amazing what a bit of lipstick will do in the right place. Eh, Joanie?

JOAN: Yes.

ARTHUR: It was nice, though. Wasn't it?

(*A marginal hesitation, again.*)

JOAN: Yes.

ARTHUR: A bit of capital and a bit of affection. I told you it was all I needed. You won't regret it, sweetie pie.

(*She lowers her head.*

Iris-out.)

INT. THE VILLAGE SCHOOL. EILEEN'S CLASS. DAY

Last lesson – story time for the seven-year-olds. But EILEEN *does not seem so relaxed as when she last told them an old favourite.*

EILEEN: The King's son climbed up the long tresses, but instead of finding Rapunzel he found the wicked witch at the top of the tower. 'Aha!' cried the witch, in a horrible, scratchy old voice – 'Aha! Your beautiful bird sits no longer in her nest. Rapunzel is lost to you for ever. For ever! You will never, never see her again! Never ever!'

(*There is mixed tension and rapture on the faces of the children.*

97

EILEEN *lowers her head, rather as Joan had done. Which provokes an immediate murmur – the children want her to finish the story.*)

EILEEN: Quiet!

(*Silence. She doesn't usually shout at them.*)

The Prince – The Prince was so heartbroken at these words that he leapt down from the tower. He did not die, but fell in a thicket of thorns at the foot of the tower. The thorns pierced his eyes and – The thorns *blinded* him and he wandered all about the forest, unable to see, eating nothing but the few roots and berries he could find by touch and smell alone.

(*She stops. The children are puzzled by her manner – so puzzled that they remain silent.*)

And so it was – And so – the poor Prince wandered about in misery for many a long year. Until he came at last to the desert where the wicked old witch had left Rapunzel. She was living there in the dry land with great wretchedness with the twins who had been born to her, a little boy and a little girl.

(*Quick shot of a couple of smirking boys.* EILEEN *looks at the class, almost challengingly. Then she seems to turn her head away, giving the final paragraph an oddly sepulchral quality.*)

The Prince heard a voice and he knew that voice. He stumbled blindly towards it and Rapunzel saw him. She rushed to him, fell on his neck and wept. Oh, she wept. She wept. Two of her tears trickled into his eyes and the eyes grew clear. And he could see again.

(*Silence. She looks at them again, her own eyes gleaming with unshed tears.*)

And they lived happily ever after.

(*A rustle of content.*

    She closes her eyes for a moment. The two simpering boys exchange glances, each daring the other until –)

BOY: Please, Miss.

(EILEEN *opens her eyes and turns a steady gaze on the boy, who loses his nerve.*)

EILEEN: Yes?

BOY: How did – I mean – them twins, Miss?

98

(*She stiffens.*)

EILEEN: What about them?

(*The other boy is egging his friend on.*)

BOY: Her warn't married, was her, Miss?

(*An excited titter from the class. And since* EILEEN *does nothing, the sound grows and spreads. And then, as it reaches a crescendo of whooping laughter, she suddenly screams at them.*)

EILEEN: Quiet!! Be quiet, damn you!

(*Shocked, frightened silence. Class and teacher absolutely still, looking at each other. Silence.*

Then, in hideous parody of all children in musicals, the class, in brisk unison, open the lids of their small desks and take out miniature replicas of all the dance band instruments. And, one-two, bouncing, they swing into 'Love is Good for Anything That Ails You' by Orlando and his Orchestra. They beat it out with exaggerated dance band panache.

EILEEN *'sings' to the impromptu orchestra. Then a hot piano takes over – the boy who had asked the question plonking his hands up and down the desk lid as though it were the piano keyboard. The others continue to gyrate with their 'instruments', until –*

Music out, abruptly. Children quickly, silently, resume their places. Fold arms behind their backs. Dead silence.)

That's better.

(*Fade.*)

EXT. THE COUNTRY, ON LONDON–GLOUCESTER ROAD. DAY

Arthur's car parked at the side of the road, driven up on to the grass. Pan across to a grassy, bumpy bank beyond a small hedge or wooden fence. ARTHUR, *out of sight from the road, and largely from us, just finishing urinating behind a solitary tree. He starts to whistle, buttoning up, and moving out of shelter. Then he stops whistling – follow his eye-line.*

Along a path that eventually leads to the road, spiralling out of some trees, comes a girl. But the way she is moving shows there is something wrong with her. ARTHUR, *eyes narrowing, stands watching. She approaches and, slowly, too slowly, passes. She should have seen him, but clearly has not. She is also strikingly attractive. Just as she passes him:*

ARTHUR: (*Suddenly*) Good afternoon, Miss!

    (*She starts. Then stops dead, turns half about.*)

GIRL: Who is there?

    (*The words are not aimed well enough. She is nearly blind.*)

ARTHUR: No you don't know me. Is – is anything the matter?

GIRL: (*Hesitant*) Nothing is the matter what – what do you want – ?

ARTHUR: My car is down there on the road – see it? I've just stopped for a – for a bit of a rest.

GIRL: (*Nervous*) I'm afraid I – excuse me.

    (*She goes to turn away, but awkwardly.* ARTHUR *watches, realizes, looks about, then goes up to her. She stands still when he speaks, looking very vulnerable.*)

ARTHUR: I beg your pardon, Miss. You can't – um – you can't see, can you?

GIRL: (*Hesitant*) Not properly. No.

ARTHUR: Isn't it dangerous – walking like this? I mean, it's very rough ground – ?

GIRL: No, I have done it so often. (*She goes to move again.*)

ARTHUR: Oh, you live – near, do you Miss? (*He is staring at her, very taken by her beauty.*)

GIRL: The house over there, behind the trees.

    (ARTHUR *looks, but cannot see anything.*)

ARTHUR: Do you want someone to walk with you?

GIRL: That's very kind, but I'm used to –

ARTHUR: (*Quickly*) I'm in no hurry, you see, driving from London to Gloucester. Could do with a stretch of the legs. It'd be a privilege, Miss.

GIRL: (*Firmer*) It's very kind. No thank you.

ARTHUR: But you haven't even got a stick –

GIRL: This is our property. I know my way.

ARTHUR: I'm not trespassing, am I?

GIRL: Yes.

ARTHUR: Oh, I'm sorry. It didn't look – well, you know, like – private.

GIRL: It doesn't matter. (*Slight smile.*) Goodbye.

ARTHUR: (*Awkwardly*) Goodbye, Miss.

    (*She seems to orientate herself, and slowly, gracefully, putting feet down carefully, moves off.* ARTHUR *watches her, very touched.*

Hold – a long time.

Then suddenly he calls out to the departing figure:)

I shall never forget this! Not ever!

(She stops, absolutely still, her back to ARTHUR. *He does not move. Then, with both of them peculiarly still, he calls out again:)*

I think you are the most beautiful young lady I have ever seen!

(Standing still, her back to him, she bows her head.)

(Shout) Please excuse me saying that! I couldn't help it!

(She still does not move. ARTHUR *speaks again, too quietly for her to hear; they are, oddly, at least twenty yards apart.)*

(Quietly) I'd cut off my right arm if I could make you see again. I'd – I dunno what I'd do if I could only – *(whisper/ hiss)* – *take your knickers off.*

(Quietly, up ahead, the GIRL *resumes her careful walk.*

ARTHUR, *tears in his eyes, watches and watches until she is out of sight.)*

(Shout) Take care! Take care!

(Then he turns, abruptly, to make his way back to the car. Picture 'turns over'.)

INT. PUB IN GLOUCESTER (FEATURED IN EPISODE ONE).
NIGHT

Again, crowded. Again, standard pub pianist thumping out a song – 'Marie, the Dawn is Breaking'. It is late.

Drift round boozy, animated faces eventually finding ARTHUR. *He is wedged in at the bar, with just enough elbow room to manage his pint. He lifts his pint to drink, and, as he does, sees* ALF, *one of the door-to-door salesmen from Episode 2.* ALF *is pushing his way to the bar.*

ARTHUR: Alf! Over here, old boy!

ALF: Oh, hello Arthur, old chap. Bit crowded, ennit?

ARTHUR: Plenty of money about, Alf. What's yours?

ALF: I dunno who's got it, then. Doesn't come my way, Arth.
That's very nice – I'll have a pint of half and half, old pal.

ARTHUR: Coming your way, Alf.

(As ARTHUR *turns to order,* ALF *surveys bar, and pianist.)*

ALF: *(Sourly)* Bloody noise.

ARTHUR: (*Over shoulder*) Too much left hand.

ALF: I dunno about that. It's the sort of tunes you get today that get up my nose. No – humour in it. Not like the old songs.

ARTHUR: You got to put a two bob piece down now to get a couple of pints. (*He is being served.*)

ALF: And who knows where it's all going to end, Arthur. Ta. Ta very much. Cheers.

(*They drink. Pianist switches to 'Tiptoe Through the Tulips'.*)

ARTHUR: How are the brushes going, Alf?

ALF: Don't ask me.

ARTHUR: Poor, is it?

ALF: I did about two hundred calls today. Two hundred bleed'n doorsteps. Took six orders. And one of them was only for a lavatory brush. (*Snigger.*) Gets right up my arse.

ARTHUR: Sheet music's as bad. Bloody terrible, in fact.

ALF: So where's all this money, then?

ARTHUR: It's my last trip with sheet music.

ALF: Honest?

ARTHUR: Gramophone records. That's the thing now. Me own little shop.

ALF: Blimey, Arth. Moving up a bit, entcha?

ARTHUR: Got a bit of capital behind me, see.

ALF: Have you? Well, good luck to you, Arth. (*He looks at* ARTHUR, *hesitant.*) You remember what you was on about last time. Month ago, wasn't it – here in Gloucester. Last time I was here.

ARTHUR: (*Evasive*) I wasn't myself, was I?

ALF: (*Disappointed*) Oh. I thought you'd got hold of something –

ARTHUR: I had. A nice bit of crumpet, Alf.

ALF: I mean, *something* – you know – a way of seeing things, like . . . Know what I mean?

(*Pause. Piano thumping.* ARTHUR *brooding, rubs his finger round his glass.*)

ARTHUR: I keep looking Alf.

ALF: Yeah – but you sounded as though you'd found it.

ARTHUR: It's all between the legs. Ennit?

ALF: Is it?

(ARTHUR *drinks, wipes his mouth with the back of his hand, a depression willy-nilly creeping up on him.*)

ARTHUR: Or in the belly. (*Sniff.*) Beer and pickles.

ALF: So that's it, then. That's all there is.

(ARTHUR *looks across at the pianist.*)

ARTHUR: (*Sadly*) Too heavy on the left. Far too heavy.

ALF: (*Doggedly*) Only, the way you was talking –

(ARTHUR *looks at him heavy-faced.*)

ARTHUR: I hadn't had it then, see. I hadn't dipped my wick.

ALF: And now you have.

(*They both sigh.*)

ARTHUR: Yes.

(*They both drink. The piano stops.*)

ALF: Any chance of – well – ?

ARTHUR: What?

ALF: Local girl, was it?

ARTHUR: Half an hour from here. Why?

ALF: Well – any chance of – well, come on – passing a bit of it
on, like?

(*Pause.*)

ARTHUR: She's not like that, Alf.

ALF: No. But she might be now. You know – once one's been
there –

(*Music starts: 'Hand in Hand' by Lew Stone band, vocals by
Al Bowlly.*)

ARTHUR: I don't promise anything, Alf. I'll see what I can do.

ALF: Bit of all right, is she?

ARTHUR: Lovely, Alf. Bloody lovely, mate.

(*Glowing a little, they drink as* ALF*'s mouth breaks from the
rim of his glass and he 'sings' 'Hand in Hand'.*

*In between verses, close mouth-shots of both men draining
their froth-flecked glasses, piggily.*

Music out. They look at each other.)

ALF: Going to have another, Arthur?

ARTHUR: Why not?

ALF: Would you like a chaser – drop of rum, or something?

(ARTHUR *sighs, heavily.*)

ARTHUR: Let's get tiddly, Alf. For Christ's sake.

ALF: Nothing to stop us, is there old mate?

(ARTHUR*'s face is as black as hell.*)

ARTHUR: Nothing at all. We can always piss it back out in the morning.
  (*Iris-out.*)

INT. WAITING-ROOM, DOCTOR'S SURGERY. DAY
With patients, as before. But little hand-bell goes almost at once, and EILEEN, *pale, face set, looking at none of the others, gets up and goes through to:*

INT. DOCTOR'S SURGERY. DAY
The DOCTOR *is elderly, hirsute. He does not get up from the narrow desk as* EILEEN *comes in. She comes part of the way in, then stops, as though wishing not to be there. The* DOCTOR *looks at her, steadily and without a smile.*
EILEEN: (*Faintly*) Can you say now, Doctor . . . ?
DOCTOR: (*Abruptly*) I'm sorry to have to tell you . . .
EILEEN: (*Anguished*) Oh, no.
DOCTOR: Yes. You are pregnant, Miss Everson.
  (*A faint emphasis on the 'Miss'.*
    Close-up on EILEEN.
    Fade.)

INT./EXT. IN ARTHUR'S CAR. DAY
As it turns into the lane leading to the cottage where Eileen lives with her father and two brothers. ARTHUR *rather pensive at the wheel. Cottage into view through windscreen.*

INT. THE COTTAGE. DAY
Where EILEEN *sits, hugging her knees, staring at nothing. Sound of car. She lifts her head for a moment, then drops it again. A moment, then* ARTHUR'*s face at the window. She does not see him. He peers in, looking at her. Hesitates, then taps on the glass. She looks up with a start, makes a tiny choking sound in her throat, goes to rush to the door, then visibly controls herself and gets up in a normal, restrained, even hesitant manner. She presses her palms together, unconsciously, then opens the door.*
ARTHUR *is on the step, grinning, but not comfortable.*
EILEEN: Arthur.
ARTHUR: Hello, sugar. Are you – alone?

EILEEN: Yes. (*Hesitates.*) They're on evening shift.

ARTHUR: What time will they be home?

(*Again she hesitates, face tightening.*)

EILEEN: About eleven o'clock.

ARTHUR: Ain't natural, is it? Working them sort of hours.

EILEEN: They're lucky to get a full shift.

ARTHUR: Depends on how you look at it, I suppose.

(*They look at each other, still in doorway.*)

EILEEN: I – I've just got in. From school.

ARTHUR: How are the little bleeders, then?

EILEEN: They – (*swallow*) Arthur.

(*Pause.*)

ARTHUR: What are we standing here for, Eileen? (*He seems nervous.*)

EILEEN: I – I don't know whether I want you to come in or not.

(**ARTHUR** *looks at* **EILEEN**, *seemingly hurt and bewildered.*)

ARTHUR: What do you say that for? Eileen – ?

EILEEN: I – (*But she stops, eyes fixed on him.*)

ARTHUR: Oh, now, love –

(*He reaches for her. She steps back.*)

EILEEN: You'd better come in.

ARTHUR: Yes.

(*Space between them, they go in.*

   ARTHUR *hovers, but is forced, by her demeanour, to sit apart from and opposite to her. Silence. They look at each other.*)

(*Evasive*) I haven't been able to get down this way. I just haven't been able to manage it.

EILEEN: (*Flat*) Nor to write.

(*He shifts uncomfortably.*)

ARTHUR: No.

EILEEN: Why haven't you written, Arthur?

ARTHUR: I know I'm in the wrong. I know I should have done but I'm here now – enn I?

(*She looks at him, steadily.*)

EILEEN: And what are you here *for*, Arthur?

(*He looks down, then up.*)

ARTHUR: You, my love.

EILEEN: (*Tense*) Am I?

ARTHUR: What?

EILEEN: Your love.

(*Pause.*

    ARTHUR *finding it hard, something like 'the truth' is shaping itself inside him.*)

ARTHUR: Now that – I know this doesn't sound very nice, Eileen – but now that I can see you, sitting there – I – yes. My love.

EILEEN: And when I'm not in front of you?

ARTHUR: Don't let's talk like this, Eileen.

EILEEN: What way shall we talk then, Arthur?

ARTHUR: I don't want to talk at all.

EILEEN: (*With an edge*) What *do* you want to do?
    (*He looks at her, and tries a grin.*)

ARTHUR: Kiss you.

EILEEN: (*Mockingly*) Is that all?
    (*His smile dies.*)

ARTHUR: To tell you the truth, I haven't . . .

EILEEN: (*Interrupting*) The truth, yes. Please tell me the truth.
    (*Fractional pause.*)

ARTHUR: I was going to say, I can't stay very long, anyway.

EILEEN: Why did you come?

ARTHUR: Like I said, to see you.

EILEEN: But only for a little while.

ARTHUR: Well – I can't st–

EILEEN: A few minutes?
    (*Pause.*)

ARTHUR: I didn't say that. Not just – no, I'm not popping in and then popping out. What's the matter wiv you? Just because I didn't . . .

EILEEN: What's the matter with me? Do you really want to know?

ARTHUR: (*Shifting about*) I mean . . . we're grown-ups and all that – there was no sort of, sort of, whatdyacallit – commitment.

EILEEN: *Are* you married, Arthur?

ARTHUR: (*Indignant*) What d'you go and ask me *that* for?
    (*Pause.*

    She looks at him. He tries to hold her gaze and then his eyes slide helplessly away.*)

EILEEN: (*Flat, but with certainty.*) Yes. You are.

(*Silence. And his silence is eloquent.*)

ARTHUR: (*Eventually*) You – you haven't got such a thing as – Eileen, do you think you could make us a cup of tea?

(*She looks at him then, slowly, painfully slowly, her eyes fill with tears.* ARTHUR *watching, can scarcely bear it.*)

(*Thickly*) Oh, don't do that or you'll set me off.

EILEEN: (*Controlled, just*) What have you got to cry about, Arthur?

ARTHUR: (*Choked*) I dunno (*almost a sob*) but it feels like everything.

(*She watches him a moment. Then, getting up abruptly*)

EILEEN: I'll put the kettle on.

(ARTHUR, *fighting a lump in his throat, watches her busy herself. Then, after a moment, puts his hands to his face and weeps, almost without restraint.*

Wordless, lips tight, EILEEN *carries on, preparing pot, boiling kettle, setting out two cups. Let it occupy natural time, this domestic activity, so that it seems to take a long space, and a weird one.*

ARTHUR'*s crying, meanwhile, subsiding. He controls himself eventually. But his face is dead, his eyes without lustre.*)

It ought to stand a bit longer but you'd better have a cup now. Do you take sugar?

ARTHUR: Yes. Two spoonfuls. Please.

(*She puts in sugar, milk, pours tea, hands him a cup. An activity he watches as though it were some alien ritual. They sip tea, not now quite looking at each other.*

Then, suddenly, very matter of fact:)

EILEEN: I'm going to have a baby.

(*Chink-chink of cup on saucer as* ARTHUR'*s hand jerks, then trembles.*)

ARTHUR: (*Trembling*) How – how do you know? I mean – I mean, is that definite?

EILEEN: Quite definite.

(*Pause. Weirdly, they both struggle to sip at their cups of tea.*)

ARTHUR: Does anyone else know? Your dad, er –

EILEEN: No. Only the doctor.

(ARTHUR *gets up, sits down, gets up again.*)

ARTHUR: Pardon me, Eileen. But – excuse me, Eileen – but do

you intend – I mean, are you going to try to get rid of it?
(*Pause.*)

EILEEN: To *what*? (*No anger.*)

ARTHUR: Get rid of . . . (*He then realises how dreadful that phrase sounds.*) No. That's not how – I mean – Do you want to have the, the – baby, Eileen?

EILEEN: Please sit down.
(*He does, immediately.*)

ARTHUR: Yes.
(*She puts her cup down and seems to study him. He twitches a bit.*)

EILEEN: Have you already got children?

ARTHUR: No. No – I – no.

EILEEN: If you tell me any more lies, I will stick a knife in your back. (*Said without raised voice, and therefore chillingly.*)

ARTHUR: Christ, Eileen.

EILEEN: The truth. Please.

ARTHUR: Cross my heart and – (*his voice trails off*) – no. Eileen, no. We haven't got any kids.

EILEEN: But you do live with your wife?

ARTHUR: I – (*He stops, helpless.*)

EILEEN: (*Calmly*) Yes. I see.
(*Her calm, her quiet pain, suddenly jerks* ARTHUR *to his feet again, with an anguished cry.*)

ARTHUR: What are you going to do!

EILEEN: There's nothing very much I can do. What are *you* going to do?

ARTHUR: Me? (*He swallows, in terror, and sits down again.*) Yes, what the bleed'n hell am *I* going to do?

EILEEN: I shall lose my job.

ARTHUR: (*In horror*) Will you?
(*She almost laughs.*)

EILEEN: Miss Everson, the infant teacher, and her baby.

ARTHUR: No. They won't have it, will they? They won't stand for that.

EILEEN: And I shall have to move away.

ARTHUR: Will you? Yes – I suppose so. Oh, Christ.
(*Pause.*)

EILEEN: Serves me right, doesn't it?

ARTHUR: (*Twisting his head away*) Don't say that! Please don't!

EILEEN: I believed you, Arthur. Silly me.

ARTHUR: I . . . (*He stops.*)

EILEEN: Yes.

ARTHUR: I believed myself!

EILEEN: Yes.

(*He looks at her, almost in awe.*)

ARTHUR: Do you *understand* – ?

EILEEN: Yes.

ARTHUR: My God. I think you do! I think you really do!

(*Fractional pause.*)

EILEEN: I wanted you, you see.

ARTHUR: (*Brightening*) Did you, love?

EILEEN: Oh, yes.

(ARTHUR's *whole manner is changing. He is touched by wonder.*)

ARTHUR: And you still do, don't you, Eileen. You – still – do.

(*She holds his gaze, tilts her head, and speaks almost proudly.*)

EILEEN: Yes. I still do. Very much.

ARTHUR: (*Almost to himself*) Blim-ey!

EILEEN: (*Falters*) What's the matter?

ARTHUR: I – never in all my life . . . Not once. I've never heard a woman talk like that. Just like that.

(*She lowers her head a little.*)

EILEEN: (*Faint irony*) It's not decent. Is it?

ARTHUR: It – it – (*He can hardly get it out.*) It's bloody marvellous!

EILEEN: (*Utterly matter-of-fact*) I spend most of my time thinking about it.

(ARTHUR *literally gapes at her.*)

ARTHUR: Thinking about . . . about –

EILEEN: About that second time.

ARTHUR: When your dad and them was on nights –

EILEEN: Yes.

(*His eyes are too bright. He is totally excited.*)

ARTHUR: Gawd – it was nice – it was that! – in that big soft bed.

EILEEN: But –

(*She waits. He hangs on the word.*)

ARTHUR: But what? But what? Eileen –

EILEEN: But you went away.
   (*He deflates.*)
ARTHUR: (*Sigh*) Yes.
EILEEN: So that's that, then. Isn't it.
   (*He frowns, staring at her, trying to formulate something.*)
ARTHUR: Say we was married, me and you –
EILEEN: (*Again, faint mockery*) Ah.
ARTHUR: No. Just for the sake of argument. Say we was.
EILEEN: Well?
   (*He shifts about, looks away.*)
ARTHUR: I'm going to go all round the houses.
   (*She waits.*)
   Well – there's a story I . . . Do you mind if I have a fag,
   Eileen?
EILEEN: No.
   (*He fumbles nervously.*)
ARTHUR: You don't smoke, do you?
EILEEN: No.
   (*He drags in the smoke, hungrily.*)
ARTHUR: There's this story I heard. And it's true, really true. In
   the band, well-known band, there's a lead man singer and
   a lead woman singer –
EILEEN: What's this got –
ARTHUR: (*Urgently*) Shh! A minute. A minute. And – just listen
   a little bit – and they have this engagement at one of the
   big West End hotels. Now, then. (*He looks at her anxiously.*)
   They gave the liftman a five-pound note to stop the lift
   between floors and – and turn his back and shut his eyes.
   (*He waits.*)
EILEEN: (*Eventually*) Do people do things like that?
ARTHUR: (*Excited*) Like what, Eileen? Like what?
EILEEN: Well – (*Her eyes flicker away, and then back to him,
   suddenly bright*) – make love in a lift like that?
ARTHUR: You mean kissing – do you?
EILEEN: (*Disappointed*) Oh – is that all?
ARTHUR: (*Delighted*) There's a good little girl! Oh, Eileen.
   Eileen. You knew what I was on about – Would *you* ever
   do that? What *they* did, I mean – ?
   (*She looks at him, her eyes narrow.*)

EILEEN: Between which floors, Arthur?
> (*Startled little pause, then he slaps his thighs, laughing so much.*)

ARTHUR: By God, Eileen . . . by God . . . you're a gel, you are – Hoo! Hoo!
> (*Music bounces in over his laughter. She remains stiff but very, very alert.*
>
> *Music: 'Oh You Nasty Man' by Ray Noble; singer Dorothy Carless.* EILEEN *'sings'. As music changes tempo, with strong drum beat and no words,* EILEEN, *in rhythm, begins an elaborate striptease in front of* ARTHUR. *When she unrolls her stockings at the end of the music, she looks up, brazenly, at* ARTHUR. *She stands, almost fully unclothed, in front of* ARTHUR, *looking now – without the parodied support of the music, so to speak – extremely vulnerable. She makes a small gesture of defence, or perhaps it is an appeal. And* ARTHUR, *making a small noise in his throat, rushes to enfold her.*
>
> *Fade.*)

EXT. GRASSY BANK, TREES AND PATH ALONGSIDE LONDON–GLOUCESTER ROAD. DAY
Back to the spot where the blind girl walked.
Moving in from long shot, slowly. Picking up first one, then another, then several uniformed policemen.
Music: 'Pick Yourself Up', Lew Stone band, driving and bouncing in at the end of long shot, with a shock.
Policemen are bent over, picking and scratching about in the long grass and bushes beside the path. Music out before vocal begins, abruptly.
Close-shot: one of the policemen as he straightens, with something in his hand, and calls, excitedly:

POLICEMAN: I got summat here, sergeant! Packet of fags.
> Empty packet of fags.

SERGEANT: (*Calls*) What make be they?

POLICEMAN: Craven A.

SERGEANT: Does not harm the throat.
> (*Wipe.*)

EXT. STREET (PERHAPS BY GRAPHICS). DAY
Newspaper placard, behind wire grid: 'Blind girl found strangled'.
Pan to the ACCORDION PLAYER *playing, on pavement, 'There is a*
Green Hill Far Away'.
ACCORDION PLAYER: (*Mechanically, as he plays*) Thank you very
    much sir, thank you very, very much madam, thank you
    very, very much sir, thank you very, very much –
    (*Dissolve.*)

INT. POLICE STATION, COUNTRY TOWN, OXFORDSHIRE.
DAY
Usual plain room. On a table a cloth is spread, upon which are
various bits and pieces: a button, the empty packet of Craven A
cigarettes, some scraps of paper, a broken pocket comb, a hairpin, a
bus ticket.
POLICEMAN: Yes, sir. That's the lot. That's everything, sir.
SUPER: Mmm. Not very much, is it?
POLICEMAN: It's not a busy spot, sir. Nobody stops there.
SUPER: (*Sharp*) Somebody did!
POLICEMAN: Yes, sir.
    (*They both look at the cloth.*)
SUPER: (*Eventually*) You'd think they'd have more sense –
    letting a girl who can't see walk about like that. In *this* day
    and age.
POLICEMAN: The mother says she never went on the road, sir.
SUPER: But anybody could have seen her.
POLICEMAN: Not unless they knew she were there.
SUPER: What's that?
POLICEMAN: Well – you can't see the path from the road, sir.
    (*Pause.*)
SUPER: Mmm.
    (*Pause.*)
POLICEMAN: So he'd have to know it was there . . . or . . .
SUPER: Or stumble across it by accident. And find her, alone.
POLICEMAN: That's right, sir. She wouldn't see him, poor soul.
SUPER: A strong man. And a girl who can't see.
POLICEMAN: Sir. Terrible, sir. Hanging's too good.
SUPER: A very strong man. (*Sniff.*) The bruises round her neck
    are – well – (*He stops.*)

POLICEMAN: (*Quickly*) Yes, sir.
    (*Fractional pause.*)
SUPER: More like King Kong.
    (*They both nearly smile.*)
POLICEMAN: King Kong with a car, though.
SUPER: Not necessarily. Oh, no.
POLICEMAN: Unless it were local. Though I don't . . .
SUPER: Or one of the tramps. There are more of them on the
    road than ever before. And it *is* the London road, bear that
    in mind.
    (*Pause.*)
POLICEMAN: Does this stuff go on to Oxford, sir?
SUPER: (*Irritated*) In time. In all good time, constable. *I* want to
    have a good look at it myself first. (*Broods.*) But there's not
    much to go on here, I'll be damned.
POLICEMAN: It mightn't look much now – but –
SUPER: Pennies from heaven. Yes, yes, I know, don't teach
    your granny to suck eggs, my boy.
    (*Wipe.*)

INT. EILEEN'S CLASSROOM. DAY
*The last few children going through the door at end of another school
day. One* BOY *lingers – adoringly.*
BOY: Dost want me to help lock cupboards, Miss?
    (*She smiles at him, distractedly.*)
EILEEN: No, no. Run off home, there's a good lad.
BOY: (*Disappointed*) Miss.
    (*Turns to go, all but collides with* HEADMASTER *coming in
    through door.*)
HEADMASTER: Steady!
BOY: Oo – sorry, zir. I –
HEADMASTER: Unless you want the cane, my boy, you'll look
    where you are going.
BOY: Zir.
    (*And he backs out cautiously, almost bowing.*
       EILEEN *is putting some books into a high cupboard at back
    of class.* HEADMASTER *looks at her for a moment, rather
    furtively. She turns, books in hand, slight frown, picking up the
    merest trace of lasciviousness from the little old man.*)

HEADMASTER: Everything all right, Miss Everson?

EILEEN: Yes, headmaster. Perfectly.

> (*She puts last books away. But he is still there. They look at each other.*)

HEADMASTER: I – ah – you aren't rushing to get away for a few moments, are you?

EILEEN: No – not exactly.

HEADMASTER: Nobody picking you up, then? (*She looks at him.*)

EILEEN: No.

HEADMASTER: Ah – not the gentleman with the car?

EILEEN: No. Why?

HEADMASTER: (*Quickly*) Oh, no reason, no reason. I – ah – I would, however quite like a word with you if I may, Miss Everson.

EILEEN: Yes, of course.

HEADMASTER: In confidence.

> (*She stiffens slightly.*)

EILEEN: Have the boys been up to their –

HEADMASTER: (*Quickly*) No, no. Nothing to do with the pupils. At least not with their behaviour.

> (*Fractional pause.*)

EILEEN: (*Tense*) Something to do with me?

HEADMASTER: I've known you now for a very long time, Eileen, and I –

EILEEN: (*Interrupting*) Oh, dear!

HEADMASTER: What's the matter?

EILEEN: That's the sort of sentence which usually means trouble.

HEADMASTER: Oh. Does it?

EILEEN: Yes. (*Half laugh.*) Like 'Let me be perfectly frank for a moment' or 'I hope you won't mind me saying, but . . .'

> (*Pause.* HEADMASTER *looks at pictures on the walls, embarrassed.*)

HEADMASTER: *That* one was there when *I* was a child, you know. And I haven't looked at it, I mean *looked* at it, for – oh, nigh on twenty or thirty years, when I taught Standard One.

> (*It is a month-by-month picture, with a little verse beneath each segment.*)

EILEEN: Well – the months *do* stay pretty much the same.
HEADMASTER: (*Sadly*) One of the few things that does.
(*Pause.*)
EILEEN: What did you want to – to say, Mr Warner?
(*He looks at her, then, strangely, covers his eyes with one hand.*)
HEADMASTER: (*Slowly in tones*)

    January snowing
    February rain
    March with winds a-blowing
    April sun again
    May a world of flowers
    June with dancing leaves
    July long, lazy hours
    August golden sheaves
    September, apples redden
    October, winter's near
    November, skies all leaden
    December, Christmas cheer!
    (*Tense little silence.*)

EILEEN: Yes. It's strange how little things like that can stay in the mind.
HEADMASTER: (*Obscurely moved*) But you see, Eileen, I can remember you saying those lines as one of my little girls (*points to desk*), standing right there at the front of the class with a bit of blue ribbon in your hair.
(*Pause.*)
EILEEN: Dr Bartholomew is one of the school governors, isn't he?
(*The* HEADMASTER *turns away to look at the various pictures, again tears spring to his eyes.*)
HEADMASTER: (*Upset*) 'September, apples redden.'
EILEEN: Ah, yes. The apple.
(*He turns swiftly.*)
HEADMASTER: I'm not, I hope, a blasphemous man, Eileen, but I do often think that the picture we are given of Eve in Genesis is not altogether a fair one. Indeed, when I look round and about – and even into my own heart, yes – I think it much, much more likely that it was Adam who offered the fruit to Eve.

115

EILEEN: (*Shocked*) Mr Warner – you – you've got tears in your . . .

(*She stops, abruptly, wishing she had not said it. He wipes at his eyes with an old and now trembling hand.*)

HEADMASTER: Be that as it may –

EILEEN: (*Ashamed*) I beg your pardon.

(*In order to control himself, he turns half away again to the drawings on the wall.*)

HEADMASTER: Where does it all go to, I wonder?

EILEEN: (*Very tense*) What are you – ?

HEADMASTER: These children. Look – there's a tree one of them has drawn, and it's like a diamond. With different sorts of fruit on the same branch.

EILEEN: A greengrocer's tree. (*Her laugh is tight and forced.*)

HEADMASTER: No. no. A tree out of The Garden. And that's how they *see* things, you know. I think they really do see things in a way that – in a way that they eventually lose. Not only lose, but even forget they ever had.

EILEEN: Yes, so why – (*Again, she stops abruptly.*)

HEADMASTER: No – do go on. Please say it.

EILEEN: This is not really the time or the place, and it sounds unkind – but – oh, excuse me – but if you understand all that, about a child's mind – why – (*Again she stops.*)

HEADMASTER: (*Dully*) Why do I *hit* them so often?

(*Fractional pause.*)

EILEEN: (*Quietly*) Yes.

HEADMASTER: So that they can learn enough to keep a job in the pits, Miss Everson. What do they want with visions, or trees shaped like diamonds? Or any memory at all of the Garden of Eden? (*Sniff.*) Cheap music will do, cheap music. And beer. And skittles.

EILEEN: Oh, but that's – that's –

HEADMASTER: (*Bleakly*) Dreadful. Yes.

(*Pause.*)

EILEEN: Life isn't very – grand. Sometimes. Is it?

HEADMASTER: It is – just – if you obey the rules.

EILEEN: (*Gently*) The rules, Mr Warner. But whose?

HEADMASTER: Ours is not to reason why, my dear.

EILEEN: Not ever?

HEADMASTER: Oh, frequently. Provided you pay the price, of
course. Or – evade detection.
(*They look at each other. She lowers her eyes.*)
EILEEN: Yes.
HEADMASTER: Forgive me but – are you going to get married?
EILEEN: I – (*She looks up, very direct.*) I'm afraid I don't know, I
cannot say. But not before my baby is born – there
wouldn't be time.
(*He sucks in his breath, pained.*)
HEADMASTER: The fellow needs a good thrashing!
EILEEN: Yes. He probably does.
HEADMASTER: What does your father or your brothers – what
do they intend to do about it?
EILEEN: Nothing.
HEADMASTER: (*Angrily*) Nothing! What do you –
EILEEN: (*Cutting in*) They don't know anything about it. Yet.
(*He is getting angrier.*)
HEADMASTER: It's that fellow with the car, isn't it! I know what
I'd like to do with him!
EILEEN: Please. Don't.
HEADMASTER: I suppose he's married or –
EILEEN: I don't wish to talk about it.
HEADMASTER: (*Anguished*) But what will you *do*?
(*Pause. She considers.*)
EILEEN: I realize I cannot stay as a teacher.
(*He looks at her, turns away.*)
HEADMASTER: (*Thickly*) No.
EILEEN: Do you think I could stay till the end of the month?
(*Distressed, he shakes his head.*)
I see well – that's that, then. Can I stay until the end of the
week?
(*He turns to her, quickly.*)
HEADMASTER: Oh, my dear girl! Of course you can, of
course.
EILEEN: Yes. Thank you.
(*They look at each other.*)
HEADMASTER: This is the worst day of my life.
EILEEN: Don't say that.
HEADMASTER: Ah. But it is. It *is*.

EILEEN: (*Upset*) I'm sorry. I'm terribly sorry about –
everything.

HEADMASTER: Something very, very special indeed – (*thickly*) –
very, very bright and – will go out of my life when you
leave this little school of ours. I shan't want to come here
myself.

EILEEN: Oh, now.

(*He turns away.*)

HEADMASTER: No, you don't understand. And you'd be
horrified if you did.

(*As she looks at him – indeed potentially horrified – he starts to
walk away. Then he stops, and takes out his wallet.*)
(*Embarrassed*) Please don't be offended.

EILEEN: No! Don't do that!

(*But he has already taken out four pound notes.*)

HEADMASTER: You'll find you'll need more than you think you
need. I'm afraid I can't offer more, but – now, please.
Please be sensible.

EILEEN: I'd rather you didn't.

HEADMASTER: (*Almost angrily*) Don't be foolish! (*And he grabs
her hand and thrusts the money into it.*)

EILEEN: (*Shaken*) I – Oh, Mr Warner – I shall always
remember this – you've been very, very kind.

(*The tears are back in his eyes.*)

HEADMASTER: Something very special, and very bright, my dear.

EILEEN: (*Making light*) Now, now, Mr Warner. You're flirting
with me, sir.

(*He looks at her a long time, very seriously, during which music
starts, very quietly: 'I Love You Truly', by Al Bowlly.*)

HEADMASTER: (*Almost a whisper*) I know trees that are shaped
like diamonds. *I've* never forgotten.

EILEEN: (*Tense*) I think I –

(*She stops.
Music gets louder, and the* HEADMASTER *'sings' softly to her.
At the end of the song they stand looking at each other.*)

EILEEN: (*Gently*) Nobody ever, ever stops – yearning, Mr
Warner.

HEADMASTER: (*Recovering*) Then they jolly well better had,
Miss Everson.

EILEEN: No. I don't think so.
(*Silence. He holds out his hand.*)
HEADMASTER: (*Dignified*) Good afternoon, my dear.
EILEEN: G–good afternoon.
HEADMASTER: (*Abrupt*) Please try to take very special care of
yourself.
EILEEN: Yes, I will.
(*He looks at her, seems about to speak, then turns and walks
away. Something about his exit disturbs her. She stares after
him. Hold. She bites her lip. A door shuts in the distance.*

Move slowly in big close-up of EILEEN.)
(*Just audible*)
January snowing
February rain
March with winds a-blowing.
(*Silence.*

Pull out slowly.

*She turns to the blackboard and easel. Picks up a stick of
chalk, and writes, in big plain letters: 'Goodbye children'. The
chalk goes squeak, squeak.*

And then, after looking at it, rubs it out.)
Close your eyes. Stand on one leg. And count up to ten,
ve-ry slow-ly. (*A sardonic expression.*)
(*Iris-out.*)

EXT. THE GLOUCESTER–LONDON ROAD. DAY
Arthur's car chugging homewards.

INT./EXT. IN THE CAR. DAY
ARTHUR *at the wheel, whistling happily. He stops whistling as the
road turns into a familiar (to us) stretch. Close-up of* ARTHUR.
Wavery dissolve to:

EXT. FLASHBACK TO THE PATH BY THE ROAD. DAY
ARTHUR: I beg your pardon, miss. You can't – um – you can't
see, can you?
GIRL: (*Hesitant*) Not properly. No.
ARTHUR: Isn't it dangerous – walking like this. I mean, it's very
rough ground – ?

119

GIRL: No, I have done it so often.
(*Wavery dissolve.*)

INT./EXT. IN THE CAR. DAY
ARTHUR *peering about in his car, looking for the spot he had stopped before. He slows.*

EXT. THE ROAD BY THE MURDER PATCH. DAY
Arthur's car crunches twig and gravel as it pulls into the side of the road. A moment. Then he gets out of the car, crosses the verge, goes over the wooden fence, up on to the grassy bank. He looks about, all about, looking for the blind girl.
ARTHUR: (*To himself*) Where are yer, my lovely?
(*He sees no one, and so, looking about once more, settles by a tree, looking down on the path. He takes out a packet of Craven A cigarettes, lights one, puts head back against the tree, blows out smoke and relaxes.*
   Slow fade.)

INT. THE COTTAGE IN THE FOREST. NIGHT
The three miners – her FATHER *and two* BROTHERS *– watch with stupefied gloom as* EILEEN *folds up her few clothes and puts them neatly into a cheap suitcase. Nobody says anything for a while. Then:*
DAVE: Aye. That's all very well, our Eileen.
(*Silence. She carries on packing.*)
DAD: (*Eventually*) But tha' costn't goo tonight, Eileen.
EILEEN: No, Dad. Not tonight.
DAD: Well, then!
EILEEN: First thing in the morning. On the first bus to Gloucester from Five Acres.
DAD: To London, is it?
EILEEN: Yes. I'll get the train to Paddington.
DAVE: But thow ootn't be safe up there!
EILEEN: Don't be silly.
MAURICE: (*Upset*) Dave's right, our Eileen. You bent used to't. Anything could happen to tha'.
EILEEN: I know how to look after myself.
DAVE: (*Angrier*) But dost! You ant got nowhere to stay or anything!

(*She shuts the lid of the case and looks at them.*)

EILEEN: Look – I'll write to you tomorrow night, one letter for all of you – I won't lose touch or (*her voice quavers slightly*) or anything silly like that. I'll find a room very easily. I've got enough for more than a month.

DAD: (*In pain*) Things is dear up there, mind.

DAVE: Ay – 'um be! You can pay up to two pounds a week for a room, without any meals or nothing.

EILEEN: Don't be silly!

MAURICE: That's right mind, Eileen. Tom Wintle went up to the band contest and him said –

EILEEN: Tom Wintle couldn't even find his way round Gloucester, Maurice!

DAD: Holt on, holt on. *You* ant never bin up to London bar thik once.

EILEEN: There's no use in arguing about it. My mind's made up.

DAVE: Aye. That's all very well!

DAD: How ool we manage here, on our own? Have you thought of that!

EILEEN: Oh now, Dad. You know you'll be all right.

DAD: I don't know't at all! And we shall miss your bit of money, o' butty.

(*Silence.*)

EILEEN: (*Strained*) I'm sorry, I'm very sorry.

DAVE: Sorry don't get the victuals!

MAURICE: (*Quickly*) Highsht, Dave!

DAVE: Highsht theeself!

(*They look at each other, flaring up, then, sheepishly turn to* EILEEN.)

EILEEN: You two.

MAURICE: (*Pleading*) You byunt going because of that, be ya Eileen? Cos of the rows and –

EILEEN: (*Quickly*) Of course not, Maurice.

DAVE: (*Awkwardly*) Only it chunt serious, look.

EILEEN: I know it isn't Dave. No – I love both of you. But I hope you won't quarrel so much. Think of Dad.

DAD: (*Heavily*) I wish *you* ood, o' butty. I don't want tha' to goo.

121

EILEEN: (*Moved*) Oh, Dad.

DAVE: It's thik bloke, yun it? Thik Arthur, with the big talk.

EILEEN: No. It's for me. It's for myself.

MAURICE: There's nothing wrong is there, Eileen? With you, I mean.

(*She smiles at him, the one most like herself.*)

EILEEN: Nothing, Maurice. You're not to worry about anything like that.

DAD: We shall be wuss off, though, you can't get round that, Eileen.

EILEEN: I'm not trying to . . .

DAD: And I can't shift as much coal as I could. Where's the money coming from, o' but?

EILEEN: Dad . . .

DAD: No, no you *tell* me.

EILEEN: You can't expect me to . . .

DAD: (*Cutting in*) This is your home. Here!

MAURICE: Don't poke your finger at her, Dad. We shan't get anywhere like this.

DAD: I byunt poking my finger!

EILEEN: Look . . .

MAURICE: What's that, then? Your big toe?

EILEEN: Now look . . .

DAD: (*To* MAURICE) Cheeky bugger!

DAVE: Holt on! Holt on!

EILEEN: (*Decisively*) Listen to me! Please!

(*They stop and look at her.*)

I have made up my mind. And I have the right to make my own life in my own way.

DAD: Yes, but . . .

EILEEN: I've done my bit in this house.

DAVE: Nobody's saying you ant.

EILEEN: I've cooked for you and washed for you, and cleaned this house from top to bottom *and* brought in my share of the money.

(*Silence.*)

DAVE: That's all very well!

EILEEN: Don't keep saying that. Why do you keep saying that? Don't you *understand* what I am saying! I have the right –

the right – to go if I want to go. I'm over twenty-one, I've
worked for my living. I've done my duty. And-I-want-
something-else.
(*The three men look at each other.*)
DAD: (*Feebly*) If it was going away to get married, then . . .
EILEEN: Then it would be the same!
(*Silence.*)
MAURICE: Good luck to you, Eileen.
DAVE: Aye. We'd all wish tha' that.
EILEEN: I know you do.
(*Silence.*)
DAD: So long as we know you're all right. Please God.
(*Fade.*)

INT. ROOM AT POLICE STATION. NIGHT
ARTHUR *sits by himself at a plain table, very morose. A*
POLICEMAN *stands at the door, trying not to look at* ARTHUR.
ARTHUR: (*Eventually*) You're all going to be very sorry. I can
tell you that! Make bloody fools of yourselves!
(*The* POLICEMAN *darts his eyes away quickly.* ARTHUR *glares
at him. Then* ARTHUR *reaches for a cigarette, strikes a match.*)
Do you want a fag, copper?
(*The* POLICEMAN, *rather nervously, shakes his head.*)
Cat got your bleed'n tongue, has it?
(*No response.*
    ARTHUR, *worried, blows out smoke. Sound of steam train in*
distance.
    Wipe.)

INT./EXT. RAILWAY CARRIAGE. THIRD CLASS. DAY
EILEEN *in seat by window, cheap suitcase on rack, an old woman
and three men knee-to-knee. She is looking at a* Radio Times, *and
dreamily out of the window.*
She concentrates on the contemporary Radio Times. *Let's us see
some of its goodies, so to speak. Then puts it down to stare out of
window again.*
The PASSENGER *opposite has had his eye on the magazine. He
plucks up courage.*
PASSENGER: Beg your pardon, Miss . . .

EILEEN: (*Coldly*) Yes?

PASSENGER: (*Nervously*) I was wondering if you'd mind if I had a look at that *Radio Times*.

EILEEN: Yes . . . but there's nothing much in it.

SECOND PASSENGER: As usual. (*Smiles and chuckles.*)

FIRST PASSENGER: Only I wanted to see if they were broadcasting the big fight. From the Albert Hall.

SECOND PASSENGER: The *Henry* Hall is more in my line. (*Smiles and chuckles.*)

(*A speculative look replaces the smile on* EILEEN*'s face.*)

EILEEN: Yes. I quite like his dance band . . .

SECOND PASSENGER: Crisp. Very crisp.

EILEEN: Being in the business myself. In a way.

(*They all look at her. She swallows, and smiles.*)

My . . . my husband is a songwriter, you see. I'm going up to London to join him as a matter of fact.

(*The Forest of Dean is falling away mile by mile.*)

THIRD PASSENGER: That's what I like about these long journeys. You never know who you are going to meet.

(*Realizing, too late, that she has no wedding ring,* EILEEN *is trying to hide her left hand. But the* OLD WOMAN *notices.*)

OLD WOMAN: Nor what tales that' bist going to hear.

(*The* SECOND PASSENGER *winks at* EILEEN. *She smiles back, rather brazenly.*)

EILEEN: I can't wait to get back to London, actually. Always something going on.

SECOND PASSENGER: Life begins at Oxford Circus.

OLD WOMAN: If you've got no work to do.

EILEEN: (*Laugh*) Or if you haven't!

(*The men look at her speculatively. She goes to pull her skirt down, then leaves it.*

Start urgent, driving, bouncing music: 'Radio Times': Henry Hall, with singer Val Rosing and chorus.

The train plunges into a tunnel, music bouncing. It emerges; they look at each other and the SECOND PASSENGER *begins 'singing' along to Val Rosing. The others provide the chorus.*

EILEEN *'sings' the final verse, then bouncy music fades. Clack-clackety-clack.*

Eyes look at eyes then dart away again. English people in a

railway carriage. Long whistle. Close-up of EILEEN: *the*
plangent sound disturbs her.
    Picture 'turns over'.)

CAPTIONS
Paddington Station, 1935. Merging into detailed, affectionate
drawings of famous London landmarks: Nelson, Eros, Palace,
Broadcasting House, Marble Arch, Big Ben – ending up with
Oxford Circus and crowds, crowds, lights, signs, traffic.
Music over: a raucous chorus of 'Life Begins at Oxford Circus' –
Jack Hylton Band.
Irising from captions to:

EXT. STREET. NIGHT
Theatrically, a single spot falling out of darkness and brick upon
scared-looking EILEEN, *clutching her suitcase, alone. Chorus carried*
over to just take this in.
Silence.
Iris-out to:

INT. JOAN'S AND ARTHUR'S BEDROOM. NIGHT
JOAN *jerking up in bed, alarmed, as* ARTHUR *creeps in.*
JOAN: Arthur – ?
ARTHUR: It's all right. It's only me.
JOAN: But where have you *been*? Oh, Arthur, you said you were
    coming back at –
ARTHUR: (*Snort*) Where've I been? Where've I been? In the
    bleed'n nick – that's where I've been!
    (*Startled pause. She pulls the light cord. They blink in the light.*)
JOAN: (*Alarmed*) Arthur?
ARTHUR: Did you read about that blind girl that was done in in
    Oxfordshire? The cops said it was in all the papers.
JOAN: Yes, I – but what –
ARTHUR: (*Proudly*) They thought as *I* did it!
    (JOAN *stares at him, frightened.*)
JOAN: Wh-who thought . . . ?
ARTHUR: The cops. (*His anger returns.*) Silly thick-headed
    rozzers! They've had me in a police station for four bleed'n
    hours, Joan.

125

JOAN: (*Sick*) But what for, Arthur? Why? Arthur?

ARTHUR: What for? Because I stopped to have a jimmy riddle, that's what for! I would have been home at the time I said if they hadn't – cor blimey. I *would* have to have a pee right on the very spot where this girl was done in!

JOAN: But – are you telling the truth? Is this another of your jokes, Arthur?

ARTHUR: Joke! Some bloody joke, ennit? Third-degree, I had.

JOAN: But *why* – just because –

ARTHUR: They thought I was the murderer returning to the scene of the crime, didn't they?

JOAN: Oh, Arthur! How awful!

ARTHUR: Took 'em all that time to get that dozy sod in Gloucester, from the shop. Good thing for me, Joanie. I was making my last call at the time that poor bitch was being choked to death.

JOAN: Oh, my God.

ARTHUR: If I hadn't had a whatdyacallit – alibi – they'd have had the rope round my neck as sure as God made little green apples. It's enough to give you the creeps!

JOAN: What a thing to happen!

ARTHUR: I mean, whoever did it – well, he had his way with her first, didn't he? I *mean*.

JOAN: And they thought *you'd* do a thing like that?
    (*Pause. He looks at her.*)

ARTHUR: Ridiculous. Ennit? Lovely young girl like that.
    (*Pause.*)

JOAN: How do you know what she was like?

ARTHUR: They showed me her picture, didn't they? Poor little thing. Nor they wouldn't even give me a cup of tea.

JOAN: Poor Arthur. You poor old love.

ARTHUR: Yeah. I need a bit of comforting, don't I? Not half I bloody don't!
    (*Close-up on* JOAN. *Slow mix to:*)

INT. SMALL ROOM IN CHEAP HOTEL, LONDON. NIGHT
Very small, rather sparse, with dirty curtains, a narrow bed and chest of drawers with some of the knobs off. A notice on the inside of the door: 'No guests etc.' EILEEN *looking about. A woman with*

steel-grey hair and severe spectacles on a chain on her way out.

HOTEL OWNER: I suppose you've got your own soap and towel, Miss?

EILEEN: I – a towel, yes. I didn't think about soap.

HOTEL OWNER: Oh well, you can buy some in the morning, can't you?

EILEEN: Yes, of course.

HOTEL OWNER: There is a bath and washbasin at the end of the passage. It is available for the use of the guests between eight o'clock and half past ten in the mornings, eight o'clock and ten o'clock in the evenings.

EILEEN: Oh, thank you.

HOTEL OWNER: Except Sunday evenings, of course.

EILEEN: Of course.

HOTEL OWNER: That's all, I think. There is a bolt in the door you can latch from the inside. (*Almost a smile.*) Goodnight.

EILEEN: Goodnight. And – thank you. Thank you very much.
(*The door shuts.*
   Expressionless, EILEEN *looks around the little room. It seems very drab and cramped. And then, unexpectedly, she smiles with pleasure and excitement, and clasps herself with delight. She puts her suitcase on the bed, to open it. Click, click go the catches. Then she stops, hearing distant music through the curtained window. Someone outside is playing 'The Old Rugged Cross' on a piano accordion. She gives a pleasurable sigh.*)
London!
(*Fade.*)

INT. JOAN'S AND ARTHUR'S BEDROOM. NIGHT
A blackness so black that at first nothing can be seen. Slowly, almost imperceptibly, lighten until indistinct shapes can be seen. Camera, moving gradually to closer and closer shot of ARTHUR, *awake, sitting up, eyes gleaming in the gloom, his wife's steady, near-whistle of breathing beside him, asleep. Now only* ARTHUR's *darkened face fills the screen.*
Music (gentle): Lew Stone Band intro to 'Easy Come, Easy Go', the singer, eventually, will be Al Bowlly.
Hold face during gentle band intro. Slow, slow mix (music continuing) to:

EXT. THE GRASSY BANK BESIDE LONDON–GLOUCESTER ROAD.
DAY
The BLIND GIRL *not quite 'looking' at* ARTHUR, *beautiful,*
vulnerable.
Music continues. Slow mix to:

INT. JOAN'S AND ARTHUR'S BEDROOM. NIGHT
ARTHUR. *Music. Slow mix to:*

INT. THE COTTAGE, FOREST OF DEAN. NIGHT
EILEEN *on sofa, at her most attractive.*
Music: Slow mix to:

INT. JOAN'S AND ARTHUR'S BEDROOM. NIGHT
ARTHUR *starts 'singing'. The remarkable thing about the song is the*
way Al Bowlly's tone and inflection seems to deny the lightness of the
words: it may be 'Easy Come', one feels, but it is never 'Easy Go'.
The music fades. JOAN *turns in the bed.*
JOAN: (*Waking*) Arthur?
ARTHUR: Yes.
    (*She looks at him.*)
JOAN: Can't you sleep, love?
ARTHUR: (*Hollow*) No.
    (*Pause. She murmurs, sleepily*)
JOAN: Everything's all right. Just relax, eh?
    (*Pause.*)
ARTHUR: (*Thickly*) Joan?
JOAN: (*All but asleep*) Mmmm – ?
ARTHUR: Put your arm round me. Please put your arm round
    me.
    (*But she is already asleep.*
        Music: to non-vocal version of 'Hand in Hand'.
        Fade out.)

4 'BETTER THINK TWICE'

GRAPHICS
*Back street London, at night. 1935. Lamps, doorways. A woman
waiting on street corner. Sleazy. Drifting to 'Café' sign.
Music over: 'Pennies From Heaven' on piano accordion.
Mix through to:*

INT. CAFÉ. NIGHT
*Marbled counter, tea-urn, cakes and rolls under rather grubby glass
domes on counter.* PROPRIETOR *behind counter, fat, with striped
half-apron.*
EILEEN, *hesitant, is at counter, looking at the glass domes.*
PROPRIETOR: Yes, Miss?
EILEEN: A cup of tea, please. No sugar.
PROPRIETOR: Tuppence, Miss.
   (*She looks almost wistfully at the food. He picks up her look as
   he turns the lever on tea-urn.*)
   Anything else you'd like?
EILEEN: How much are the – those sausage rolls?
PROPRIETOR: The big ones is thrappence and the little ones is
   tuppence.
EILEEN: Oh. Are the little ones half as big as the big ones – or a
   little bit bigger?
PROPRIETOR: What?
EILEEN: Only if they're just half as big they should be three
   ha'pence.
   (*The* PROPRIETOR *hands over the big cup of tea with a
   sardonic movement and expression.*)
PROPRIETOR: Well, they ain't, ducks. They're tuppence.
   (EILEEN *looks at him, half challengingly, then suddenly seems
   to wilt.*)
EILEEN: All right. I'll have a little one then. The biggest little
   one you've got.
PROPRIETOR: All the same size, lady.
EILEEN: No they're not. That one on the end there – I'll have
   that one.

PROPRIETOR: (*Amused*) That's not a big little one. It's a little big one.

EILEEN: (*Flaring*) Then they're not all the same size!

(PROPRIETOR *looks at her. He suddenly realizes the issue is important.*)

PROPRIETOR: A lawyer, are you, Miss?

EILEEN: No. Just hard up.

PROPRIETOR: Who isn't?

EILEEN: Well – *you* aren't, for one. Not if you charge tuppence for a sausage roll that ought to be three ha'pence.

PROPRIETOR: Here you are, my love. The biggest little one.

EILEEN: Thank you. Thank you very much.

PROPRIETOR: Which is fourpence altogether, less a ha'penny for letting your tea get cold. Threepence ha'penny, please.

EILEEN: Oh, but – well, are you sure?

PROPRIETOR: Or do you want to argue about it?

EILEEN: No. Thank you. Thank you very much.

(*She gives him the money.*)

PROPRIETOR: (*Amused*) You've got about twelve minutes to eat it up and drink your tea.

EILEEN: What?

(*He turns and taps a notice behind him.*)

PROPRIETOR: 'Unaccompanied ladies are not served after ten p.m.' That's when the pubs turn out, see.

EILEEN: (*Shocked*) Oh – do you mean? – do you think *I* –

PROPRIETOR: Now, now. Just pulling your leg. I can see you're not one of *those* women –

EILEEN: (*Flustered*) I didn't know this was *that* sort of place.

PROPRIETOR: It isn't. But it's that sort of street. I shouldn't hang about outside if I was you. Not at this time of night, love.

(*She looks anxiously at him, then takes her tea and roll to little table.*

Move in closer and closer to EILEEN *as, worried, thoughtful, she sips her tea and eats the roll, like one conserving every crumb.*

EILEEN *looks in her purse, as one who knows it is almost empty. Then she becomes aware that a* CUSTOMER *in the café, eating, is staring at her: a hard, hopeful, sexual stare.*

130

Begin music: 'I Only Have Eyes For You', band intro.

Their eyes lock. EILEEN *looks away, annoyed, then looks back again, with the faintest hint of speculative interest. The customer 'sings' 'I Only Have Eyes . . .'.*

(EILEEN, *meanwhile, carefully chews her little sausage roll, then delightedly wipes her lips with a lace handkerchief. But by the end of the song, the 'singer' has approached her table. She looks up with a frown.*)

EILEEN: What do you want?

CUSTOMER: (*Awkwardly*) I – ah – couldn't help hearing your remarks about the – sausage rolls, Miss.

EILEEN: I wasn't aware that I was speaking to *you*.

CUSTOMER: No, no. Of course not. Pardon me. I think I've made a mistake.

EILEEN: (*Coldly*) Yes. I think you have.

(*The* CUSTOMER *turns away, then, half in bravado, speaks again.*)

CUSTOMER: Only – I'm not short of a penny or two, y'see.

EILEEN: What sort of a girl do you think I am?

CUSTOMER: No offence, I hope. None intended.

EILEEN: None taken.

(*The* CUSTOMER *goes to return to his table, sees the* PROPRIETOR *looking at him, he stares, then goes out of café.*)

PROPRIETOR: Goodnight, sir.

(*But he has sloped away, furtively. The* PROPRIETOR *smiles at* EILEEN.)

See what I mean, Miss? I should go on home if I were you. At this time of night.

EILEEN: Yes. Thank you. I've finished my *huge* sausage roll!

(*She pushes back her chair.*)

PROPRIETOR: Don't let me hurry you, mind.

(EILEEN *goes up to counter, speaks in low voice.*)

EILEEN: You don't need a woman to help serve or wash up or anything like that, do you?

PROPRIETOR: (*Startled*) What?

EILEEN: I'm a good worker. And I've got no ties.

PROPRIETOR: No, I don't. I'm sorry. I don't. What's the matter then?

EILEEN: I'm an unemployed coalminer who can't sing.

131

PROPRIETOR: Oh, I see. I thought you were a comedian.

EILEEN: No, no. There are too many of those about.

(*Pause. The* PROPRIETOR *puts two sausage rolls in a paper bag.*)

PROPRIETOR: You can deliver these for me, if you like.

EILEEN: Where to?

PROPRIETOR: To wherever you're going, my love.

(*Pause.*)

EILEEN: (*Moved*) Thank you. That's very – thank you, sir.

PROPRIETOR: (*Embarrassed*) Keep your pecker up, eh?
Goodnight, Miss.

EILEEN: G-good night. And – yes. Goodnight.

(*She turns, in her suddenly abrupt way, and goes, fighting down tears.*

The PROPRIETOR *looks after her, and sighs. As he does, iris-out to:*)

EXT. STREET OUTSIDE. NIGHT

Begins on PROSTITUTE *in shop doorway, waiting. Footsteps. She steps out.*

PROSTITUTE: Like a nice time, dear?

(*The* CUSTOMER *from the café half stops.*)

CUSTOMER: I might.

PROSTITUTE: My place is just round the corner.

CUSTOMER: How much?

PROSTITUTE: A pound for a short time. Two pounds for a little bit more – a really nice time. You won't be sorry.

CUSTOMER: Just round the corner, is it?

PROSTITUTE: (*Taking his arm*) That's right, lovey.

CUSTOMER: (*Disengaging*) No – I'll walk behind you. I'm known around here.

PROSTITUTE: Suit yourself. All the same to me.

CUSTOMER: (*Hanging back*) I don't think I –

(*Sound of other footsteps.*)

PROSTITUTE: Don't be shy. I know you'll have a good time.
You can stay all night for three pounds, love.

(EILEEN *coming up alongside.*)

CUSTOMER: No! I – goodnight! Sorry!

PROSTITUTE: (*Snarl*) Please your bloody self.

(EILEEN, *overhearing all this, veers sideways to avoid them.*
The CUSTOMER, *knowing that* EILEEN *has heard, looks*
sideways at her, as PROSTITUTE *retreats back into doorway.*)
CUSTOMER: (*To* EILEEN) She had bad teeth.
   (EILEEN *quickens her stride. But so does the* CUSTOMER. *She*
   stops. He stops.)
EILEEN: If you don't go away I shall call a policeman.
CUSTOMER: I don't know what you're talking about.
   (*She glares at him and turns, walks, faster – then runs. A* MAN,
   further along, calls at her.)
MAN: What's the hurry, sweetheart?

INT. EILEEN'S ROOM. NIGHT
In the cheap hotel. EILEEN *comes in, out of breath, shuts the door,*
bolts it, leans against it, composes herself. Then she looks at the paper
bag.
EILEEN: Thank God. Oh, thank God.
   (*She moves into the room, sits on the bed, bites hungrily into one*
   of the rolls. As she bites, tap-tap on her door.)
EILEEN: (*Alarmed*) Who is it?
HOTEL OWNER: (*Off*) Miss Everson? It's me. Mrs Corder.
   (EILEEN *puts sausage roll back into bag, and the bag under*
   pillow.)
EILEEN: (*Mutter*) Oh no. Not now. Please not now.
MRS CORDER: (*Off*) I'd like a little word with you, please.
   (EILEEN *opens the door.*)
EILEEN: I was about to go to bed, Mrs Corder. Can't it wait
   until –
MRS CORDER: I'm afraid it can't. I tried to catch you when you
   went out but you seemed *deliberately* not to hear me as I
   called.
EILEEN: Why ever would I do that?
MRS CORDER: I think perhaps that you need to be reminded
   that your bill is now overdue.
EILEEN: (*Pretended surprise*) Overdue? Oh, but –
MRS CORDER: You are now half way through your fifth week
   here, Miss Everson.
EILEEN: Crikey! How time flies!
MRS CORDER: (*Unsmiling*) You paid the first four weeks in

133

advance. I explained to you at the time that in this hotel we always expect settlement at least *one* day in advance. You are now four days in arrears.

EILEEN: Please don't worry about it, Mrs Corder.

MRS CORDER: Oh, but I'm *not* worried about it. I simply want you to settle your bill, Miss Everson.

EILEEN: What – now? This minute?

MRS CORDER: If you would. Yes. Please.

EILEEN: You're not very trusting, are you?

MRS CORDER: Trust has nothing to do with it.

EILEEN: But you can *trust* me another two days, can't you? Until Friday, I mean.

MRS CORDER: Friday?

EILEEN: Pay day.

(*Slight pause.*)

MRS CORDER: Are you saying that you have found yourself a job?

EILEEN: Where do you think I've been all day? Walking the streets?

MRS CORDER: And you will be paid on Friday – ?

EILEEN: I think that's the usual procedure, Mrs Corder.

MRS CORDER: (*Tartly*) And *my* usual procedure is not to give credit.

EILEEN: What? Not even when it's due?

(*Fractional pause.*)

MRS CORDER: I shall expect you to settle by six o'clock on Friday. Is that understood?

EILEEN: It is understood. Thank you.

MRS CORDER: Thank you. Goodnight.

EILEEN: Goodnight.

(*She waits until the door is shut, tense, then turns, despairing, into the room. She puts her hands to her face.*)

PROSTITUTE: (*Out of vision*) Don't be shy. I know you'll have a good time. You can stay all night for three pounds, love.

(*She takes her hands down from her face. Close-up of* EILEEN, *thoughtful.*

Fade.)

134

INT. AN EMPTY SHOP. LONDON. DAY

A small room behind a creamed-over window, with a counter, a door to the back, a door to the street and nothing much else.

ARTHUR *and* JOAN *stand looking at it.*

JOAN: (*Dubiously*) It's not very grand, Arthur. Not much space, actually.

ARTHUR: Oh, I dunno. Gramophone records don't take up much room, you know. And empty places always look smaller than full ones – have you noticed?

JOAN: No.

ARTHUR: (*Aggressively*) Well, they do. It's what they call an optical delusion.

JOAN: Illusion, Arthur.

ARTHUR: You think you know everything, don'tcha!

JOAN: No – but I'm wondering whether the whole thing isn't an illusion. Or a delusion, if you like.

ARTHUR: (*Alarmed*) What do you mean?

JOAN: The shop. The whole idea.

ARTHUR: Now look – !

JOAN: Please, Arthur. We haven't signed anything yet. It's not too late to think again.

ARTHUR: But it'll be a little gold mine, Joanie! You mark my words.

JOAN: I've got a funny feeling, that's all.

ARTHUR: We've been over and over and over it. We can't go wrong. People is buying gramophone records nowadays. More and more of 'em. And that's *fact*, that is. Plain straightforward fact, my girl.

JOAN: Why did *this* shop have to close down, then?

ARTHUR: *Because* –

JOAN: No – but *why*?

ARTHUR: (*Exasperated*) Because the loony that ran it was selling *sheet music*, wasn't he? It's like I said! Why don't you listen?

JOAN: We shall lose all the money, Arthur.

ARTHUR: Here we go.

JOAN: We shall. Every penny of it.

ARTHUR: Money, money, bloody money. Is that all anyone ever thinks about!

JOAN: It's a good job for you I *do* think about it.

ARTHUR: But you can't back out now. You can't let me down. You've *agreed*. The money is to be mine.

JOAN: The money is to be *ours*. My father didn't scrimp and save all these years . . .

ARTHUR: Here we go!

JOAN: Right's right.

ARTHUR: Why are you such a mean cow?

JOAN: (*Shocked*) Arthur!

> (*He purses his lips at her, mockingly, and puts out his arms.* JOAN *backs away.*
>
> Music: 'We'll Make Hay While the Sun Shines' by Billy Merrin and his Commanders.*)

ARTHUR: Give us a kiss then.

JOAN: Why can't you be serious?

ARTHUR: We could get down behind the counter, eh?

JOAN: Is that all you think about?

> (ARTHUR *begins to 'sing' as Sam Browne's voice comes in over the music.*)
>
> (*Pushing him away*) For goodness' sake, Arthur. Leave me be.

ARTHUR: Let's christen our little shop, old girl.

INT. PUBLIC BAR. LONDON PUB. NIGHT

A rough-looking place. TOM, *a morose-looking man, is tinkering on the piano, trying to make a tune. There are about a dozen men and two ageing tarts scattered about the bar. The* BARMAN *has metal shirt bands like bangles on his arms to hold up his shirt sleeves. He shouts across, ill-tempered.*

BARMAN: If you can't play, Tom, shut the bleed'n lid! You're bruising my bleed'n earholes.

TOM: Nobody could play this thing.

BARMAN: Well you can't that's for sure!

> (*Meanwhile, very hesitant, unsure,* EILEEN *has come in. She all but sidles up to the bar. One of the women looks at her sharply.*)

EILEEN: (*Faintly*) Excuse me.

BARMAN: Yes?

EILEEN: How – how much is a – glass of lemonade?

BARMAN: It's so long since I sold one, I don't know. (*Laughs.*)

To you – tuppence.

EILEEN: Oh. Yes. Then – yes. I'll have a glass of lemonade, please.

(BARMAN *looks at her quizzically.*)

BARMAN: You sure you've come to the right place, ducks?

(*She lowers her head.* BARMAN *half shrugs and gets her a glass of lemonade.*)

TOM: Have a drop of port in it, dear.

EILEEN: (*Stiffening*) Pardon?

TOM: That's a very nice drink, for a lady. Port and lemon is.

BARMAN: Leave her alone, Tom.

TOM: I'm only offering to pay for it, enn I?

BARMAN: She's not that sort of . . .

EILEEN: (*Vigorously*) Thank you. Thank you very much.

TOM: What? You'll have one?

EILEEN: Yes. (*Swallow.*) Please.

BARMAN: I see. One word, lady. The rozzers look in at about nine o'clock.

EILEEN: Pardon?

TOM: The cops, love.

EILEEN: Oh. But . . .

TOM: Don't you worry about it. Don't you worry about a thing. We're just having a little drink together, eh?

BARMAN: (*Surly*) That's one and five.

TOM: Service with a smile, eh, guv'nor?

EILEEN: (*Flustered*) I don't think – I don't know whether I ought to . . .

TOM: I been and gorn and got it nah.

BARMAN: You don't have to have it, dear.

TOM: Mind your own, guv.

EILEEN: (*Almost shrill*) Sorry. So sorry!

(*She turns and literally runs from the bar. The elderly* WHORE *who has been watching cackles with glee.*)

WHORE: Out of your league, Tommy boy!

TOM: (*Snarl*) Shut your face, you old bag.

BARMAN: 'Ere! 'Ere! Any more of that and you're *out*, mate.

(*Fractional pause.*)

TOM: (*Changed tone*) She was a bit of all right, though, wasn't she?

BARMAN: (*Wistful*) Not half.

TOM: What do you reckon she was up to, then?

BARMAN: Short of a few bob, I expect.

TOM: (*Lasciviously*) Them's the best sort. Amachewers. And if you hadn't stuck your nose in –

BARMAN: Gettaway. She wouldn't let the likes of *you* touch her.

TOM: Oh, I dunno. I'm quite a natty chap, you know.

BARMAN: But you can't play the bleed'n piano.

TOM: Those ivories don't want tickling, old pal. They want replacing.

BARMAN: You'd make the same sort of racket on a Stradivarius.

TOM: That's a violin!

BARMAN: What?

TOM: That's a violin, you silly sod. A Stradivarius is a *violin*.

BARMAN: I don't care what it is, you can't –

(*He stops suddenly.* TOM *turns to see what he is looking at.*
EILEEN *has come back into the bar, eyes wide in white face.*
Fractional pause.)

TOM: Changed your mind, have you?

EILEEN: I – (*She nods, dumbly.*)

BARMAN: (*Gently*) This one is on the house, love. Just drink it down and go home, there's a good girl.

(*He slides the port and lemon towards her.*
Start music as she looks almost wildly at the two men, seizes the glass, and swallows half of it in one go.
Music: 'Better Think Twice' – Carroll Gibbons and the Savoy Hotel Orpheans.)

EILEEN: Ach – it tastes like poison.

BARMAN: Then don't try another. There's them as it doesn't suit.

TOM: You never know what you like until you try it.

(*Fractional pause. Music intro. continues.*)

EILEEN: (*Hard*) That is true.

BARMAN: Don't you be so sure.

(EILEEN *looks steadily at* TOM, *who bows slightly, on cue, and then 'sings' to the Harry Bentley vocal.*
On the record, the vocal is followed by some 30 seconds of Carroll Gibbons at the piano. TOM *moves over to the piano and mimes Gibbons' playing, swivelling on stool as in a Hollywood musical.*)

As piece ends he returns to bar.)

EILEEN: The second drop doesn't taste so bad.

TOM: Give her 'nother one, guv'nor.

BARMAN: Steady on, now.

EILEEN: (*Forced brightness*) I might as well. Mightn't I.

TOM: Atta girl. Give her another. And we'll rest our plates.

EILEEN: Pardon?

TOM: Sit down, ducks. We'll sit down.

BARMAN: (*Cold*) One and fivepence. Twice. That's two and ten.

TOM: Gawd. Your prices. (*Puts down money.*)

BARMAN: If you don't like 'em, you know what you can do.

(TOM *winks at* EILEEN.)

TOM: Money's no problem, old fruit. I might even buy you one if *you* talk nice.

BARMAN: I'd rather drink my own slops.

TOM: Sounds as though you already do, mate.

(*Glowing a bit, he leads a stiff* EILEEN *to a little table with wrought-iron legs.*)

EILEEN: (*Nervously*) Haven't you got a drink?

TOM: Oh, yes. On the piano, darling.

(*He goes back to the piano. She watches him, stiff, tense, eyes narrowing.* TOM *has a cocky walk. He picks out the opening bars of 'In Dublin's Fair City' with one finger, deliberately annoying.*)

BARMAN: (*Shout*) Leave off, will you!

(TOM *prances back to* EILEEN *with a smirk.*)

TOM: (*To* EILEEN) Testy bugger, ent he?

EILEEN: (*Tight*) Is he?

(TOM *looks at her, half-amused.*)

TOM: You want to relax a bit, you do.

EILEEN: Do I?

TOM: I mean, I'm not going to eat you, am I?

EILEEN: What – what do you want to do to me?

(*Fractional pause.*)

TOM: You must be joking.

EILEEN: (*Miserably*) Can you lend me two pounds – or –

TOM: Lend you? You *are* joking.

EILEEN: I – I'd give it you back.

(*He looks at her hard.*)

139

TOM: We'll think about it a bit. There's no hurry.

EILEEN: (*Faint*) No.

(*Pause.*)

TOM: Caught a bit short, are you?

EILEEN: Sort of. Yes.

TOM: That's nothing to be ashamed of, love. Not nowadays. Haven't you got a job?

EILEEN: Can't find one.

TOM: Who can? The whole bloody country's going to the dogs. (*Every sentence is being squeezed out of her with enormous difficulty.*)

EILEEN: What do you do for a living?

TOM: Me? I'm in the music business, enn I?

EILEEN: (*Tense*) Are you? Doing what?

TOM: (*Laugh*) No, darling. I'm a plumber.

EILEEN: Oh.

TOM: A very good one an' all. Got two young lads working for me. Doing very well in my line of work. I don't have to whistle for the odd bob or two, believe you me.

EILEEN: So – so you *could* lend me some money.

TOM: 'Neither a borrower nor a lender be.'

EILEEN: I need it very badly –

TOM: What's your name?

(*She looks at him.*)

EILEEN: Lulu.

(*He starts to smile, then suppresses it.*)

TOM: That's a very – nice name.

EILEEN: I don't like it very much. Makes me sound cheap.

TOM: Oh, nobody'd ever say that, Lulu. Look at that fat tart over there – now that's what I call cheap.

(*As* EILEEN *looks.*)

WHORE: (*Shout*) Who are you looking at!

(EILEEN *turns back quickly, and closes her eyes, bile in her mouth.*)

TOM: Here – are you all right?

EILEEN: I feel a bit sick.

TOM: How much have you had to eat today?

(*Pause.*)

EILEEN: Nothing.

TOM: (*Between teeth*) For Christ's sake.

EILEEN: I can't afford it. I'm stony.

TOM: A girl who looks like you didn't oughter go hungry, or anything like.

(*She half smiles.*)

EILEEN: That's what I thought when I caught the train to London.

TOM: Where are you from?

(*Fractional pause.*)

EILEEN: Bristol.

(*About to drink,* TOM *nearly chokes.*)

What's the matter?

TOM: Lulu from Bristol City.

EILEEN: What about it?

TOM: Just struck me as funny, that's all. Don't you know what your Bristols are?

EILEEN: What?

TOM: Your titties. Bristol City – titty. See?

EILEEN: Oh.

TOM: And very nice they are, too. Lulu.

EILEEN: Please.

TOM: Oh, I see. Prim and proper, like, are we?

EILEEN: You don't have to talk so loud.

TOM: (*Comical whisper*) No, I don't. That's true.

(*She almost smiles. He looks, looks at her.*)

You're very nice looking, Lulu.

(*She looks down, coiling her hands.*)

EILEEN: (*Softly*) Thank you . . .

(*Pause. He moistens his suddenly dry lips.*)

TOM: What did you come in this place for?

(*She does not answer.*)

Did you think some bloke was going to give you a couple of nicker – just like that? For nothing?

(*Pause.*)

EILEEN: (*Hollowly*) No.

(*He is looking at her intently.*)

TOM: I mean, that's nearnuff a week's wages for some girls.

EILEEN: Yes.

TOM: I mean, you've got to give something back in return.

Entcha?

(*Pause.*)

EILEEN: Yes.

(*Pause.*)

TOM: I mean –

(*Fractional pause.*)

EILEEN: Yes. (*And then she looks him full in the face.*)

TOM: I know how you feel, and all –

EILEEN: (*Sharper*) Do you?

TOM: Well, I can imagine it. But I'm a decent sort of bloke. When you come right down to what counts.

EILEEN: Are you married?

TOM: (*False laugh*) Married? What – me?

EILEEN: Yes. I thought you were.

TOM: (*Nastily*) Oh, I see. Been around a bit, have you?

EILEEN: I've had dozens. (*There is a new, strange, hard brightness in her eyes.*)

TOM: What's all the fuss about, then?

EILEEN: No fuss, darling. (*She drains her drink.*) Here. Get me another.

(TOM *looks at her.*)

TOM: You're not a tease, are you?

EILEEN: A tee-ee-ese?

TOM: (*Frown*) I mean, I'm not spending a penny piece on you if –

EILEEN: If what?

(*Too pert. He stares at her.*)

TOM: And you'll also get my fist in your chops.

(*Pause.*)

EILEEN: (*Changed tone*) I'd like another drink. Please.

TOM: Certainly, darling. Same again?

EILEEN: Yes, please. Only not – but with not so much lemonade?

TOM: Quite right. You're sweet enough already, eh?

(*He goes to the bar with a chortle, two glasses in his hand.* EILEEN *watches him, like a snake watching a mongoose – or the other way round.*)

EILEEN: (*To herself*) Oh, Arthur.

(*She looks up, startled, to find the fat* WHORE *hissing at her.*)

WHORE: Why don't you piss off, Snow White!

EILEEN: (*Gulp*) What?

WHORE: Get out of here if you don't want to get a bashing.

EILEEN: Who from?

WHORE: The girls, that's who from.

(*But she sees that* TOM *is looking round at her, and slinks away. Shocked, numbed,* EILEEN *closes her eyes for a moment.*)

TOM: (*Returning*) What's *she* want?

EILEEN: I don't know.

TOM: Told you to get out – did she?

EILEEN: (*Shudders*) Something like that.

TOM: Hang on.

(*Face dark, he goes over to the* WHORE. *We see him lean in to talk to her, almost lovingly. But the* WHORE *looks fearful in the extreme. She seems to be saying she 'Didn't mean it.' A last smiling threat, and* TOM *returns.*)

She won't bother you no more.

EILEEN: Wh-what did you say?

TOM: Better those nice little ears didn't hear.

EILEEN: But why did she – talk to me – like that?

TOM: Blimey. You *are* green. Entcha? Cos you was in her stamping ground, that's why. Fat old sow.

(EILEEN *winces. He notices.*)

Pardon my French. Cheers!

EILEEN: (*Flat*) Cheers.

(*Brief intro: 'And So Do I': the street singer.*
They look at each other, then TOM *'sings' very tenderly.*)

EILEEN: Did you say something?

TOM: Have you got somewhere? You know.

(*Fractional pause.*)

EILEEN: I – no. Not really.

TOM: Where do you stay, then?

EILEEN: In a – I've got a room. But it's not suitable for – for –

TOM: I might be able to help you there.

EILEEN: What?

TOM: If you play your cards right.

(*She looks at him.*)

EILEEN: What do you mean?

143

TOM: I've helped a girl or two now and again.

(EILEEN *studies his face. Her expression changes.*)

EILEEN: You're not a plumber.

TOM: Girls down on their luck, I mean. You know. A helping hand.

EILEEN: I'm not a tart.

TOM: I didn't say you were, darling. 'Course you're not.

EILEEN: (*Quavering*) Please – I – oh, dear God – I feel sick.

TOM: (*Alarmed*) Now, now. You've got hold of the wrong end of the stick.

EILEEN: I'm willing to – to – you know –

TOM: Kiss and cuddle.

(*She swallows.*)

EILEEN: (*Half nods*) For two pounds. But only once. Never again. Really.

TOM: That's all right, darling. That's what I thought. Look at me.

(*But she is looking sideways.*)

No – come on. Give me the once over with them dazzling eyes.

(*She looks at him.*)

Now – I'm not a bad-looking bloke. Am I?

(*Pause.*)

EILEEN: No.

TOM: So just pretend we're – you know. Friends, like.

EILEEN: (*Shakily*) Yes. Friends. (*Strangled laugh.*) Good Companions.

TOM: Except instead of giving it away – well –

EILEEN: I get two pounds. The Forty Shilling Tailor.

(TOM *blinks, then sniggers.*)

TOM: And you might even – well, enjoy it.

(*Pause.*)

EILEEN: Yes. I might.

(*And she holds her gaze.* TOM *puts his hand on her knees.*)

TOM: That's my little darling.

(*She hesitates, then puts her hand on top of his hand. Stiff. And sick.*

  Picture 'turns over'.)

INT. TOM'S FLAT. NIGHT
Up-to-the-minute 1935.
EILEEN *puts down a glass figure of a naked woman.*
EILEEN: Very nice. Absolutely top-hole.
TOM: I've got taste, I have. Do you want another drink?
　　(*Her speech is a bit slurred.*)
EILEEN: Another drinkie? Yes. Why not.
TOM: A cocktail.
EILEEN: A cock . . . tail. (*She giggles, and sways.*)
TOM: Try an Americano.
EILEEN: A yankie doodle dandy?
TOM: Campari and sweet vermouth and soda. Nice and pink
　　and bitter.
EILEEN: That's me.
TOM: What?
EILEEN: Nice and pink and bitter.
TOM: Oh now, angel. Don't talk like that.
EILEEN: Let's – let's pretend we are in the films. On the – on
　　the shilver screen. Pardon. The silver screen.
TOM: Why not? Anything you like, Lulu.
EILEEN: (*Snigger*) Lulu.
TOM: 'S a nice name, toots.
EILEEN: Where does all the money come from?
TOM: For this?
EILEEN: This flat must be ten pounds a week.
TOM: (*Tapping head*) From my wits. I live on me wits. I'm a
　　clever chap, I am.
EILEEN: And girls.
TOM: What? Oh. Yeah. A couple. Two or three. I looks after
　　them. No – really I do. That's the truth, Lulu.
EILEEN: So you're not a plumber?
　　(*He gives her the drink he has mixed.*)
TOM: Cheers.
EILEEN: Bottoms up. Is that right?
TOM: (*Cackle*) Soon will be.
　　(*Pause. She looks at him, with contempt.*)
EILEEN: I'm worth more.
　　(*Fractional pause.*)
TOM: More than what?

EILEEN: If I'm going to do it, I'm worth more than two pound notes.

(*Pause. He fingers his glass.*)

TOM: (*Quietly*) Get your dress off.

(*Pause.*)

EILEEN: C-can I finish my drink please – ?

TOM: Certainly.

(*A terrible silence. She sips her drink under the force of his stare. The moment is stretched – and stretched – and stretched.*

One tear forms, hovers, and trickles down her cheek. His expression does not change. She sips drink. Trembling.

Gently start music: intro to Carroll Gibbons's 'Pennies From Heaven'.)

(*Between his teeth, at last*) Come on. Come on.

(*Fractional pause, then* EILEEN *'mimes' to the vocals of Anne Lenner.*

Music out abruptly at the end of song.)

Finished?

EILEEN: Finished. But –

TOM: (*Hard*) Yes?

EILEEN: Can I have the money, please?

(*He takes out his wallet and peels off two pound notes.*)

TOM: There's more where that came from. If you're a good girl.

EILEEN: Where – where shall I put it?

TOM: On the mantelpiece.

(*And she does.*)

EILEEN: Shall I – ?

TOM: Yes.

(*Slowly, painfully, she starts to undress.*

Start music: the street singer's version of 'Pennies From Heaven', and TOM *'sings' the words.*

Music out, abruptly, at the end.

She is standing before him in her underwear.)

EILEEN: I'm – a bit shy.

TOM: That's love-ly. That's really lovely, Lulu.

(*As he steps forward to caress and slobber, the lights start to dip.*

Music: 'Indian Love Call' by Maurice Winnick, with Sam Costa and woman vocalist. In his arms, EILEEN *'sings' the opening lines.* TOM *'singing' Costa caresses her and replies in*

146

*song. In semi-darkness he pulls off her bra. The duet continues
as they sink to the carpet, virtually out of shot.)*

EXT. LONDON STREET. DAY
The HIKER *is playing, on his piano accordion, 'There is a Green
Hill Far Away'. But his 'thank you very, very much' is missing this
time. In fact, he seems very upset. His fingers falter before he gets to
the end. He starts again, but:*

POLICEMAN: Come on. Come along now. We can't have that
　　here.

HIKER: Off-officer?

POLICEMAN: What is it, laddie?

HIKER: (*With difficulty*) N-n-nothing, sir.

POLICEMAN: Move along, then. Move along.

HIKER: I w-want a cup of tea, sir.

POLICEMAN: So do I, mate.

HIKER: If I t-tell you something – will you l-let me have a cup of
　　tea?

POLICEMAN: Tell me what?

HIKER: And a – and a bun.

POLICEMAN: What's on your mind, Charlie?
　　(*Pause.*)

HIKER: N-nothing, sir.

POLICEMAN: (*Suspiciously*) Here. What have you been up to?

HIKER: No. I haven't. I haven't!

POLICEMAN: Bloody little twerp.

HIKER: (*Scurrying away*) Sorry, sir. Sorry, sorry.
　　(*The* POLICEMAN *watches him go, hands behind back in a
　　classic pose.*)

POLICEMAN: (*Calls*) And don't let me catch you round here
　　again!
　　(*Tilt up to windows above street.*)

INT. TOM'S FLAT. DAY
*He sits, smoking, tense, holding the glass figure in his hands. From
the door off, into a bedroom, the sound of a woman's cry of pain.*
TOM *puts glass figure down. Stands. Draws on cigarette. In a
moment, the door opens and a* DOCTOR *comes out, carrying a bag.*

TOM: Is she all right?

147

DOCTOR: She will be. Only about fourteen weeks gone. Let her rest today. She'll be sore. And she'll probably be sick.

TOM: Thanks. (*He hands over an envelope.*) There's no need to count it.

DOCTOR: (*Sniff*) Wouldn't dream of it, old chap.

TOM: Want a drink?

DOCTOR: At *this* time of day? No thanks!

TOM: Goodbye, then.

(*Holds out hand. The other pretends not to notice.*)

DOCTOR: Good day to you.

(TOM *goes to door with him.*)

TOM: Where's – the – ah – ?

DOCTOR: The foetus? Don't worry about it. It's gone.

TOM: Yes. Sorry. Thank you.

DOCTOR: Goodbye.

TOM: Toodle-oo.

(*Door shuts. He turns back into room, and starts to whistle. Close shot of glass figure of naked woman. Iris-out to:*)

INT. ARTHUR'S RECORD SHOP. DAY

ARTHUR *behind counter, arms stiff, the tips of his fingers on the counter. Waiting. And oddly, counting under his breath.*

ARTHUR: – nine hundred and twenty-two, nine hundred and twenty-three, nine hundred and twenty-four, nine hundred and twen–

(*Ping! Little bell as door opens. He smiles.*)

Yes, sir. What can we do for you, sir.

YOUTH: Needools.

ARTHUR: Beg pardon?

YOUTH: Box of gramophone needles.

ARTHUR: (*Disappointed*) Loud. Soft. Or standard.

YOUTH: It's for me military band records.

ARTHUR: Then it's loud you want. If it was me, it'd be soft.

YOUTH: Don't getcha.

ARTHUR: (*Sniff*) I don't like military bands.

YOUTH: We shall need 'em one day.

ARTHUR: What for?

YOUTH: The next war, mate. That's what for.

ARTHUR: Blimey. You're a cheerful cove, entcha?

YOUTH: It's gotta come, entit? I mean.

ARTHUR: Here you are. Loud needools. Who against? That's a tanner.

YOUTH: The Yanks. That's who against.

ARTHUR: That'll be the day.

YOUTH: Has to be, don't it? They're taking over. We won't stand for that. Not England.

ARTHUR: Anything else?

YOUTH: Nah.

ARTHUR: Got some good new records, you know.

YOUTH: Like what?

ARTHUR: Bing Crosby.

YOUTH: There – see what I mean?

ARTHUR: Lew Stone, then. With Al Bowlly. That's British right down to the little hole in the middle.

YOUTH: Got any marches? Pom-pom.

ARTHUR: I – ah – can order anything you want.

YOUTH: Nah.

ARTHUR: You sure?

YOUTH: Need-ools is dear nuff. Ta-ta, guv.

ARTHUR: Ta-ta.

(*Ting!*)

Bloody idiot. Wants a little 'ole in his bleed'n head. (*He looks round his shop, and sighs.*) Come on, come on. Where are they all? (*Pause.*) One – two – three – four – five – six – before I get to a hundred this time – seven – eight – nine – (*He stops, too gloomy to go on. The phone goes.*) Jubilee Records, hello? Oh. Hello, Joan. Depressed? What me? No – no. Had a very good day, in fact. No, honest. Got rid of a lot of that stock. No, that's the truth. Was there anyfink? What? Any*thing*, then. Yes. Well, I've got to go. Got three or four waiting to be served. Yes. Usual time. Goodbye, pigeon. Cheerio. (*He puts the phone down as though it were a bomb. Fractional pause.*) One – two – three – four – five – and – six, seven – and eight – nine – *out!* Out. Bloody out. Done. Finished.

(*Pause. He puts his hands to his head. Ting! And takes them down quickly.*)

Good afternoon, sir.

TOM: Afternoon. Your noo here, entcha?

ARTHUR: Been here a fortnight, sir.

TOM: Only I'm just around the corner – haven't noticed it before.

ARTHUR: (*Cheering up*) Well, it takes time, true enough. Any new business takes time to – be *noticed*, as you say.

TOM: Want some gramophone records.

ARTHUR: (*Beam*) That's what we're here for. Anyfink – any*thing* in particular?

TOM: Dance bands.

ARTHUR: Oh, yes. Dance bands. That's the stuff. Lew Stone. Henry Hall. Carroll Gibbons. Jack Payne –

TOM: All new stuff?

ARTHUR: Straight off the presses. No dogs neither.

TOM: Dogs?

ARTHUR: Dud 'uns. Flops.

TOM: Oh. Yes.

ARTHUR: It's a term we people in the music business use.

TOM: I heard something on the wireless the other night. Pop! Your heart – no –

ARTHUR: 'Pop! Goes Your Heart'.

TOM: That's the fellow.

ARTHUR: Lew Stone, that is. With vocal by Alan Kane. Nat Gonella and Alfie Noakes on trumpets. Joe Crossman clarinet, Lew Davis trombone –

TOM: I don't want to buy the bloody band, do I?

ARTHUR: Sorry sir. I gets carried away, like.

TOM: Well, I'll have that one, anyway. And – whatsit – 'Roll Along Prairie Moon'.

(ARTHUR *nearly cries with joy.*)

ARTHUR: You – want – 'Roll – Along – Prairie – Moon'?

TOM: Christ, I can if I want to – can't I?

ARTHUR: No, no – I'm de-lighted. It shows you got real taste, if you don't mind me saying so.

TOM: No, I don't mind.

ARTHUR: Which vocal do you prefer? Fred Latham? Al Bowlly?

TOM: (*Hesitant*) What do you think?

ARTHUR: Well, now. Al Bowlly is the – definitely, he's the most
    tender and you might say smooth.
TOM: Which one do the ladies like?
ARTHUR: Ah, now. Al Bowlly is the one for the ladies, bless
    'em. He makes 'em weak at the knees.
TOM: I thought doing it standing up did that.
ARTHUR: No, no. They do it standing up so they don't get one
    in the oven.
    (*They snigger.*)
TOM: You got taste and all, haven't you?
ARTHUR: Well, sir. You know what they say. Give me a bit of
    the best that's going and *then* you can take me out and
    shoot me.
    (*They laugh.*)
TOM: All right. Better make it Al Whosit.
ARTHUR: How about 'What A Little Moonlight Can Do'? That
    goes round and round very well too.
TOM: OK. OK. You pick out – mmm – half a dozen of the best
    ones. Dance bands. You seem to know what you're talking
    about.
ARTHUR: It's a pleasure, sir. A very great pleasure.
TOM: I'm not short of a penny or two.
ARTHUR: Then I won't stint – right?
TOM: Right. But no rubbish, mind. I won't have rubbish.
ARTHUR: And I don't stock it neither.
TOM: No offence, old boy.
ARTHUR: None taken. I admire your standards.
TOM: You got to know what you want nowadays. Otherwise
    you're a down and out. Things aren't like they used to be.
ARTHUR: I've seen grown men playing with yo-yoes!
TOM: I won't let a grown man play with *my* yo-yo.
    (*They laugh.* ARTHUR, *during all this, has swiftly collected
    together ten records.*)
ARTHUR: Look – I hope I haven't overdone it –
TOM: No. That's all right.
ARTHUR: But it's one pound seven and tenpence, sir.
TOM: All right. Can't be helped. Bit heavy, though.
ARTHUR: I'm shutting up in half an hour. If you live round the
    corner –

TOM: Bring them round, you mean? Yes. That's good. Ta.

ARTHUR: And then you won't mind doing business again.

TOM: Fair enough. It's sixteen Vernon Court. Third floor, that is. Down Rednall Street. Two turnings down.

ARTHUR: Oh, yes. Right you are. In about – thirty-five minutes or so. Do you want to pay now or –

TOM: When you bring them.

ARTHUR: Righty-ho.

TOM: In case you drop one. Fly, I am.

(*Laughing, he goes out of the shop. Leaving* ARTHUR *a picture of delight. He all but hugs himself. Then lifts phone, dials, humming 'Roll Along Prairie Moon'.*)

ARTHUR: Joan? Arthur. I shall be a bit late. Got a delivery – wait a minute, *dear* – got to deliver a huge pile of records to this bloke round the corner – Yes! How many? Two dozen, if you must know. You see – What? – You see, I told you it would take a little time. I was right all along – I don't know how late, do I? Might take a bit of time. He might ask me in. Business is business, so – what is it? Shepherd's pie. Well. Keep it in the oven. I love you. Bye – pigeon.

(*This time he puts the phone down much more happily.*
Wipe.)

INT. TOM'S FLAT. NIGHT

TOM *takes off his tie and rolls it up on two of his fingers. He is half-humming, half-singing 'Pop! Goes Your Heart'. He is alone.*
The bell goes. He puts the rolled tie next to the glass figure and lets in ARTHUR.

TOM: You found it, then. Come on in.

ARTHUR: Ta very much.

TOM: Put them on that table.

ARTHUR: Yes. I've – here? – yes – I've put the two you specially asked for on the top. 'Pop! Goes Your Heart' and 'Prairie Moon'.

TOM: Thanks. Let's hear one of them.

ARTHUR: Where's yer gramophone? Oh, yeh. I'll wind it up.

TOM: You don't have to. Just put the record on.

ARTHUR: (*Impressed*) No? Keep it wound up, eh?

TOM: Which one have you got?

ARTHUR: 'Pop! Goes Your Heart'. The one you wanted, sir.

TOM: Good. Let's hear it, then. There's a new needle in.

> (ARTHUR *fiddles*.
> *Music from gramophone: 'Pop! Goes Your Heart' – Lew Stone and his Band. Vocals by Alan Kane. Recorded 26 January 1935*.)

ARTHUR: There we are, sir.

TOM: Want a drink?

ARTHUR: What, cup of tea d'you mean?

TOM: (*Laughs*) Teetotaller, are you? No. A *drink*.

ARTHUR: Oh. Well. Yes. Ta.

TOM: Whisky. Gin. Rum. Beer.

ARTHUR: Blimey. Got your own bar, eh? Well – a whisky would be very nice.

> (*Music continuing as* TOM *pours whisky*.)

TOM: The Yanks put ice in it!

ARTHUR: Bloody heathens.

TOM: Cheers.

ARTHUR: Cheers. And the very best of health, sir.

TOM: Now, then. How much do I owe you?

ARTHUR: One pound seven and tenpence, sir.

TOM: And if we say tuppence for delivery – eh?

ARTHUR: No need for that, sir. Blimey.

TOM: Can't expect you to trot about for nothing. (*Listening*.) That's nice and bouncy.

ARTHUR: A very good number. Real polish.

TOM: I was reading something in the *Daily Express* the other day. The labourer is worthy of his hire, it said. I thought that a very good thing to write.

ARTHUR: Makes sense, I suppose. It's a good arrangement, this number. Lew Stone does all his own arranging, you know. There's some band leaders can't even read music.

TOM: So I make it one pound eight.

ARTHUR: Well, that's very generous, sir. Very gentlemanly.

TOM: One pound.

> (*He 'cracks' a pound note between his fingers, and puts it on table. Then counts out four florins*.)

Eight shillings.

> (ARTHUR *scoops it up*.)

ARTHUR: Thank you very much.

TOM: Finish your drink first, old chap.

ARTHUR: Yes. Ta. Going down very welcome, too.

TOM: It's a nice song.

ARTHUR: Very nice tune.

TOM: That sort of music takes you right out of yourself.

ARTHUR: Every time. That's why I'm in the business I'm in.

(*The record finishes with a swish-swish as the arm carries on past the tracks.* TOM *lifts it off.*)

TOM: Well, that was hot stuff. And very true to life.

(ARTHUR *finishes his drink.*)

ARTHUR: I think you'll like the others, too. And thank you very much. I hope to be able to serve you again.

(*He holds out his hand.* TOM *and* ARTHUR *shake hands.*)

TOM: I don't see why not, old chap.

ARTHUR: I hope so, hope so.

(TOM *opens the door for him.* ARTHUR *goes, almost bowing.*

Whistling 'Pop! Goes Your Heart', TOM *turns back into the room.*

The door off to bedroom opens. EILEEN, *in silky nightdress, looking a bit sick, stands in doorway.*)

EILEEN: Tom?

TOM: Hey. What are you doing, Lu? I told you to stay in bed.

EILEEN: You were playing some music.

TOM: Yeh. Did you like it? I had some new records delivered. Nice bloke.

EILEEN: It was a bit loud. I was – I thought it was in my head. I –

TOM: Here – are you all right, love – ?

EILEEN: I didn't know whether I was awake or still asleep or –

TOM: But you're all right.

(*Fractional pause.*)

EILEEN: (*Dead*) Top hole.

TOM: Well, you will be by tomorrow.

EILEEN: Yes. I will be, tomorrow.

TOM: Go back to bed.

EILEEN: Tom?

TOM: What is it, sugar?

(*Pause.*)

EILEEN: Nothing.

TOM: (*Irritated*) That's fine then, ennit? For Christ's sake, buck yourself up. You didn't *want* the baby did you? What good's it to a girl like you.

EILEEN: No good. To a girl like me.

TOM: You want to show a bit more gratitude.

EILEEN: Sorry.

TOM: Twenty-five quid, that's what it cost me.

EILEEN: Yes. Sorry.

TOM: I'll bring you some fish and chips later.

    (*She looks at him, queasy, and retreats back into bedroom.*)

    (*To himself*) Miserable cow.

    (*Iris-out.*)

INT. SHEPHERD'S PIE WITH ARTHUR AND JOAN AT HOME. NIGHT

ARTHUR, *eating with relish, contemplates a golden future, to a rather dubious* JOAN.

ARTHUR: And there's no reason why – in time –

JOAN: Empty your mouth first, Arthur.

ARTHUR: For goodness' sake!

JOAN: Well, I don't want to see what you're chewing.

    (*Chew–chew–swallow.*)

ARTHUR: I was saying. There's no reason why I shouldn't *branch out* in time.

JOAN: (*Cautiously*) Branch out?

ARTHUR: We'll never make a fortune with one little shop. It's not much bigger than a shoe-box.

JOAN: You've got to learn to walk before you can run.

ARTHUR: (*Chew*) That's right. Pooh-pooh everything.

JOAN: Oh, Arthur. Can't you ever stop and think?

ARTHUR: I *know* I'm going to do all right with the shop.

JOAN: But not so far.

ARTHUR: *Because* we've just opened. But today is the pointer.

JOAN: All from one or two sales.

ARTHUR: You know something? You got no vision.

JOAN: I can see my hand in front of my face. I can tell what's real from what's make-believe.

ARTHUR: And I can see a – yes, a *whole chain* of record shops.

JOAN: Ar-thur.

ARTHUR: Some of them selling gramophones and the wireless
sets –

JOAN: Why not pianos?

ARTHUR: Yes, and even the old joanna too.

JOAN: Or a mouth-organ.

(*Comically, he stops chewing and looks at her. She laughs.*)

ARTHUR: All my life – (*He realizes his mouth is still full, so has to
stop to chew and swallow.*)

JOAN: I'm only joking, Arthur.

ARTHUR: All my life I've wanted somebody with me who can
see what I can see.

JOAN: Don't be so –

ARTHUR: Somebody who doesn't scoff and jeer and turn her
nose up. Who likes what I talk about and who wants me in
bed and who . . .

JOAN: Oh. We're back to *that*, are we?

ARTHUR: It all goes together. It makes something what you call
A Wife.

JOAN: Or mistress.

ARTHUR: Yes. Or a mistress.

JOAN: Which is what you'd like.

ARTHUR: Which is what I'd – (*Then sudden, comical reversal.*) –
No. I didn't say that. I didn't say that at all.

JOAN: You don't have to say it. It's written all over you.

ARTHUR: Let me eat my tea in peace.

JOAN: But it *is*, Arthur. You always seem to be *yearning* for
something I don't know how to put it – but I know what I
mean.

ARTHUR: I mean, I been working hard all day. On my feet.

JOAN: I just wish you were a bit more contented. That's all.

(*Silence. They eat.*)

ARTHUR: I mean –

(*But he again falls silent. They pick over their food, disgruntled.
Start music: Henry Hall's 'How's Chances'. Dare to take a
lot of band intro, as they look at each other. Slow chew-chew,
rhythmic, comic.*

Then – JOAN *bumps in with male vocal (Dan Donovan) , an
amusingly middle-class English rendering of American words.*)

After, the music bounces on. ARTHUR *and* JOAN *eat, locked away from each other.*)

JOAN: Is – is the food all right, dear?

ARTHUR: Not bad.

(*Silence.*)

JOAN: If the shop does well – *really* well – then of course you can expand. In time.

(*Pause.*)

ARTHUR: 'S very nice, actually. I always have liked the way you do a shepherd's pie, Joanie.

(*Fade.*)

INT. THE PUB (AS BEFORE). NIGHT

BARMAN: Hello, hello. Look what the rain's brought in.

(TOM *and* EILEEN *approach bar, very wet.*)

TOM: Gawdluvaduck. It's *bouncing* down out there, ennit, Lu!

EILEEN: Raining pouring.

BARMAN: That's because we ain't had none.

TOM: A port and lemon, guv. And a drop of the hard stuff for yours truly.

(*He slaps down half a crown.*)

BARMAN: That'll wet you in as well as out, eh?

TOM: Bleed'n rain.

(*She is very tense and anxious.*)

EILEEN: Excuse me. Is there a Ladies?

BARMAN: Out the back, love. Through that curtain. First door on your left.

EILEEN: Thank you.

TOM: Don't be long.

EILEEN: No.

(TOM *to* BARMAN, *or for* BARMAN.)

TOM: And don't forget to pull 'em back up!

(*She breaks her stride and flashes him a look of hatred.*)

BARMAN: Bit crude, entcha?

TOM: Oh, it's only my way. You know me.

BARMAN: She don't like it, though.

TOM: What? Her? She's a bloody sex maniac, mate. Like a snake, the way she wriggles about.

BARMAN: (*Fascinated*) Yeh?

TOM: She's going to go on the game, like. You know.

BARMAN: Geddaway.

TOM: Oh, it's what *she* wants. Nothing to do with me.

BARMAN: She won't stick it. No. And it's a crying shame, that's what it is. A girl like that.

TOM: There you are. Some want to keep it, some want to give it, and some want to charge for it. 'Sonly a business, I suppose.

BARMAN: And a rotten one.

(*Fractional pause.*)

TOM: Where's your dog-collar, mate?

BARMAN: I don't blame the girls.

TOM: Whose fault is it, then?

BARMAN: The ponces'.

(*Fractional pause.*)

TOM: I suppose so. Whoever they are.

BARMAN: Layabouts. Riff raff. Scum. That sort of bloke.

TOM: Ever met any, then?

BARMAN: You tell me.

(TOM *turns away.*)

TOM: Ach – you been reading the *News of the World* for too long.

BARMAN: *Reynolds News*. That's my paper.

(*But he has to serve somebody else.*

TOM *sits at a little corner table, and runs his finger along the rim of his glass, morose. Hold.*

Move away to the bar: ARTHUR *comes in, day's work done.*)

ARTHUR: Pint of half n' half.

BARMAN: Still raining, then?

ARTHUR: Cats and dogs.

BARMAN: That's because we haven't had any.

ARTHUR: Bad for business, though.

BARMAN: So's everything nowadays.

ARTHUR: I've had four people in all afternoon.

BARMAN: What – a shop or – ?

ARTHUR: Record shop. Round the corner. New place.

BARMAN: Oh, I know. Used to sell sheet music and –

ARTHUR: Not me. That was the bloke who used to have it.

BARMAN: Went bust, didn't he?

(ARTHUR *pays, drinks.*)

ARTHUR: Shut up, for Christ's sake.

(BARMAN *laughs.*

EILEEN *returns from Ladies, crossing bar to Tom's table.*
ARTHUR, *facing into bar itself, does not see her.* EILEEN, *eyes fixed straight ahead, does not see him.*)

TOM: Took your time, didn't you?

EILEEN: Sorry.

(TOM *looks at her, then puts his hand on her knee.*)

TOM: Come on, now. Don't look so worried.

EILEEN: I've made a mistake, Tom. I think I've made a mistake.

TOM: Don't be silly. You can always pack it in if it don't suit.

EILEEN: Then why start?

(*Fractional pause.*)

TOM: Nice food. Good clothes. What you want, when you want. Nice flat. You name it.

EILEEN: And end up like what?

TOM: End up how you like. Nobody is forcing you.

EILEEN: Feels like it.

TOM: You want to pay me back, don't you?

(*She doesn't answer.*)

Look – I'm going to leave you now. It's up to you, then, ennit? If nothing happens, nothing happens. But if – (*He shrugs*) – you've got the key to that nice little room. If you use it, then you stay there. It's as simple as that. If you don't, then bring the key back to me, pay me what you owe and we'll say ta-ta with no bad feelings. Right.

EILEEN: But I don't see –

TOM: (*Cutting in*) Don't be daft, eh? It's up to you, like I say. Your own place. Your own ways. And money in your purse. *And* it's something you're good at.

EILEEN: (*Half-pleased*) Am I?

TOM: Blimey, you're a wonder, sweetheart. No kidding.

EILEEN: But I'm not very – experienced.

(TOM *gets up to go.*)

TOM: And how do you *get* experienced, Lulu? I'll see you, eh? Either at my place or –

EILEEN: Yes.

TOM: Remember the rules.

EILEEN: Yes.

TOM: Good hunting.

EILEEN: Yes.

TOM: Ta-ta, then.

> (*She doesn't answer. He hesitates, then goes.*
>
> *She sips, almost gingerly, at her drink.* EILEEN *dabs her lips, and, at last, looks around the bar. Zoom (as her startled eyeline) to* ARTHUR, *turning from bar. They gape at each other. Full 'One Enchanted Evening'-style trill or whatever –*
>
> *Song starts without intro: 'Fancy Our Meeting', sung by Al Bowlly.*
>
> *Settle on* ARTHUR – *as he 'sings' he slowly moves towards* EILEEN, *and she slowly moves towards him.*)

EILEEN: Arthur.

ARTHUR: Eileen. What – good God! – What are you doing here?

EILEEN: Arthur. Oh, Arthur. You are such a swine, Arthur.

ARTHUR: Eileen – I haven't been able to stop thinking about you. Honest.

EILEEN: Take me out of here.

ARTHUR: What?

EILEEN: Take me somewhere, for God's sake. You swine.

ARTHUR: Don't say that. Don't belittle me.

> (*But she is laughing, happily.*)

EILEEN: You dirty rotter, Arthur. You cad.

ARTHUR: (*Grin*) I know. I know. (*Expression changes.*) 'Ere! Why are you dressed up like this?

> (*She looks at him, lowers eyes, then pouts provocatively.*)

EILEEN: Three guesses.

> (*Long pause. Study* ARTHUR: *his face changes several times. Finally:*)

ARTHUR: (*Hoarse*) No. Not really? Eileen?

EILEEN: Except I call myself Lulu now.

ARTHUR: But – but – how could you – how!

EILEEN: I don't know. I still don't know.

ARTHUR: You're a *schoolteacher*! I mean –

EILEEN: And I used to tell them fairy tales, Arthur. The frog and the princess. The mirror on the wall.

(*He stares at her, then grabs her by her arm.*)

ARTHUR: Come on. Come along with me.

EILEEN: You mean, you want to buy?

ARTHUR: Shut up! Else I'll wash your mouth out, you dirty little bitch!

(*Tamely, she lets herself be pulled out of the pub by an angry* ARTHUR.)

EXT. OUTSIDE ARTHUR'S SHOP. NIGHT

Close in – ARTHUR *opening door. The window has a shutter.*

EILEEN *stands back, half reluctant, confused.*

ARTHUR: Well, *I* don't know where else to go, do I? It's sticking, this key.

EILEEN: I've got to hide, Arthur. I've got to find somewhere to hide.

(ARTHUR *finally gets door open.*)

ARTHUR: Don't talk so bloody ridiculous.

(*They go through to:*)

INT. ARTHUR'S SHOP. NIGHT

ARTHUR *switches on the overhead light. They both look about the little shop.*

EILEEN: (*Flat*) Gramophone records.

ARTHUR: (*Proudly*) Hundreds of 'em. Almost any dance tune you can name. Any *good* dance tune.

(*Silence. They look at each other.*)

EILEEN: You gave me the wrong address.

ARTHUR: (*Embarrassed*) What?

EILEEN: There's no such place as you wrote on the back of that envelope.

(*He flaps his arms a bit, then:*)

ARTHUR: Put yourself in my shoes, Eileen!

EILEEN: Oh, I have. I know I can't rely on you, Arthur. Not for anything.

ARTHUR: That's right. Blame everything on me.

(*She has to laugh – almost.*)

EILEEN: Oh, Arthur!

ARTHUR: I know, I know. I can hear myself say things sometimes, and – oh, God. I'm a wash-out. A real, bleed'n

161

wash-out, Eileen. Everything I want or hope for – it all comes down to *this* poky hole and having me words corrected and buggering you up and – What about the baby? What's happened?

(*Slight pause.*)

EILEEN: It's been got rid of.

(*He stares at her, then without defence, starts to cry.*)

ARTHUR: I haven't – I didn't – think about it, not at all – not a bit – but now – oh, dear God, why does the – why isn't it all like I wanted it to be – the world – why did you have to – to –

(*But he can't go on. He covers his face with his hands. She watches, waits, then – brutally matter of fact:*)

EILEEN: My pimp arranged it.

(*He takes his hands away from his face.*)

ARTHUR: What?

EILEEN: He said I couldn't go out at nights if I had a yowling brat to keep me at home.

(*Pause.*)

ARTHUR: Beg pardon. But I think I'm going to slap you one, right in the chops.

EILEEN: So long as you don't smudge my lipstick.

(*Fractional pause.*

Then ARTHUR, *rather as though holding a huge teddy bear, suddenly wraps his arms round her.*)

ARTHUR: You poor little devil. You poor girl.

(*At last, she lets herself go, weeping on to his shoulders. Eventually:*)

EILEEN: Get me out of it, Arthur.

ARTHUR: (*Earnestly*) I will if I can. God knows, I ought to. Just – here, sit down on me one and only chair – and tell me all about it. Everything.

EILEEN: Where will you sit, though?

ARTHUR: On the counter.

(*He does so. They look at each other.*)

EILEEN: I couldn't get a job.

(*Pause.*)

ARTHUR: No, well –

(*Pause.*)

EILEEN: I had left too much of my money with Dad because –
  oh, never mind why. I paid for a room at a – well, not a
  very posh hotel or anything silly – and then – (*she shrugs*) –
  my money trickled away. I couldn't pay my bill. I didn't
  even have enough for a decent meal. I couldn't go home. I
  couldn't or perhaps wouldn't find *you*. I was pregnant.
  And I couldn't couldn't couldn't get a job, except twice I
  washed up at a restaurant.
ARTHUR: (*Distressed*) And this is supposed to be the greatest
  country in the world!
EILEEN: (*Sincerely*) Oh, but it is, Arthur.
ARTHUR: I'd rather be a Yank.
EILEEN: (*Surprised*) Pardon?
ARTHUR: (*Seriously*) They got the best songs.
EILEEN: What's that got to do with it!
ARTHUR: I want to – (*He stops.*) I know it sounds daft Eileen –
  but I want to live in a world where the songs is –
  (*Again he stops, and looks at her, as though for help.*)
EILEEN: Where the songs come true.
ARTHUR: Yes.
  (*Fractional pause.*)
EILEEN: Poor Arthur.
  (*He looks at her quickly to see if she is being sarcastic. It seems
  she is not.*)
ARTHUR: I'd like to smash up every record in the shop. And
  tear up every song that has ever been written.
EILEEN: They still wouldn't come true.
ARTHUR: Truer than *this*, I bloody hope.
EILEEN: So I heard this girl in the street talking to a man,
  offering herself – for money. And I went back to my room
  and I thought about it and – there seemed something –
  inevitable about it. Do you know what I mean?
ARTHUR: Well, you got guts. I'll say that.
EILEEN: I went into that pub. I – there was this man – he
  bought me a drink.
ARTHUR: He would, wouldn't he? The rotten bugger.
  (*Pause.*)
EILEEN: And I did it with him for two pounds.
  (*Pause.*)

163

ARTHUR: Well, you got to eat (*sniff*) I suppose.
(*Pause.*)
EILEEN: And – one thing fetched another.
ARTHUR: It would. Wouldn't it.
EILEEN: This bloke – he paid to get rid of – He bought clothes and – Now he says I owe him fifty pounds. And if I don't get it –
ARTHUR: He's got you, then. Hasn't he?
EILEEN: Looks like it. He's given me the key to a room in Manton Street I can use it for – you know. And pay him twenty-five pounds a week for it.
ARTHUR: God Almighty.
EILEEN: Or I can pay him back. But I have to do it tonight. By tonight.
ARTHUR: Does he threaten to do anything to you if –
EILEEN: What do you think!
ARTHUR: (*Sigh*) Yes. But if you pay the fifty pounds.
EILEEN: And if elephants had wings. (*Pause.*) What shall I do?
ARTHUR: Can't you go back home? He'd never find you. Not owt at the back of beyond.
EILEEN: I can't. I don't know why. But I can't.
ARTHUR: But why ever not?
EILEEN: Because I was already dead there. This way feels like dying – but I'm still alive, in a way. I can see everything, feel everything – do you understand?
ARTHUR: Did you – um – did you *like* doing it? For money.
(EILEEN *hesitates.*)
EILEEN: It wasn't as bad as I thought it was going to be.
ARTHUR: (*Vaguely excited*) By God, you *are* a gel!
EILEEN: (*Quickly*) But I'd rather pick and choose. I don't want to be a – I want to own myself, my own body. I know I'm wicked, but I'm still – *proud*.
ARTHUR: I think you are beautiful.
EILEEN: Do you?
(*Pause.*)
ARTHUR: Let's – um – shall we – ?
(*They examine each other.*)
EILEEN: If you've got two pounds.
ARTHUR: (*Shocked*) Eileen!

164

EILEEN: I can't afford not to, can I? And the name is Lulu.
  Please.
ARTHUR: That's disgusting. Haven't you got any shame!
  Gorstrikea light!
EILEEN: I don't think I have.
ARTHUR: What?
EILEEN: Got any sense of shame.
  (ARTHUR *licks his lips, eyes bright.*)
ARTHUR: Blimey, Eileen –
EILEEN: Lulu.
ARTHUR: We're the same sort, you and me. We ought to stick
  together.
EILEEN: But I can't rely on you, Arthur.
ARTHUR: Listen to me!
EILEEN: I am. I am. Very carefully.
ARTHUR: I'm choking to death. I'm up to here with it all! I
  should have hung on to you no matter what. But I wanted
  me own record shop!
  (*She starts to laugh.*)
  I know. I know. It's enough to make a bleed'n cat laugh.
EILEEN: You'll *never* be satisfied, Arthur. Not somebody like
  you.
ARTHUR: Don't say that!
EILEEN: You're like the children in my class.
ARTHUR: But you're sweet on me, entcha? You still want me –
  eh? Eileen? Tell the truth.
EILEEN: Yes. I do.
  (*Start swift, bouncy music: 'I've Found the Right Girl': Jack
  Jackson Band, Jackson singing.*)
  And I'll go anywhere with you, or do anything with you.
  I've burnt all my bridges, Arthur. I'm not going home, I'm
  not going to walk the streets, either. And I'm damned if
  I'm going to go hungry! Lulu I am, Lulu I stay.
  (ARTHUR *gives her a swift little kiss and then holds her at arm's
  length, to 'sing'.*)
EILEEN: So what are we going to do?
ARTHUR: Trouble is, I'm hard up.
EILEEN: I can always pick up a bob or two. Now I know how.
ARTHUR: I haven't even got me car, any more.

EILEEN: We'll get another. One day.

ARTHUR: 'Course we will!

EILEEN: So – what shall we do? Where shall we hide?

ARTHUR: I've got eleven pounds seventeen and fivepence.

EILEEN: And I've got three pounds.

ARTHUR: (*Excited*) We can – we can live for a fortnight on that.

EILEEN: It's a start, anyway.

    (*Silence. They look at each other.*)

ARTHUR: What? Just go? Just go and – (*looks round the shop*) – leave everything? Just like that?

EILEEN: Just like that.

    (*Pause.*)

ARTHUR: All right.

    (*Pause.*)

EILEEN: Are you sure, Arthur? Have you got the guts?

ARTHUR: I ain't got no guts at all.

EILEEN: Don't worry. I've got enough for both of us.

ARTHUR: That's what I'm banking on.

EILEEN: Then – let's get out of here. Shall we?

ARTHUR: Yeh. But – hang on a minute –

EILEEN: What are you doing?

    (*He has picked up some records.*)

ARTHUR: 'On a Little Bamboo Bridge'. 'Marie'. 'You Sweet So and So'. 'Dancing with My Shadow'. 'September in the Rain'.

    (*Pause. She waits, held by the expression on his face. He throws them on the floor, then jumps on them, frenzied. She starts to laugh. Panting, he gets some more.*)

    'You Couldn't Be Cuter'. 'Isn't it Heavenly'. 'Hand in Hand'. 'Yes, Yes, My Baby Said Yes'. 'Indian Love Call'.

    (*Smash! Crash! Splinter!*)

EILEEN: 'My Sweetie Went Away'. 'Moon over Miami'.

ARTHUR: 'Down Sunnyside Lane'. 'What a Little Moonlight Can Do'.

    (*Smash! Crash!*)

EILEEN: (*Gurgle*) 'The Clouds Will Soon Roll By'.

ARTHUR: (*Pant*) 'April in Paris'.

    (*Smash!*)

EILEEN: (*Near scream*) 'Roll Along Prairie Moon'. (*She has

raised the record above her head, ready to hurl it against the
wall.)
ARTHUR: (*Shout*) No! Wait!
    (*He grabs hold of her wrists. They wrestle. They fall to the floor,*
    coiled together, on top of the broken records. The struggle turns
    into the passionate preliminaries to love-making.
       Music over: 'Roll Along Prairie Moon', Al Bowlly version –
    intro.)

GRAPHICS
ARTHUR*'s face only, a white oval in a screen that changes colour*
again and again: black, purple, red, orange, yellow, green, blue,
violet, black, purple, red. Arthur 'sings' 'Roll Along Prairie Moon'
as imperceptibly, ARTHUR*'s face turns, slowly, into the full moon.*
The colours merge into a velvet black, star-dotted sky. Silence.
Fade out.

5 'TIPTOE THROUGH THE TULIPS'

GRAPHICS. SUNNYSIDE LANE. DAY
There is a small police car outside Joan's and Arthur's.
Over street scene: opening bars (non-vocal) of 'You're Laughing At
Me' by the Lew Stone Band. Mixing through to:

INT. JOAN'S LOUNGE. DAY
A POLICE INSPECTOR, *in a grey suit, puts his cup of tea down,*
shaking his head. He also looks at JOAN's *crossed legs.*
INSPECTOR: I'm afraid it's all a bit of a puzzle, ma'am. I can't
pretend it ain't.
JOAN: (*Anxious*) But something's jolly well got to be done,
Inspector. Somebody, somewhere, must know something!
My poor husband can't just disappear off the face of the
earth, just like that – !
INSPECTOR: We haven't been idle. Far from it.
JOAN: I mean, this isn't Chicago or – this is London. People
don't vanish into thin air, for goodness' sake!
INSPECTOR: But all our enquiries – every one's a dead end, as
I've told you. Nobody saw anything that night. And
nobody heard anything.
JOAN: I find that very hard to believe. The shop was all upside
down – every gramophone record was in pieces. It was an
awful mess.
INSPECTOR: (*Sigh*) But there was no sign of forced entry, you
see Mrs Parker. And that was why the constable on that
particular beat failed to hear or notice anything unusual.
Whoever made that horrible mess, ma'am, made his entry
by means of a key, ma'am. That's what I – ah – want
another little chat about, if I may.
JOAN: You're surely not hinting that *my husband* did it himself,
are you?
(*Pause. They look at each other.*)
INSPECTOR: Whoever got into the shop got in with a key.
JOAN: That's preposterous! What you are suggesting is out of
the question, Inspector. Really – if that's all you can say –

INSPECTOR: I have to do my job, Mrs Parker. I'm only looking
   from every possible angle. I don't want to upset you.
JOAN: I mean, why would Arthur *do* such a thing?
   (*She re-crosses her legs in agitation. The* INSPECTOR *eyes them.*
   She notices, and pulls at her skirt.)
INSPECTOR: (*Quickly*) He wasn't in any trouble, was he?
JOAN: Trouble? What sort of trouble?
INSPECTOR: Well – for instance, ah, financial difficulties.
JOAN: (*Hotly*) Certainly not!
INSPECTOR: I beg your pardon.
JOAN: The shop wasn't doing all that well. But that was because
   it had only just opened. He wasn't in debt, or anything like
   that. We'd paid for all the stock.
INSPECTOR: I see.
JOAN: He loved music. All the songs. He could never, ever have
   smashed up all those gramophone records. Not in a
   million years.
INSPECTOR: He wasn't – please do forgive me for asking – but –
   ah – he wasn't mixed up with – ah – anybody else, er –
JOAN: Anybody else?
INSPECTOR: A lady friend, or –
JOAN: No!
INSPECTOR: I see.
JOAN: (*Agitated*) There wasn't Another Woman. Ab-so-lute-ly
   not. He only had eyes for me.
INSPECTOR: I should think so, too.
JOAN: What?
INSPECTOR: (*Awkwardly*) Begging your pardon, Mrs Parker.
   You're a very handsome young woman.
   (*Awkward, comical little pause.*)
   I'm very sorry. I got carried away.
   (*He coughs into his hand, then blows his nose. She stares down*
   at the carpet. Then – eventually:)
JOAN: (*Quietly*) Everything was top-hole between us, Inspector.
   I can assure you of that.
INSPECTOR: Yes. Of course.
JOAN: We were a very, very happy couple.
   (*But there is a forlorn note in her voice. He looks up.*)
INSPECTOR: And he hadn't been feeling – *ill*, or – behaving in

any way unusual – any way whatever – ?
(*Longish pause.*)

JOAN: (*Tense*) Loopy. Do you mean?

INSPECTOR: Not necessarily loopy. Under strain.

JOAN: (*Hesitant*) No. I – I don't think so.

INSPECTOR: (*Quickly*) For example, did he ever do or say
anything – anything at all – that, well, made you raise your
eyebrows or stop and wonder –

JOAN: I – (*But she stops.*)

INSPECTOR: It would be very helpful. If we are ever going to
find him. And this is all in confidence, you understand.

JOAN: (*With difficulty*) Perhaps he – perhaps he wasn't
altogether himself.

INSPECTOR: In what way?

JOAN: I don't think I – do you have a woman police officer at
the station, Inspector?

INSPECTOR: Well – yes. Of course, yes. By all means.

JOAN: (*In discomfort*) Is she – married?
(*He snorts, then controls himself.*)

INSPECTOR: No, madam. She is not the – marrying kind. She –
(*he sniggers*) – well, she looks a bit like a horse.
(*But* JOAN *does not laugh.*)
No. I don't mean that, of course. If you want her to come
and . . .

JOAN: Are *you* a married man, Inspector?

INSPECTOR: Ho, yes. I have a better half, ma'am.

JOAN: And you *did* say we could talk in confidence – ?

INSPECTOR: I can see that something is troubling you. Now
take my advice, Mrs Parker. If you want us to help find
your husband and get to the bottom of this little mystery –

JOAN: Yes. (*But she is starting to wring her hands.*)

INSPECTOR: Believe me, every little helps. And you really
shouldn't hold anything back, you know.

JOAN: I don't want Arthur to get into any sort of trouble.

INSPECTOR: But perhaps he already is.

JOAN: Then you think –

INSPECTOR: I don't think anything. We've got nothing to work
on at all. All we know is that he is missing and that his
shop was left in a complete jumble.

JOAN: (*Unhappily*) Yes.

INSPECTOR: So anything you can tell us about his – ah – his state of mind or his –

JOAN: (*Abrupt*) He asked me if I would stop – (*Then she stops. Pause.*)

INSPECTOR: (*Gently*) Yes?

JOAN: (*Near whisper*) If I would stop wearing a certain item of clothing while I was in the house.
(*Comical pause.*)

INSPECTOR: I don't think I quite understand.
(*Pause.*)

JOAN: (*With difficulty*) A certain garment. A – certain item of – underwear.
(*Pause.*)

INSPECTOR: An upper or a lower garment would that be, madam?

JOAN: Do I have to say?
(*And suddenly while he stares at her, she bursts into tears, covering her face with her hands.*
Unsure of what to do, the INSPECTOR *lurches to his feet and hovers over her.*
Start music: 'The Echo of a Song' by Roy Fox with Al Bowlly.)

INSPECTOR: (*Gruff*) Now, now – don't upset yourself – there, there – I *do* understand – You don't have to say anything else.
(*She sobs.*)
I take it, madam, that you are referring to your knickers.

JOAN: (*Sob*) He – won't be locked up, will he?

INSPECTOR: (*Grimly*) A man like that is capable of anything! This puts an entirely different complexion on the whole affair. He sounds a very sick chap, indeed.

JOAN: (*Howl*) Oh, poor Arthur!
(*The* INSPECTOR *mimes the words as Al Bowlly begins to sing.*)
Oh, no. I want him back. I want him found. I shall always stand by my Arthur.

INT. ROOM IN LODGING HOUSE, LONDON. DAY
A bed, a table, a dresser, two chairs, a stove, sink.

Begin on ARTHUR *at the table, face heavy with concentration, and unshaven, trying to fit a piece of (wooded) sky into a jigsaw. It doesn't fit.*

ARTHUR: (*Eventually*) This bleed'n sky. It's very hard – it's all blue, except for a bit of white. Cloud and that.

EILEEN: (*Flat*) Blue skies. Nothing but blue skies.

ARTHUR: What?

EILEEN: Wish it was.

(ARTHUR *glares at her, then scrabbles the pieces, fed up.*)

ARTHUR: Bloody jigsaws. Wish I hadn't found it.

EILEEN: That's about the only thing that *has* turned up, Arthur. One jigsaw. One box of Liquorice All-sorts.

ARTHUR: (*Sniff*) Must have been a bloody millionaire, the bloke that left stuff like that behind.

(*A tube train passes, as though on the other side of the wall. Things tremble and shake.*)

Probably owned the underground, an' all.

EILEEN: God! What a dump!

ARTHUR: We can't complain – eh, what are you doing?

EILEEN: Putting some lipstick on.

ARTHUR: (*Irritated*) I can see that, can't I. What are you putting it on *for*?

EILEEN: To go out.

(*Fractional pause.*)

ARTHUR: Where to?

(*She finishes lipsticking.*)

EILEEN: Anywhere, to go out anywhere. Just so long as it's out of this place.

ARTHUR: And what about me, then?

(*She looks at him so steadily that he almost averts his eyes.*)

EILEEN: Look in the mirror, Arthur.

ARTHUR: I know, I know. I haven't shaved.

EILEEN: Mirror, mirror, on the wall! Who is the fairest of – !

ARTHUR: (*Snarl*) Shut up, will ya!

(*She looks at him, then starts to powder her nose.*)

All right. I'll have a shave, then. But we got no money, love, so I don't know where you think you're going to go.

EILEEN: I'm sick of being poor!

(*She snaps shut her powder compact with a venomous click!*)

173

ARTHUR: I'll find something soon, don't you worry. Perhaps even tomorrow, eh?

(*She brushes some powder off her clothes.*)

EILEEN: Yeh. Perhaps.

ARTHUR: Now look, Eileen – you're beginning to sound like my wife –

EILEEN: I'm not surprised. Poor woman.

ARTHUR: Here we bloody go. What is it about women? Do your mothers teach –

EILEEN: I hardly ever knew my mother, poor soul.

ARTHUR: I didn't mean –

EILEEN: She worked her fingers to the bone – and for what? For a life at the daily tub and the kitchen stove and sewing and darning and – oh, what's the use. She was dead at forty-five.

ARTHUR: I wasn't talking about *your* mother, was I?

EILEEN: We've only got one life, Arthur.

ARTHUR: Yes. I know we have. Blimey, Eileen, you don't half –

EILEEN: (*Interrupting*) And I was quite content with mine. I mean, I didn't *think* about it. I just accepted it. Monday and then Tuesday and then Wednesday, all the way, every week, every year –

(*A tube train roars and rattles by.*)

ARTHUR: Like a bleed'n train. Yes, I know.

EILEEN: But you changed all that.

ARTHUR: (*Pleased*) Did I? Yeh – well – I suppose I did.

EILEEN: You told lies. You were selfish and dishonest –

ARTHUR: Here! Hold on!

EILEEN: And you acted as though the songs were real – as though you yourself had written them – as though they *allowed* you to – to – get away with . . .

ARTHUR: (*Uneasy smirk*) No – I draw the line at murdering people, love.

EILEEN: Do you?

ARTHUR: For Christ's sake!

EILEEN: Well, you killed off *my* old life, that's for sure.

ARTHUR: Fanks very much That's nice, ennit?

EILEEN: No – I'm *glad* you did. Truly. When you – made love to me and all that – I dunno. I became very – I saw things

174

differently. I just had to get away. I just *had* to see
something else. (*Looks around.*) Something more.

ARTHUR: It's a dump, I know. But we won't stay here –

EILEEN: But we will if we don't get some money.

ARTHUR: We was mad to smash up them records. I could have
sold 'em off easy.

EILEEN: I want nice things, Arthur.

ARTHUR: And you shall have 'em, my sweet.
(*She is looking at him steadily.*)

EILEEN: But I don't want to wait. There isn't time.

ARTHUR: (*Snort*) What do you mean – there isn't time?

EILEEN: I *know* there isn't. Don't ask me how, but I just *know*.
(*Something about the way she says this – something almost
sepulchral – makes him stop and stare.*)

ARTHUR: You give me the shudders, gel. Don't say things like
that.

EILEEN: Call it a woman's intuition.

ARTHUR: (*Comically, fearfully*) All right, all right. I'll shave, I'll
smarten myself up a bit. I'll try a bit harder.

EILEEN: (*Smile*) Finish your jigsaw, Arthur.

ARTHUR: Wha?

EILEEN: I'm going out on my own.

ARTHUR: Eileen – !

EILEEN: No. Don't worry. I'll be back – eventually.
(*He stares at her.*)

ARTHUR: You're – you're not going to – to –
(*She turns, brightly.*)

EILEEN: Are the seams of my stockings straight, sweetie?
(*Piano trill, then* ARTHUR *'sings' to 'Fats' Waller's 'You're
Laughing At Me'.*)
We need the mon-ey, hon-ey.

ARTHUR: (*Hotly*) Not by. You selling yourself!

EILEEN: Are you going to stop me?
(*They stand at challenge. He suddenly lowers his eyes and turns
away, drooping.*)

ARTHUR: (*Mumble*) No.
(*She looks at him, then kisses him.*)

EILEEN: Don't looks so forlorn, lovey dove. It doesn't *mean*
anything.

(*Then, deliberately, she puts her tongue in his ear.* ARTHUR*'s
eyes gleam again.*
      Wipe.)

CAPTIONS
*Chilling pen and ink drawings, detailed, of a line of tramps, cripples
and down-and-outs waiting to get into a Salvation Army hostel.
Music over (no words): 'Pennies From Heaven' on piano accordion.
Dissolving into:*

INT. THE HOSTEL. NIGHT
*Accordion fading, as camera pans slowly in semi-darkness along beds
placed almost end to end in a big bleak room with high windows.
Snores, grunts, burbles and obscure mumbles.
Settling, ultimately, on the* HIKER, *his accordion under bed. He is
flat on his back, staring up at the ceiling. He sucks in his breath with
a half sob, half shudder, and turns over to face a cadaverous* TRAMP
staring intently at him from the next bed.
TRAMP: (*Hiss*) Can you play that ding?
HIKER: W-what?
TRAMP: Dat accordy-ion. Know how to play it, matey?
HIKER: Yes.
TRAMP: And me, and me. And me.
HIKER: What?
TRAMP: I can play it. I know how to play it. By golly, I do, I do.
      (*The* HIKER *lifts his head, stares at him, then drops back
      again.*)
HIKER: I'm not arguing. Am I?
      (*The* TRAMP *suddenly clashes his teeth together.*)
TRAMP: No. And you'd better not, matey. That's all I can say.
      You'd better bloody not.
VOICE: Shut up!
TRAMP: (*Hiss*) And don't you tell me to shut up, soldier.
HIKER: I d-didn't say – it wasn't me –
TRAMP: Because I'm a killer, I am.
      (*Silence. The* TRAMP *loses interest. But the* HIKER *stares and
      stares at him. Then:*)
HIKER: (*Eventually, whisper*) Are you?
      (*The* TRAMP *works his jaws, but takes no notice.*)

176

D-did you k-k-k – (*He can't get it out.*)

TRAMP: K-K-Katie. (*And sniggers.*)

HIKER: (*Whisper*) Did you, though? Did you?

TRAMP: (*Suddenly, comically, very formal*) I beg your pardon?

HIKER: (*Restraining excitement*) Did you k-kill anybody? Like.
you said.

TRAMP: Oh, I expect so.

HIKER: (*Moan*) Don't you *care*?

(*Pause, a malicious glint comes into* TRAMP'*s eyes.*)

TRAMP: It don't trouble me one bit, old pal. I swots dem down
like flies.

HIKER: Did they bite? Did they scratch?

TRAMP: Go to sleep, you silly sod.

(*And others mumble and murmur.*)

HIKER: I can't s-s-sleep. I'm not like you. I can't. I keep seeing
her f-f-f- I see her face all the time: All the time.

TRAMP: Whose face?

VOICE: Bloody hell. Get some sleep!

HIKER: (*To* TRAMP) Shh! Shh. Shh.

TRAMP: Don't you shh me, you bugger.

HIKER: No, no. I didn't m-mean – No. It don't matter.

TRAMP: I don't believe you.

HIKER: Oh, yes. She was b-blind. She was – (*He stops.*)

TRAMP: I don't believe you can play dat ding. No. You can't.

HIKER: Hymns.

TRAMP: What?

HIKER: I can play hymns.

TRAMP: Poon. I can play 'I was a Wild Colonial Boy'.

HIKER: (*Reflective*) No. I don't know that. I never heard that
one.

TRAMP: Oh, it's a lovely tune, all right.

(*Some mumblings and murmurings of protest about the noise.
Pause. Somebody breaks wind. Snores.*)

HIKER: (*Whisper*) Oh, I think of her. I think of her all the t-time.

(*Slowly move into big close-up of* HIKER, *distressed.*
*Begin sound of massed accordions: the Primo Scala
Accordion Band playing 'Serenade in the Night'.*
*Jump cut: change of lights. All the down-and-outs standing
by on and in their beds are playing piano accordions. Then – as*

part of what is now a big production number (!), the HIKER
'sings' the haunting serenade.

*Finale on crescendo of accordion music from the grinning
down-and-outs. Lights fading. Sound fading. Picture fades.*)

EXT. ROAD IN HYDE PARK. DUSK
*Pan along. On benches, well spaced, three or four women sit, or
sometimes move away, obviously prostitutes. Men, too, linger,
hesitate or stride past on the prowl, shopping for pre-Wolfenden sex.
Finding, eventually,* EILEEN, *alone on a bench, looking carefully to
the right, and to the left. (Slow build to this scene.)*
*Further along the carriageway, shining against the trees, a pale
Rolls-Royce, with a running board, is, so to speak, kerb-crawling.*
Closer shot EILEEN *watching it, eyes beginning to narrow with
interest. (Slow – slow – as in a thriller.)*
*Faintly, start Charlie Kunz version of 'In the Middle of a Kiss'
before vocal.*
*The trees reflect, scuddingly, in the darkening windscreen, observing
the driver.*
Music continuing (non-vocal).
EILEEN: (*Intensely, to herself*) Come on, then. Come on. Come
on.
(*The car stops, about ten, fifteen yards from her. She is
uncertain whether to go to it or not.*
Music stops.
The car flashes its lights, once. EILEEN, *still hesitant, rises
from the slatted bench and tippetty-taps towards it. But
suddenly, and just as she reaches it, a smile clamped on her face,
the driver seems to lose nerve, and the car accelerates away in a
squeal of tyres.*
*She gapes after it, stands, shrugs, and slowly walks back to
the bench.*
*Change angle: someone is watching her from behind a tree
from this position. We see* EILEEN *from a rear-to-side view.*
*Camera judder – walking style – across the dusk-laden grass.
She turns, startled:*)
Oh – you startled me.
(*We see now it is an adolescent youth, in a dark blue blazer,
very nervous. Call him* MICHAEL.)

MICHAEL: Sorry, Miss. (*But he just stands there.*)

EILEEN: (*Rather irritated*) Well – what do you want?
(*The youth is in a paroxysm of nerves.*)

MICHAEL: P-p-pardon – I mean – what, Miss?

EILEEN: (*Gentler*) I said, what do you want?
(MICHAEL *almost shuts his eyes in panic.*)

MICHAEL: I wondered if – if I might – if I could sit down, Miss.

EILEEN: What? Here?

MICHAEL: Beside you – Miss. To to to talk for a minute. Just a just a little while, Miss. (*Then yearningly*) Please.
(EILEEN *examines him, almost tenderly.*)

EILEEN: If you want to, yes. It's not my bench, is it?

MICHAEL: (*As he sits, with comic alacrity*) I – it's a very nice evening, isn't it?

EILEEN: (*Solemnly, amused*) Yes. It is. Very nice.
(*Pause. He looks sideways at her, desperately.*)

MICHAEL: I like the dusk. There is something about the light as it – as it fades and dies. Isn't there?

EILEEN: Yes. It will soon be dark, though.
(*Pause.*)

MICHAEL: I – ah – I was wondering –
(*Pause.*)

EILEEN: Yes?

MICHAEL: (*Abrupt*) How much do you charge, Miss?

EILEEN: (*Only half-amused*) For what?

MICHAEL: I – I hope you don't think I'm – well – I'm –

EILEEN: You're what?

MICHAEL: That I'm *rude*.
(*She laughs.*)

EILEEN: No. But I *do* think you're very *young*. What's your name?

MICHAEL: Pete – Michael. It's Michael. What's *your* name?

EILEEN: Lulu.

MICHAEL: (*Pleased*) Really?

EILEEN: Really.
(*An awkward silence.*)

MICHAEL: (*Eventually*) You see, I've got a ten-shilling note – Lulu.
(*She laughs out loud.*)

EILEEN: And I should take care of it if I were you!
  (*He suddenly grabs at her hand.*)
MICHAEL: Please! Don't laugh – please – I'm sorry – I've been
  looking at you for more than an hour and – I – and I –
  (*He stops, and hangs his head.*)
EILEEN: You're still at school, aren't you?
MICHAEL: I – (*deflated sigh*) yes. But I'm nearly seventeen.
EILEEN: And you've never slept with a lady, have you? (*She
  hesitates on 'slept'.*)
MICHAEL: No. But – (*He sucks in his breath*) – I've thought
  about it! By golly, I've thought about it!
EILEEN: What would Mummy and Daddy say if they knew
  that?
MICHAEL: Crikey – you can guess. But – (*his face changes*) – oh,
  it's so, it's such a dream of mine – Lulu – if I could, if
  you'd let me, just – put my hand on your – (*gulp*) knee or –
EILEEN: No, no. You'll have a girlfriend before long. You don't
  want to spoil it, do you?
MICHAEL: I'd give you ten shillings for a – a proper kiss. You
  know, like they do it in the pictures.
  (*She looks at him.*)
EILEEN: Everybody has to wait, you know.
MICHAEL: I bet you didn't!
EILEEN: Oh yes I did. Believe you me.
MICHAEL: Do – do you – like doing – like making love – I
  mean –
EILEEN: I don't think you should be asking things like that. Do
  you?
  (*He gropes awkwardly, suddenly, for her knee.*)
MICHAEL: If I could *touch* – touch you –
EILEEN: You are trembling.
MICHAEL: I know. I know. It's as though – all my blood is
  pumping harder and harder and – oh, please – I'd –
EILEEN: Take your hand away.
MICHAEL: Please!
EILEEN: Listen to me –
MICHAEL: Just let me . . .
EILEEN: No – listen! I know what you're feeling. But you'll spoil
  everything you are dreaming about if you start off like *this*.

180

MICHAEL: (*Savagely*) All right then! You can have my watch
and my fountain pen as well!

EILEEN: Oh, you poor boy!
(*Pause. He trembles so much that he clamps his arms together.*)

MICHAEL: (*Awed*) I'm wicked. I know I am. And I can't help it.
I can't stop. Can't.

EILEEN: Have you been up here before? In the trees?

MICHAEL: (*Faintly*) Yes.

EILEEN: Watching the prostitutes? Just watching?

MICHAEL: Once or twice. I – not talking, though. I've never
plucked up courage to – talk, before now.
(*Fractional pause.*)

EILEEN: Yes. It takes courage. It takes a lot of courage.
(*Something in her voice makes him look.*)

MICHAEL: You don't have to do what you do, do you? You
sound quite – or – normal –

EILEEN: (*Laugh, edgily*) Normal!

MICHAEL: Are you unhappy – is that why? Don't you care?

EILEEN: No, I don't care very much.

MICHAEL: But you're so beautiful!
(*She looks at him, and, astonishingly, her eyes glitter with
tears.*)

EILEEN: Thank you.

MICHAEL: If I were a bit older –

EILEEN: Ah. No.

MICHAEL: – If I were – and had a job and things – I'd – I'd –

EILEEN: Save me?

MICHAEL: Yes!

EILEEN: Just so long as you could sleep with me.

MICHAEL: (*Confused*) What?

EILEEN: (*Sardonically*) You wouldn't *save* me for nothing,
would you?

MICHAEL: I mean it! I really do!

EILEEN: All right, then.

MICHAEL: P-pardon?

EILEEN: I'll let you sleep with me, and you can save me. You
can keep your ten bob. And your watch. Your fountain
pen. All you have to do is look after me, and serve me, and
– cherish me. When shall we start?

(*Pause.*)

MICHAEL: There – there's no need to be nasty, you know.

(*Pause.*)

EILEEN: You mustn't think, you see, that words come from between your legs.

MICHAEL: That's a rotten thing to say.

(*She gets up.*)

EILEEN: Good night, sonny.

MICHAEL: No, wait. Please wait a minute!

EILEEN: What for?

MICHAEL: I shall have five pounds next Tuesday. It's my birthday. Will you be here? In the park?

EILEEN: You'll be seventeen? Sweet sev-en-teen.

MICHAEL: Will you? Will you please? At – at about six o'clock – no, half past?

EILEEN: Is that what you want for your birthday?

MICHAEL: Will you, though? Please, Miss?

EILEEN: We'll see.

(*And she tip-taps away.*

Start music: 'I've Found The Right Girl' by Jack Jackson.

MICHAEL *'sings' with a dance on and around the park bench. Tap-dance clickers in shoes.*

A brisk band section follows. There is time to zip along the carriageway, past bench after bench, passing and going ahead of EILEEN. *On the benches, prostitutes in various stages of decomposition: from young and would-be pretty to old and raddled.*

Music stops dead at sight of the Rolls-Royce coming towards camera. Settle on Rolls as it moves slowly along. Pull back. EILEEN *stops. The car stops. A moment of hesitation.*

Music: band intro (non-vocal) to 'How's Chances?' by Henry Hall.

EILEEN, *in longer shot, goes to the car, leans in, seems to talk. The door opens. She gets in and the car accelerates away into the thickening dusk.*

Fade.)

INT. INSPECTOR'S OFFICE, POLICE STATION. DAY

The INSPECTOR *on the telephone, and sipping tea from an enamel mug. Waits for an answer.*

INSPECTOR: Hello? What? Yes – you sent a note about him at the time. Arthur Parker, commercial traveller. Age thirty-five. That's the one. Yes, I know you let him go. But what I want to know is – how solid was the – what? Yes. No, you see, I have reason to believe the man is a – he might be a sexual maniac. And he's gone to ground. Yes, scarpered! This girl that was done in, the blind girl – could I see the papers on it. What? Well – look at it from my point of view. This bloke – he disappears from view after smashing up his own property – oh, yes – I goes round to the wife and she tells me things about him that gives me a funny old feeling and then the name rings a bell and I turn up the circulars and find that it's now a couple of months since you had him in for questioning down there at your station – What sort of feeling? Well, now. What if I told you that he made his wife walk round the house without any knickers on! (*A pause. He sniggers.*) Yeh! She's a bit of all right an' all! But – wasn't that what was missing in *your* bit of mullarkey? Yes – that's right, old boy. Her knickers. They weren't on the body, were they? No – but it's interesting, ennit? Yes. All right. Call me back. This afternoon. Yes. Ta-ta. Cheers.
(*The* INSPECTOR *puts the phone down. And sips his tea, ruminatively.*

    Then he gets up and takes his raincoat off the hatstand-coat hanger in the corner, ready to go out.

    Wipe.)

INT. ROOM IN LODGING HOUSE. LONDON. DAY
ARTHUR *puts in the last two pieces of 'sky' in his wooden jigsaw puzzle. We see now it is a Jubilee (1935) picture of Buckingham Palace and a parade or similar. He smiles in triumph:*
ARTHUR: There! Gotcha!
    (*But the smile quickly dies. He stares moodily at the picture.*)
    (*Flat*) God Save the King. (*Sniff.*) And God Save Me.
    (*Move in to close-up of the monarchical jigsaw.*
    Slow dissolve into:)

INT. A POLITICAL MEETING (CONSERVATIVE PARTY). NIGHT
The speaker has his thumb in his waistcoat, and beats time with his other hand, in best 1930s political style. He is flanked, on the platform, by gentlemen with primrose flower-buttons, or the like, and ladies with ornate hats. The platform rostrum is draped with a large Union Jack.

The speaker is Major Archibald Paxville, MC, MP.

PAXVILLE: And I must say it is an astonishment which I do not share. The loyalty of our people, the love they have shown for their Majesties, the fervour we have seen in the streets and in the homes of even the humblest in the realm, is something that we, at least, have always known was there! (*'Hyah! Hyah!'*)

The Jubilee of His Majesty King George the Fifth is quite properly the occasion for national joy and gratitude. But it is also something more. Much more. What we have seen may well mark the turning point, the watershed, in the affairs of this great nation of ours. There were those in the Socialist Party, and not a few in the Liberal Party too, who chose to see or claimed to see in advance – that the Silver Jubilee was a *disgrace* or a *mask* of some sort designed to take our minds away from the serious problems that are now facing Great Britain both at home and abroad. On the contrary! (*'Hyah! Hyah!'*)

Quite the opposite, ladies and gentlemen. The people have shown, the length and breadth of the land, that they are fundamentally at one! They have shown their contempt for the sour and alien creeds which would set one class at the throat of another, which would trample the country's Flag under foot, which would turn its back on our great and united Empire, and level us all down to the same drab, uninspiring and impoverished condition. The people in the streets, shoulder to shoulder in their cheers and their patriotism, in their love and their loyalty, in their enthusiasm and in their prayers, have sent a message to every political leader in this land of ours. And the message, my friends, is as clear as a bell. It is that we can overcome our difficulties if and only if we all pull together. If and only if we put rancorous division between us, feebly promoted, well and truly to one side. If and only if we build *now*, and build straight and true, on the mood of this glorious Jubilee.

(*Applause.*)

Let the carpers and the moaners hold their peace! Let us forget past bitternesses – whatever they are – and look towards a better future!

(*Start music.*)

Let us show the world, as we have always shown the world, that our difficulties, such as they are, are as nothing compared with our virtues and our strengths.

('*Hear! Hear!*'

    PAXVILLE *starts to 'sing' to Brian Lawrence vocal of Carroll Gibbons' 'On the Other Side of the Hill', keeping the gestures of 1930s political oratory.*

    As the Major, to prolonged applause, raises his arm stiffly in acknowledgement, freeze the picture.

    The still fragments into dots, as in a newspaper photograph, and the dotted news picture is set in lines of print and becomes part of the newspaper being read by ARTHUR *in:*)

INT. ROOM IN LODGING HOUSE. LONDON. DAY

ARTHUR *fed up, crinkles the newspaper, then puts it down with a sigh.*

ARTHUR: (*To himself*) Where the bleed'n hell are you?

    (*Sound of footsteps on the stair. He gets up eagerly, opens the door.*)

    Eileen, love! I thought you were never coming!

EILEEN: I know. I know. Never mind.

ARTHUR: What you got here, then?

EILEEN: A nice big bag of macaroons.

ARTHUR: Ooh.

EILEEN: Well, you said you liked them. They're made by
    Fuller's, too.

ARTHUR: We in the money then?

EILEEN: We're in the money.

    (*They look at each other. He lowers his eyes, then she kisses him.*)

185

ARTHUR: I wish you didn't have to get it *that* way.

EILEEN: It's not real. It doesn't seem real. So don't worry about it.

ARTHUR: Real enough, ennit? When you got some bloke pushing and gasping away, flopping about all over you. Christ!

EILEEN: Don't think about it.

ARTHUR: Blimey. What else am I going to think about when you're out for all hours? I'm not going to concentrate on me jigsaw, am I? I feel a right banana stuck here, I can tell you.

EILEEN: But we agreed.

ARTHUR: Did we?

EILEEN: And it excites you. Just a bit, eh? Doesn't it? Arthur?

ARTHUR: When we're in bed. But not when – not most of the time. I can't get used to the idea. I just can't swallow it. I can't, Eileen.

(*They look at each other. Then she opens her handbag and puts twelve pound notes on the table.*)

EILEEN: Does *this* help?

ARTHUR: What? You got that this afternoon? In the backs of cars?

EILEEN: Yes. And – look! Two fivers.

ARTHUR: Gawd! How many have you had!

EILEEN: This was all off one bloke. In a hotel. The one with the Rolls-Royce.

(ARTHUR *picks up the money moodily, then almost flings it down again.*)

ARTHUR: (*Sullen*) Generous, ennhe?

EILEEN: Oh, come on, Arthur.

ARTHUR: I can hardly take it in. I still can't really believe you are doing this.

EILEEN: Once you start, somehow it's – (*she shrugs*) I've stopped bothering about what it means, or what's supposed to be right and wrong.

ARTHUR: But don't it ever *disgust* you, eh? You know what I mean.

EILEEN: I thought it would.

ARTHUR: And it don't?

186

EILEEN: Not really. No.

ARTHUR: (*Suddenly, hotly*) Well it does me! You dirty bitch!
    (*Silence.*)

EILEEN: Do you want to stay in this place, Arthur?

ARTHUR: I've been in a lot worse.

EILEEN: There's a nice flat going in Ellwood Crescent. I saw
    the board up.
    (*Pause.*)

ARTHUR: We can't afford anything like that.

EILEEN: That bloke with the Rolls –

ARTHUR: (*Tense*) Yeh? What about him?

EILEEN: He said – oh, Arthur. Look at it the right way, love –
    he said he'd give me ten pounds a week. If – (*she looks at
    him*) – if I was to give him every Friday afternoon.

ARTHUR: (*Bitterly*) He thinks you're good, does he?

EILEEN: Well, I am, aren't I?
    (*They look at each other. She laughs.*)

ARTHUR: Yes. But I wish it was all mine.

EILEEN: Oh, but it is, my love. It is really.
    (*They kiss.*)

ARTHUR: A lot of blokes'd give their eye teeth to be me. I know
    that.

EILEEN: What you grumbling about, then?

ARTHUR: It's the way we were brought up, I suppose. I've
    always thought it was all right for blokes to do it, but not
    girls. Especially not for money.

EILEEN: And it's only for a bit anyway. Till we get out of the
    wood.

ARTHUR: Yes. Not for long, eh?

EILEEN: Not on your life!

ARTHUR: Perhaps we'll be able to buy a piano, even.

EILEEN: Of course we will.

ARTHUR: I could learn to play, proper.

EILEEN: And try out a song, one of your songs.

ARTHUR: If I could have had a different start in life – I know I
    got it in me. I know I have.

EILEEN: Make us a cup of tea, eh, love?

ARTHUR: All my life I've loved music, you see. I know a good
    song when I hear one.

EILEEN: Of course you do. (*She sits.*) Oof.

ARTHUR: Tired?

EILEEN: I am, a bit.

ARTHUR: Active, is he?

(*She looks at him.*)

Yeh – all right. I'll make a cuppa. I can do *that*, any road. (*While he busies himself, a bit sullen, she picks up the paper.*) Tea and fags. What would life be without a cup of tea and a fag? Blimey, it wouldn't be worth a light, would it?

EILEEN: (*Reading, mechanically*) No. It wouldn't.

ARTHUR: I've had about five cups already. I don't seem to want to put me head out through the door any more. I don't know what's the matter with me.

EILEEN: Well I'll be blowed!

ARTHUR: What?

EILEEN: Major Archibald Paxville. So *that's* who he is!

ARTHUR: What you talking about?

EILEEN: The fellow I've been with this afternoon. The one with the Rolls. There's his picture in the paper!

ARTHUR: Where? Let's see!

(*He looks over her shoulder at the photograph.*)

EILEEN: I'm *sure* that's him.

ARTHUR: (*Reads*) 'MP says we are one nation again.' Who's he kidding?

EILEEN: Fancy that, now. A Member of Parliament. A proper nob!

(ARTHUR *and* EILEEN *look at each other.*)

ARTHUR: I'll bet that's something his constituents don't know. (*They laugh. She stops.*)

EILEEN: He wouldn't like them to find out either – would he?

ARTHUR: (*Amused*) Not half, he wouldn't. (*Then he registers her expression.*) 'Ere! What are you thinking?

INT. JOAN'S HOUSE. DAY

The INSPECTOR *calls, again.*

JOAN: Are you sure? Are you quite, quite sure?

INSPECTOR: Yes, madam. All our enquiries point in the same direction. We have now established that your – ah – husband left the shop and went to a nearby public house frequented by common prostitutes.

JOAN: People saw him?

INSPECTOR: The landlord identified him from the photograph you provided.

JOAN: (*Icily*) I see.

INSPECTOR: Shortly afterwards he left this public house with a young woman.

JOAN: Was she – ?

INSPECTOR: Apparently so.

(*Her face grimly set now.*)

JOAN: Go on, Inspector.

INSPECTOR: And the two of them were seen to return to the shop. Together, ma'am.

JOAN: How do you know that?

INSPECTOR: We have finally established that this was so. The constable on the beat has been to every house, flat and shop along that street. Someone very reliable remembers thinking it just a little odd that your – ah – husband should go back into the shop at that time of the evening with – ah – such a young woman.

JOAN: (*Tight*) You mean he went there to –

INSPECTOR: Probably, madam. I'm sorry. But that seems more than likely. Doesn't it?

JOAN: Knowing him – yes!

INSPECTOR: Ah.

JOAN: What do you mean?

INSPECTOR: Begging your pardon – but you seem to suggest that – well, that that sort of behaviour is not – totally outside his character – ?

(*Pause. She looks at him. Her face is full of hate.*)

JOAN: He's only got one thing on his mind, that man.

(*Pause.*)

INSPECTOR: It is our belief now that he, and this woman, broke up the gramophone records in the shop to – simulate a robbery or – in some way to divert attention from their – ah – running away together. She, perhaps, to continue her – trade, and him – well, to live off her immoral earnings.

JOAN: Dear God – how absolutely humiliating!

INSPECTOR: You have my deepest sympathy, Mrs Parker.

JOAN: The dirty little beast!
  (*Pause.*)
INSPECTOR: (*Carefully*) I don't suppose he's ever threatened
  you in any way. Has he?
JOAN: Threatened me?
INSPECTOR: Forgive me – but I'm quite sure you are not the
  type of young lady who would *willingly* – um – divest
  yourself of certain garments when –
JOAN: (*Quickly*) The man is a rotter!
INSPECTOR: *Has* he ever threatened you?
  (*Pause.*)
JOAN: As a matter of fact he has.
INSPECTOR: Can you tell me about it?
  (*She looks at him, seeming to decide something.*)
JOAN: He came back very late one night from – from one of his
  frequent debaucheries – and I woke up to see him standing
  by my bed in the dark with his tie stretched tight between
  his hands – like this –
INSPECTOR: Good gracious.
JOAN: I asked him what he was doing. He said he was going to
  kill me.
INSPECTOR: He *actually* said that, did he?
JOAN: His exact words were 'I'm going to squeeze the life out of
  you, you' four-letter word.
INSPECTOR: What did you do?
JOAN: I talked him out of it. But only at the cost of considerable
  personal indignity.
INSPECTOR: Sorry?
JOAN: I kept him quiet by putting lipstick on my – on the points
  of my bosom. (*The* INSPECTOR *twitches.*) Yes. No one
  knows the things I have had to endure. It is time it was all
  told.
INSPECTOR: I'm glad you feel that way. Too many of those sort
  of men are protected by their victims. You're obviously a
  lady of character, Mrs Parker. I can see that *you* wouldn't
  be browbeaten.
JOAN: Thank you. Thank you very much.
INSPECTOR: Now what I want to ask you – and I want you to
  think very carefully –

JOAN: (*Nervous*) Yes?

INSPECTOR: Did your husband tell you that he had been questioned by the Oxfordshire police in connection with – in connection with anything?

JOAN: Yes. He was very angry about it. (*She looks at him. Her eyes widen.*)

Oh – but – Good God! – You don't mean –

INSPECTOR: (*Quickly*) I don't mean anything at this stage. He – you know why he was questioned? He did tell you, did he?

JOAN: It – (*swallows*) – it was about that dreadful murder. The blind girl.

INSPECTOR: Yes. Poor soul.

(*She is staring at him now.*)

It wasn't in the newspapers, of course. But – please excuse me – that lovely young girl was found without any knickers on.

(*Silence.* JOAN*'s eyes narrow.*)

JOAN: (*Eventually*) What do you mean, it wasn't in the newspapers?

INSPECTOR: We don't allow that sort of detail to be published. For obvious reasons.

(*Pause. She works her mouth.*)

JOAN: But Arthur –

(*She stops.*)

INSPECTOR: (*Tense*) Yes?

(*Slight pause.*)

JOAN: But Arthur *told* me she wasn't – that she was found without her – underwear.

INSPECTOR: *Are you sure?*

JOAN: (*With a glint*) Oh, yes. That's the sort of thing that – well –

(*He leans forward eagerly.*)

INSPECTOR: That what, Mrs Parker?

(*She looks at him, very directly.*)

JOAN: That's the sort of thing that always excites him.

INSPECTOR: Does it?

JOAN: (*Coldly*) Yes. It makes him go all wet round the mouth. The filthy beast.

(*The* INSPECTOR *quickly wipes his mouth with the back of his hand.*)

INSPECTOR: Beast is right, I think.

(*Sudden, startling crash of music.*

JOAN *rises from her chair, arms upstretched, and 'sings'* 'Anything Goes'.

As the song comes to an end:)

INSPECTOR: (*Calmly*) Please sit down, Mrs Parker. I know you are upset, but –

JOAN: No. I'm not. I just want him hanged by the neck, that's all. I want them to break his dirty neck and then bury him in quicklime.

INSPECTOR: That's the spirit!

EXT. LONDON STREET. NIGHT

The HIKER *is playing his accordion again: 'There is a Green Hill Far Away'. He is outside, or near to, a cinema, and there is a queue. They are giving him amused or rueful glances. Move along the queue, nearer to cinema, and a team of buskers is doing a complicated comic dance on sand spread on paper – rather like 'Wilson, Keppel and Betty'. Watch – then travel back along the queue. The accordion stops.*

HIKER: (*Shout*) I killed her! I killed her! I killed her!

(*People in the queue laugh, but they are now starting to shuffle forward.*)

MAN IN QUEUE: What did you do? Play her them hymns!

(*Laughter.*)

HIKER: She was blind. She was blind!

MAN IN QUEUE: Pity she wasn't deaf an' all!

(*More sniggers. The raucous sound of the buskers further up adds a garish note.*

The HIKER *is in an extraordinary condition, looking and sounding totally crazed.*)

HIKER: We're all going to hell. We're all going to b-burn in hell.

(*And then he starts to play again: 'Rock of Ages'. Faces in the queue, moving slowly forward, indifferent.*)

(*Off, mechanically*) Thank you very, very much, sir. Thank you very, very much madam. Thank you very, very much, sir. Thank you very – very – very.

(*The moving heads pass, revealing more details of the poster*

*and/or stills in the showcase on the wall: Bing Crosby in
'Pennies from Heaven'.*

Pull out. One of the BUSKERS, *weirdly garbed, angrily
approaches the* HIKER *now that the queue has passed. The*
HIKER *is still playing 'Rock of Ages'.*)

BUSKER: Here! You! Piss off! This ain't your bloody pitch!

HIKER: (*Stops playing*) Beg your pardon, sir.

BUSKER: What?

(*He is taken by surprise.*)

HIKER: P-p-punish me! You can. You sh-should.

BUSKER: (*Turning away*) Oh, for Christ's sake.

HIKER: (*Shouts*) Go on! Punish me! Punish me!

(*The* BUSKER *scurries away. Closer shot, the* HIKER. *He sighs,
looks about, unstraps his accordion, puts it down in the middle
of the pavement, and walks away.*

*People pass, look at the ornate accordion, but do not pick it
up.*)

INT. A RESTAURANT. LONDON. NIGHT
*Rather plush, with, in the background, a violinist and a pianist
doing standards such as 'Tiptoe Through the Tulips', Stephen
Foiter's 'Alexander's Ragtime Band', etc.* ARTHUR, *in a new suit,
and* EILEEN, *in a new dress, are going to have a meal – and feeling
just a little out of their depth.* ARTHUR *nervously addresses the*
WAITER.

ARTHUR: We'll both be having the – um – the melon. To start
wiv, that is.

WAITER: Very good, sir.

ARTHUR: Then the lady will have the whatdyacallit – the – this
Cod bool – um –

WAITER: Cod boulangère, sir.

ARTHUR: That's what I said. (*Sniff*) And the gent– I mean, and
me, I'll have the Dover sole.

WAITER: Thank you, sir.

(*He goes to take the menu.*)

ARTHUR: And then both of us'll have the mixed grill, please.

WAITER: (*Puzzled*) Sir? What about the cod and the sole?

(ARTHUR *looks at* EILEEN *in agony, but she can't help.*)

EILEEN: The m-mixed grill.

WAITER: Oh, but –
ARTHUR: What's the matter? Have I done something wrong?
WAITER: Not wrong, sir. No, sir, of course not.
ARTHUR: Well, then –
(*The* WAITER *leans in half-whisper.*)
WAITER: I think, sir, you'll find it a little too much.
(ARTHUR *looks desperately at* EILEEN.)
EILEEN: (*Half-whisper*) We're both – we didn't have any
breakfast, you see.
ARTHUR: (*Sweating*) That's right.
WAITER: Even so, sir –
ARTHUR: You tell us, then. (*Mock aggressive.*) It's your job,
ennit, old pal?
WAITER: If I were you, sir, I'd have the mixed grill to follow the
melon.
ARTHUR: That's what we said.
WAITER: Yes, sir.
EILEEN: (*Faint*) That would be very nice.
ARTHUR: And some wine too, please. You haven't got any here
– on this menu.
WAITER: The wine waiter will bring you the list, sir. Thank you
sir, madam.
(*The* WAITER *withdraws. They look at each other.*)
EILEEN: Oh, Arthur.
ARTHUR: Stuck-up bleeder.
EILEEN: I didn't know where to put myself.
ARTHUR: Sod it, I don't care.
(*But,* WINE WAITER *approaches.*)
Oh, yes. Ta very much. Red or white, dear.
EILEEN: (*Faint*) We're having meat, Arthur.
ARTHUR: Ho, yes. A nice bottle of red. Um, let's see –
(*He looks furtively at* EILEEN, *then at wine list.*)
Yes – this one, please. The Beaune. (*Wink.*) Give the old
dog a bone, eh?
WINE WAITER: (*Unsmiling*) Ver' good, sir.
(*Pause.*)
ARTHUR: (*Awed*) Bloody hell.
EILEEN: (*Tense*) What's the matter?
ARTHUR: It's seven and ninepence a bottle!

194

EILEEN: Never mind, Arthur. We can afford it.

ARTHUR: Yes, we can, can't we! Money talks, don't it? Why do they try and make you feel so bleed'n small?

EILEEN: They can tell, that's why. They can see we're not used to it.

ARTHUR: 'Tiptoe Through the Tulips'.

EILEEN: What?

ARTHUR: That's what they're playing. Listen.

EILEEN: Oh. Yes.

ARTHUR: And that's what we're doing. Tiptoe-ing through the bleed'n –
(*The melons arrive.*)
Oh. Thank you, yes. Very nice.

EILEEN: Thank you so much.
(*Pause. They look at each other, and start to giggle.*)

ARTHUR: (*Eventually*) I fought – I fought, you see – (*Starts to laugh again.*)

EILEEN: Who did you fight?

ARTHUR: No – no – (*snigger*) I fought that after the soup or the melon or whatever –

EILEEN: Oh. You *thought*!
(*They both explode, then comically shush each other.*)

ARTHUR: I fought that in a *posh* place you had the beginnings and *then* the fish and *then* the main course.

EILEEN: Well, I was leaving it up to you.

ARTHUR: You weren't much help, that's for sure. 'What about the cod' – my God.

EILEEN: *I* haven't been in this sort of place, Arthur. We don't have them in the Forest of Dean.

ARTHUR: No – but you been to bed with an MP, aintcha!
(*Too loud. People look.*)

EILEEN: (*Shocked whisper*) Arthur!

ARTHUR: (*Flustered*) All right, all right. Keep your voice down.
(*The wine arrives, label shown to* ARTHUR.)
Yes, very good.
(*A little poured.* ARTHUR, *trying to regain face, makes a comically elaborate ritual out of the tasting. But as he swirls the wine around his mouth, he catches* EILEEN'*s eye. The result is that he starts to laugh, making it a near miss, whether he gulps*

down the wine prematurely or spurts it out in a helpless guffaw.
He just manages to swallow, and EILEEN *turns her face away*
into the flat of her hand.)

(*Gasp*) Yes. That'll do very nicely.

(*Expressionless, the* WAITER *fills their glasses and withdraws.*)

EILEEN: We're a right pair, we are, Arthur.

ARTHUR: Sod it, that's what I say.

EILEEN: (*Laugh*) Yes, sod it. Sod everything, why not?

ARTHUR: Thank God I met you, gel.

(*They look at each other.*)

EILEEN: I like your new suit.

ARTHUR: And I like your new dress.

EILEEN: You see, we can start to live a bit, for a change.

ARTHUR: (*Moodily*) There's something abaht England, though.
They'll always make you feel out of place.

EILEEN: Who will?

ARTHUR: Them that runs things.

(*Their melons are removed. They keep a frozen silence when
being attended to. Their mixed grills arrive, and vegetables.
They are tense. At last:*)

They'll always make you feel – awkward and that. Christ,
even my wife did her best – and she was only a bleed'n
shopkeeper's daughter.

EILEEN: Do you miss her?

ARTHUR: What – that lah-di-dah old cow! This chop's a bit of
all right – what's yours like – ?

EILEEN: Very nice.

ARTHUR: No. I don't miss her, I ain't got no regrets. None at
all.

EILEEN: You talk in your sleep, though.

ARTHUR: Do I? What do I say?

EILEEN: Nothing I can make out. But you don't sound very
happy.

ARTHUR: (*Too vigorously*) But I am! I really am!

(*Pause, they chew, chew. But she looks at him, covertly.*)

EILEEN: (*Eventually*) There's no need to be frightened, love.
(*Pause.*)

ARTHUR: I been frightened all me life.

EILEEN: Then stop. Stop feeling like it.

ARTHUR: That's something I've never told a living soul.
(*Slight pause. She reaches for him.*)
EILEEN: I'll look after you. Don't worry. I'll take care of you, my love.
(ARTHUR *is moved, his eyes prickle.*)
ARTHUR: Yeh, well . . . That's something I don't really understand. *You* could have anybody.
EILEEN: (*Laugh*) I *do* have anybody!
ARTHUR: Shhhh!
(*Piano/violin stop playing.*)
EILEEN: The wine is making me squiffy.
ARTHUR: Good. But keep your voice down. That's what this country is all about –
EILEEN: What?
ARTHUR: Keeping your voice down. Whispering behind yer bleed'n hand.
EILEEN: You're right.
ARTHUR: 'Course I'm right.
EILEEN: I'm going to get what I can out of him, that Major whatsit, MP.
ARTHUR: You mind he don't bite.
EILEEN: He can afford it, the dirty old devil.
ARTHUR: They stick together, that lot. You watch what you're doing. Don't be stupid.
EILEEN: Close your eyes. Stand on one leg. And count up to ten.
ARTHUR: What you on about?
EILEEN: I'd like a baby one day, I'd like to have that baby. And then – (*She frowns.*)
ARTHUR: And then what?
(*She looks at him, puzzled.*)
EILEEN: I don't know.
ARTHUR: No, come on. What were you going to say?
(*Fractional pause.*)
EILEEN: If I say it I shall cry.
ARTHUR: If you say *what*?
EILEEN: (*Strained*) I don't know. Except –
ARTHUR: Here! You're not going to cry, are you?
(*She smiles. But her eyes glitter.*)
EILEEN: No. I'm not going to cry.

(*Start music.*

    They look at each other, hard and long and obscurely questioning, during dance band intro. to 'Hands Across the Table': Henry Hall and Dan Donovan, then ARTHUR *'sings' the sentimental song.*

    During this, their plates are collected and they get pudding.)

EILEEN: This is very nice.

ARTHUR: Yeh. It's all right, ennit? Bit sickly, though.

EILEEN: Still – we can be sick if we want to, can't we, Arthur?

    (*She says 'sick' with great force, even venom.*)

ARTHUR: We can do what we like, my sweetie pie.

    (*Fast wipe.*)

EXT. HAMMERSMITH BRIDGE. NIGHT

Dark, with lights glimmering on the river slugging along below the gilded bridge.

Move in to discover the HIKER, *without accordion, sitting on the narrow seat on the pedestrian walk of the bridge. He is huddled into himself, strangely shapeless, making obscure moaning noises.*

A MAN *passes going towards Hammersmith end. He hesitates, then:*

MAN ON BRIDGE: 'Ere – are you all right, mate?

HIKER: Mmbblmm, – wha–?

MAN ON BRIDGE: What's the matter with you? Eh?

    (*The* HIKER *lolls his head about, then focuses on the questioner.*)

HIKER: (*Angrily*) F-f-f-fu–

MAN ON BRIDGE: Hey now. None of that!

HIKER: It's a f-fine old world, sir.

MAN ON BRIDGE: Are you drunk? Is that it?

HIKER: 'Tis that. 'Tis that. It's a m-marvellous world if you
    look at it right. Lights on the w-water.

MAN ON BRIDGE: (*Embarrassed*) Here. Get yourself a cup of tea.

HIKER: Thank you very, very much, sir. Thank you very, very
    much.

    (*The* MAN *nods, and walks away, quickening his stride. In the distance, a river barge hoots.*

    Pause.

    The HIKER *throws the two pennies he has been given into the river. Plop! Then, plop!*

    Fade.)

INT. THE MUSIC SHOP, GLOUCESTER. DAY

There is a new MANAGER, *talking to a* POLICE INSPECTOR, *from Gloucester Force.*

SECOND INSPECTOR: But what happened to him, then?

MANAGER: Well, I didn't know him myself. I had a shop down in Winchester till a month ago. But he had a heart attack. Right here in the shop, so I understand.

SECOND INSPECTOR: That's nice.

MANAGER: So, you see, I can't really help you, Inspector.

SECOND INSPECTOR: There's no way you can tell, then, if this man called at the shop on that particular day?

MANAGER: What's this all about, anyway?

SECOND INSPECTOR: We're just making enquiries. And they're not routine neither.

(*'Ting' as shop door opens.*)

MANAGER: You can look at the order book. Here. If this Parker bloke took any orders for sheet music that day, then they'll be in that book. It's the same one. I've inherited it, worse luck.

SECOND INSPECTOR: Well, *that's* something. Yes thank you.

MANAGER: (*To* CUSTOMER) Can I help you, sir?

CUSTOMER: I can wait.

SECOND INSPECTOR: No, no. Carry on.

CUSTOMER: Are you sure? Right, ta. I wanted the sheet music for 'Roll Along Prairie Moon', please.

MANAGER: Oh, yes. Turning out very popular, that.

CUSTOMER: (*Snort*) Gets on my wick, personally. The wife wants it. She plays the piano at the British Legion.

MANAGER: (*Laugh*) Oh, well. There's a lot of cowboys there, all right.

CUSTOMER: Not many Indians, though. Thanks very much.

MANAGER: Thank you. (*Takes money.*) Anything else?

CUSTOMER: No. Good afternoon.

MANAGER: Good day, sir.

(*'Ting'.*)

SECOND INSPECTOR: He didn't give this man an order. Not on that day. There's nothing written down here.

MANAGER: Doesn't prove he wasn't here, of course.

SECOND INSPECTOR: Perhaps not – more to the point, it doesn't prove he *was* here. Does it?

MANAGER: (*Laugh*) The way you coppers work! I'm beginning to feel sorry for the bloke, whoever he is.

SECOND INSPECTOR: You wouldn't if you knew what he'd done.

MANAGER: Oh? What's that, then?

SECOND INSPECTOR: Look. I'm afraid I shall have to take possession of this book. I'll give you a receipt, of course.

MANAGER: Oh, but – that's not going to be very convenient, Inspector.

SECOND INSPECTOR: Scotland Yard will want to see it, you see.

MANAGER: Really, well – I – suppose – ah – yes. That's different. The book's nearly full up, anyway.

SECOND INSPECTOR: You'll get it back, in time. With our thanks.

MANAGER: That's what I like about the music business. You never know what's going to happen. (*Smile.*) One moment it's tiptoe through the tulips and the next it's whistling in the dark.

SECOND INSPECTOR: Just as well I'm tone deaf, I think. Well – thanks for your help. I'll write you a receipt, shall I?

MANAGER: No, it's all right. Not if you're tone deaf, sir.
(*They both laugh.*)

INT. BEDROOM IN FLAT. LONDON. DAY

MAJOR PAXVILLE, *in bed with* EILEEN, *falls back on to the pillows, panting, exhausted.*

PAXVILLE: (*Eventually, panting*) Dear me . . . oh, goodness . . .

EILEEN: Are you all right?

PAXVILLE: I'm – (*gasp*) – I'm not very fit, am I?

EILEEN: Fit enough. (*She stares up at the ceiling, rather blank.*)

PAXVILLE: This is about the only exercise I get, you know.

EILEEN: They say it keeps you young and happy.

PAXVILLE: Who says?

EILEEN: Not parsons, that's for sure. Nor mothers with daughters.

PAXVILLE: What are you looking at?

EILEEN: Those cherubs or angels or whatever they are carved in the plaster. All along the ceiling.

PAXVILLE: Oh, those. Pretty, aren't they? Little bare botties.

EILEEN: Is this your flat?

PAXVILLE: (*Slightly cautious*) It's – yes. I use it sometimes.

EILEEN: But it's not your home.

PAXVILLE: Questions, questions.

EILEEN: Sorry.

PAXVILLE: You're a very sweet gel. But –

EILEEN: But I mustn't be curious.

PAXVILLE: There's no need to be, is there?

EILEEN: Not if you –

> (*She stops, biting her lip. He frowns, props himself up on an elbow and looks down at her.*)

PAXVILLE: Not if I what?

EILEEN: Never mind.

PAXVILLE: What's going on in that pretty little head of yours?

EILEEN: I saw your picture in the paper the other day.

> (*He looks at her. His voice hardens.*)

PAXVILLE: Did you now? Or was it someone who looked like me?

EILEEN: Oh no. It was you, Major Paxville.

> (*He takes time. He reaches for a cigarette, and puffs out smoke.*)

PAXVILLE: Did I have my clothes on?

EILEEN: (*Smile*) I don't know. It was only head and shoulders.

PAXVILLE: Just as well, I think.

EILEEN: Are you – are you worried?

> (*He blows out smoke.*)

PAXVILLE: (*Languidly*) Do I *look* worried, my dear?

EILEEN: Yes. You do.

> (*Pause.*)

PAXVILLE: Do you think I have reason to be, then? Worried, I mean.

EILEEN: Well –

PAXVILLE: Don't be a bitch, now.

EILEEN: Not even a – a *greedy* bitch?

> (*Pause. He stubs out his cigarette.*)

PAXVILLE: I think you'd better get dressed.

EILEEN: Are you sure?

PAXVILLE: (*Harshly*) Quite, quite sure. Thank you very much.

(*She looks at him, wilts, then slides out of bed. He watches her coldly fish-like, as, suddenly awkward and fumbling, she puts her clothes on.*

    Start music.

    As EILEEN *dresses,* PAXVILLE *'sings' Jack Buch's 'You Sweet So and So'.*

    Dressed, she looks at him.)

EILEEN: Do you want me to come again?

    (*He examines her.*)

PAXVILLE: There are plenty more where you come from, my dear.

EILEEN: I see.

PAXVILLE: I hope you do. The police are not at all nice to blackmailers especially if they are *whores*.

EILEEN: Shall I telephone then?

    (PAXVILLE *stares her down.*)

PAXVILLE: What a cheap little tart you are.

EILEEN: (*Quavering*) Shall I – ?

PAXVILLE: No. Don't bother. I'll do it myself.

    (*And he reaches for the phone beside the bed. She watches him, eyes widening. When he starts to dial she gasps, turns and runs from the room. He carries on dialling. He smiles grimly as he hears a door crash shut, off. Then:*)

Hello? Ah – Preece, old fellow. It's Archie. I wonder if you know the Test Match score, old boy. Mmm. Really? Bloody weather. All right, thanks. Toodle pip.

    (*He hangs up. Then sucks in his breath, badly shaken.*)

EXT. TOWPATH. THE THAMES. DAY

Begin on some swans, bobbing on the river, between Hammersmith and Putney.

Music over: 'Pennies From Heaven' on piano/accordion.

Pull back to show some 1935-style, working-class kids at the side of the river, where stone steps meet an expanse of littered mud. They are playing 'ducks and drakes' by skimming stones across the water, and shouting.

FIRST BOY: There! Four times! Mine bounced four times.

SECOND BOY: Gitahtofit!

FIRST BOY: Four times!

THIRD BOY: It was free. I counted. Free times!

SECOND BOY: Big 'ead – he finks he can count.

FIRST BOY: I don't care, anyway. Don't bother me.

THIRD BOY: A penny is best.

FIRST BOY: Who's going to throw a penny in the river, loony!

SECOND BOY: Bet there's lot of money in there. Dropped off bridges and that.

FIRST BOY: And off the barges.

THIRD BOY: I found half a crown dahn here once.

SECOND BOY: Bleed'n liar.

THIRD BOY: No – straight up. God'strewth.

FIRST BOY: Penny – perhaps. Not half a crown, though.

THIRD BOY: Half a crown. I'm telling you. I had a bottle of pop and some fish and chips and went to the pictures. Honest.

SECOND BOY: What did you see, then?

(THIRD BOY *wipes his nose on his jersey, thinking too long.*)

THIRD BOY: *King Kong.*

SECOND BOY: You bloody liar!

(*The* FIRST BOY *makes ape-like, gambolling and grunting.*)

THIRD BOY: 'Ere! What's that, then! (*Points across river.*)

FIRST BOY: Don't say it's another half-crown.

SECOND BOY: It's – yeh – it's an old coat or something. Ennit?

THIRD BOY: Or somebody drowned.

FIRST BOY: Cor – you don't half romance, dontcha?

(*But the idea is attractive. The three* BOYS *stare at the middle of the river. Eventually:*)

SECOND BOY: 'Ere! (*Awed*) It don't half look like it. Don't it?

THIRD BOY: Toldya!

FIRST BOY: Look – it's drifting in towards the bank a bit. Let's see if it comes in!

(*They race up the stone steps to the towpath, ready to go further up river. The dark bundle on the water floats, floats, slowly on by.*

Slow dissolve.)

INT. AN EMPTY FLAT, LONDON, OVERLOOKING DIFFERENT STRETCH OF RIVER. DAY

Door opens, and in come an ESTATE AGENT, ARTHUR *and* EILEEN.

203

AGENT: And this, of course, is the ah – lounge. A sizeable and well-proportioned room, as you can see.

ARTHUR: Yes. Not bad at all.

EILEEN: Very nice.

AGENT: Two points for electrical connections.

ARTHUR: Oh, that's good.

EILEEN: You don't often get two in a room, except in the kitchen.

AGENT: Everything has been very well thought out. Note the tiled surround to the fireplace.

ARTHUR: And you can see the river.

EILEEN: Oh, yes!

AGENT: This window faces south, of course. A warm and sunny room.

ARTHUR: When it's shining.

AGENT: Quite.

ARTHUR: Which ain't very often.

EILEEN: We could have a gas fire fitted there, couldn't we?

AGENT: Certainly. There is gas in the adjoining flats. The pipes can easily be taken on through.

ARTHUR: Many after it, are there?

AGENT: You are the third couple today, actually, sir. It's a very desirable flat, as you can see.

ARTHUR: Paying through the nose, though –

(AGENT *makes a gesture.*)

AGENT: There's such a demand for property nowadays. It *is* very nicely situated.

EILEEN: The rent is monthly – is it?

AGENT: Well, actually – the landlords prefer *this* class of property to be – quarterly. On a three-year agreement, as I said.

ARTHUR: That's a lot to find in one go.

EILEEN: We can manage it, dear.

(*The* ESTATE AGENT *coughs, discreetly.*)

ARTHUR: Suppose so.

AGENT: Perhaps you'd – rather talk about it amongst yourselves and –

EILEEN: (*Suddenly*) We'll take it!

(ARTHUR *looks at her, then:*)

ARTHUR: Yes. Well – yes. No point in beating about the bush, is there?

AGENT: None at all, sir. If you're sure.

ARTHUR: When I makes up my mind I makes up my mind.

EILEEN: My husband is a songwriter, you see.

AGENT: Really?

ARTHUR: There's room in here for a piano, any road.

EILEEN: And inspiration through the window.

ARTHUR: What? 'River Stay Away From My Door'?
(*They laugh.*)

AGENT: Would I know any of your songs, sir?

EILEEN: I don't think –

ARTHUR: (*Loudly*) 'Lover, Come Back to Me'.

AGENT: Really? Did you write that, sir?

ARTHUR: (*Smirk*) Not under my own name, of course.

EILEEN: (*Half-laughing*) Do we have to come and sign anything – er –

AGENT: This eager heart of mine is singing.

EILEEN: Pardon?

AGENT: Lo-ver come back to me-ee-e.

ARTHUR: Nice, ennit? Even if I do say so myself.

AGENT: Beautiful. Beautiful.

EILEEN: Arthur – we have to go soon.

ARTHUR: What?

AGENT: If you could pop in before half past five to sign the lease and – (*cough*) – the first quarterly payment, I'm afraid –

ARTHUR: By all means, old chap.

EILEEN: That's definite, then, is it? I mean, it's ours if we come in and sign this afternoon.

AGENT: It won't be anyone else's, madam. Not once you've jolly well signed.

ARTHUR: And then there's 'Tiptoe Through the Tulips'.

AGENT: (*Frown*) Oh, but –

ARTHUR: Which is one I wish I had written.
(*The* AGENT *laughs, uncertainly.*)

EILEEN: (*Firmly*) Come on, Arthur. We must go.

ARTHUR: All right, dear. Thank you very much. (*To* AGENT) We'll see you later.

AGENT: Good, good. Yes. Can I give you a lift – ?

ARTHUR: No. It might get stuck between floors.

AGENT: Pardon?

EILEEN: Come *on*, Arthur –

ARTHUR: Toodle-oo, then.

AGENT: Goodbye. Yes.

EILEEN: Goodbye. Thank you.

(*She steers* ARTHUR *out.*)

ARTHUR: (*Retreating*) 'Roll Along Prairie Moon'. That's one of mine.

(*They have gone.*

AGENT *stares after them. His face twitches momentarily, as if in pain.*)

AGENT: (*Hiss, to himself*) Muckin' bighead.

EXT. OUTSIDE BLOCK OF FLATS, BUSY PAVEMENT. DAY

ARTHUR *and* EILEEN *come out on to the pavement, grinning.*

NEWS-SELLER: News. Star. Standard. News. Star. Standard.

ARTHUR: Well, I feel as though I have written 'Prairie Moon'. I *might* have done, eh?

EILEEN: If somebody else hadn't done it first.

(ARTHUR *notices the news placard: 'Blind Girl Murder: Man Sought'.*)

ARTHUR: Hang on.

NEWS-SELLER: News. Star. Standard.

ARTHUR: Give us a *Star*, mate. Ta.

EILEEN: Let's walk a bit, shall we? I feel as though I haven't had any fresh air for a month.

ARTHUR: It's air, all right. But it ain't fresh.

EILEEN: I love the smell of London – What's the matter? Arthur?

(*He is looking at the paper.*)

ARTHUR: Good Christ all bloody mighty.

EILEEN: (*Alarmed*) Arthur?

ARTHUR: I'm – (*gasp*) – I'm going to be sick – Eileen – oh, God! – Eileen!

EILEEN: Arthur! Whatever is it! What's the matter!

(*He is swaying with shock.*)

ARTHUR: (*Croak*) Read what it says. Read the – dear Christ in heaven!

206

(*She grabs the paper off him. On a third of the front page, over a big picture of a grinning* ARTHUR.

'*Have you seen this man? Song salesman hunted in blind girl murder.*'

She blanches and looks up at him mouth open.)

NEWS-SELLER: (*Off*) News. Star. Standard. News. Star. Standard.

(*Sharp cut.*)

EXT. RIVER. DAY

Two POLICEMEN, *the* BOYS, *and a small throng of onlookers on the bank. One of the* POLICEMEN, *paddling out a little way. Pulls at the bundle. The Accordion Player (the* HIKER) *is dragged on to the mud, taking human shape very slowly.*

The other POLICEMAN *orders the people to keep back. They press in, silent, to gape. Closer shot of the sodden corpse.*

Cut to screaming gulls, and distant hoot of barge.

Dissolve.

INT./EXT. PARKED CAR. SUNNYSIDE LANE. DAY

A PLAIN-CLOTHES POLICEMAN – *but still obviously a policeman – watches Arthur's house across the street, arm resting on window. He does not blink, does not move.*

Wipe.

INT. THE ROOM IN THE LODGING HOUSE. NIGHT

Curtains are open, shifting slightly in the air from partly open window, illuminating the silhouetted furniture.

Scratch and flare of a match. Someone is sitting by the door, waiting. Obviously a policeman, lighting a cigarette.

Sudden rushing sound of District Line train, and blue flashes beyond window. The light falls in flashes of garishness across the completed jigsaw on the table.

Dissolve:

EXT. THE RIVER. NIGHT

Close in. The water chopping and dancing, darkly. A few lights gleaming on it. Pulling slowly back and back, until – cut.

EXT. THE TOWPATH. NIGHT

Crunch-crunch-crunch on the gravel as EILEEN *walks, alone, carrying a parcel or bundle wrapped in newspaper. She hesitates, stops. Someone is walking towards her. She quickens her stride again. The two figures pass darkly.*

A little further on, she stops, looks back, watches the other figures recede, crunching into the dark. Then she walks back, slowly looking all about. She stops. Waits. Then:

EILEEN: (*Timidly*) Arthur – ? Where are you?

> (*A frightened voice comes from the dark bushes – Barnes side of Hammersmith Bridge.*)

ARTHUR: (*Off*) Over here! Behind the bushes.

> (EILEEN *looks about again, then cautiously goes over to the big, dark bush, disappearing behind it. Their voices off screen now.*)

EILEEN: I got the fish and chips.

ARTHUR: Thank Christ for that. I'm famished.

EILEEN: Oh, Arthur, what are you going to do?

ARTHUR: What am *I* going to do – ?

EILEEN: What are *we* going to do?

ARTHUR: I dunno. Do I?

EILEEN: Oh, Arthur.

ARTHUR: Jump in the bleedin' river, I suppose.

> (*Crunch-crunch-crunch.*)

EILEEN: Shhh!

> (*A* MAN *and his dog pass. The dog sniffs, piddles, lingers.*)

MAN: Here, boy. Come on. Come on!

> (*Crunch-crunch-crunch. The* MAN *and his dog go on their way. Silence. Move slowly closer to the big bush.*)

ARTHUR: (*Off*) This bloody fish. It's dead, stone cold.

> (*Slow dissolve into:*)

EXT. THE TOWPATH. DAWN

Start music through the slow dissolve.

During song, move behind bush: ARTHUR *and* EILEEN, *coiled together uncomfortably, asleep in a tangle of grass and twigs.*

A singer (off) 'sings' 'Painting the Clouds with Sunshine'.

ARTHUR *wakes into horror and then* EILEEN *does too.*

Pull slowly away. Graphics over sun and clouds.

EXT. POLICE STATION, LONDON. DAY
Police going in and out. Move to the array of notices on case on brick wall:
WANTED FOR MURDER,
a photograph
ARTHUR PARKER.
Mix to:

EXT. HAMMERSMITH BRIDGE. DAY
ARTHUR's *face looking out on river. But he is doing this only to hide his face as someone passes on the pedestrian walk of the bridge.*
EILEEN: All right. Come on.
ARTHUR: (*Moan*) Somebody'll see me. That's for sure. They'll recognize me.
EILEEN: You can't stay here, now can you?
ARTHUR: Watch out!
    (*He has to turn away again to look at the river.*)
PEDESTRIAN: Excuse me.
EILEEN: (*Tense*) Yes?
PEDESTRIAN: You wouldn't have a light on you, would you?
    (*He is looking at* ARTHUR.)
EILEEN: Sorry. We don't smoke. Neither of us.
PEDESTRIAN: Oh. Right. Ta. (*Walks on whistling.*)
ARTHUR: I shall shit meself before we get to the other side.
EILEEN: For goodness' sake! Stop it, will you?
ARTHUR: But what shall we do? Where shall we go?
EILEEN: We daren't go back to the room. Just in case.
ARTHUR: Well, we can't sleep on the bleed'n streets. Can we!
EILEEN: Oh, stop whining, for God's sake.
ARTHUR: Come on, Eileen. Don't be a cow. I mean, I'm bleed'n innocent, enn I? I wouldn't kill anybody – would I? How do you expect me to take it?
    (*She grips his arm.*)
EILEEN: We've got to get out of London. That's what we're going to do.

(A spurt of fear from ARTHUR.*)*

ARTHUR: Stick by me, love! Whatever you do, don't leave me!
    (And he has to turn and face the river again.
      Long shot the two on the bridge.)

INT. JOAN'S LOUNGE. SUNNYSIDE LANE. DAY
The INSPECTOR *calls.*

JOAN: No. He hasn't written. He hasn't telephoned. I've not
    heard a single word, Inspector.

INSPECTOR: I don't think you will, neither. But of course you
    will tell us if – and you will try and find out where he is if
    he telephones.

JOAN: *(A bit hesitant)* Yes.
    (He looks at her.)

INSPECTOR: You don't sound very sure, madam. That's not
    very wise, if I might say so.

JOAN: I'm – but how can you be so *sure* that my husb – that
    Arthur – did this awful thing?

INSPECTOR: Ah. You think we are wrong, do you?

JOAN: I didn't say that. But –

INSPECTOR: He tried to kill *you*, didn't he?

JOAN: I – I think he was – I won't have to *say* that, will I? I
    wouldn't like –

INSPECTOR: A wife cannot give evidence against her husband,
    madam.

JOAN: Thank heaven for that!

INSPECTOR: It's only natural for you to have doubts. You must
    have been – well, fond of him at some time or other.
    (Start music, softly.)

JOAN: *(Moved, suddenly)* Fond of him? Yes. Yes, I was. He –
    Arthur had a – *(She stops, and presses a tiny handkerchief to
    her mouth.)*

INSPECTOR: *(Uncomfortable)* Don't mind me, ma'am.
    *(*JOAN *goes to a little table, and picks up a photograph of
    Arthur that had been placed flat, in rejection.*
      *Music now swells: 'The Moon Got in my Eyes', Carroll
    Gibbons and Anne Lenner.* JOAN *'sings' to the wistful romantic
    song.*
      She lays the photograph flat again and stares into space as

the music slowly subsides.)

INSPECTOR: The point is, Mrs Parker, that his best chance by
far is to give himself up.

JOAN: What? And hang?

INSPECTOR: There'll be a trial first won't there? I mean, he'll be
able to put his side of things.
(*She looks at him.*)

JOAN: Why did you take his shoes away?

INSPECTOR: I'd rather not say at the moment, if you don't
mind.

JOAN: Was it to match it against a footprint or something? Was
that why?

INSPECTOR: (*Evasively*) We have to carry out a lot of
investigations on this sort of case, madam.

JOAN: And they fitted. Didn't they? His shoes fitted.
(*Pause.*)

INSPECTOR: Well, as I say – you've been most helpful, madam,
as I'm sure you will be again if – ah – if he attempts to get
in touch with you. (*He has stood up.*)

JOAN: I wonder if he's still with that woman? I wonder where
he's gone?

INSPECTOR: You have no idea at all? You're quite, quite sure?

JOAN: (*Flat*) No. None. None whatsoever.
(*Wipe.*)

INT. A CINEMA
*On the screen, Laurel and Hardy slapsticking towards the end of
their little film. We see and hear one of their routines, pulling back
into a laughing row of faces and* EILEEN, *smiling, wanting to forget.
And then* ARTHUR, *fretting, stubble on his cheeks.*

ARTHUR: (*Hiss*) It's coming to the end!

EILEEN: Put your hanky over your face. Blow your nose or
something –
(*Gales of laughter. 'The End' on the cinema screen. The lights
come up on a rococo tower on either side of the screen.*

ARTHUR *puts his handkerchief to his face, but has to half
stand with* EILEEN *as some people exit along their row. As they
slide back into their tip-up seats:*)

ARTHUR: Do you reckon it's dark yet?

EILEEN: Must be, nearly.

ARTHUR: Cor – have we got to sit through this lot all over again.

EILEEN: (*Smiles*) It's only three times.

> (ARTHUR *is looking so comically furtive that the* MAN *next to him eyes him, carefully.*)

ARTHUR: (*Out of the side of his mouth*) Here – this geezer's looking at me . . .

> (EILEEN *leans forward to look. The* MAN *quickly averts his eyes.*)

EILEEN: No he isn't.

ARTHUR: (*Urgently*) Change places. Change places?!

EILEEN: Oh, not again. Please. It's worse than musical chairs.

ARTHUR: For God's sake, Eileen. Change with me.

EILEEN: (*Irritated*) Come on, then.

> (*Clatter, clatter.*
>
> *The lights dip for the news – a 1935 Movietone or similar. Watch some of this then settle on* ARTHUR's *troubled gaze, the spiralling beam of the projection light flickering and shifting above him in the resonant cinema darkness.*
>
> *Mix.*)

EXT. OUTSIDE CINEMA. DUSK

People coming out of cinema, ARTHUR *and* EILEEN *among them. It is raining.* ARTHUR's *head has almost disappeared into his turned-up jacket collar.*

They walk along a row of parked cars. They pass one, then ARTHUR *scurries back. He beckons urgently.* EILEEN *looks about, then comes back to the car –* ARTHUR *is opening the door and clambering in.*

INT. THE CAR. DUSK

ARTHUR: (*Panting*) The key's in the bloody door. I could see it dangling. Who'd have thought it?

EILEEN: Arthur – ! Hurry up then! Hurry!

> (*He is pressing the starter button – cough, choke, cough.*)

ARTHUR: Bloody thing won't – ah! Thank God! Where's the lights? Oh. Here. Hang on.

> (*The car noses out of the line, and then, with a bang! from the exhaust, accelerates away.*)

EXT. COUNTRY ROAD. NIGHT
The car slows, turns off into a lane. It bump bump bumps on to grass verge. Lights flick across a wooden gate, field, hay barn. Lights go out. Engine stops.

EXT. COUNTRY ROAD. DAY
Move towards barn. Cock crows. Sunshine. Cows in field.

INT. THE HAY BARN. DAY
ARTHUR *and* EILEEN *curled up, uncomfortably, in the hay. Shafts of sunlight through glassless window. Sound of cock crow.*
EILEEN *wakes, stares about.*
EILEEN: Arthur?
    (*She shakes him.*)
ARTHUR: (*reluctant*) Wha – whassamatter – ?
EILEEN: You'd better wake up.
ARTHUR: Ooh, my neck – I'm so stiff – Gawdamighty.
EILEEN: I'm starving hungry.
ARTHUR: How about a nice cup of tea. Oh, yes! (*Feels chin.*)
    And a shave. This hay stuff makes all yer pores prickle, don't it?
EILEEN: We'll have to find somewhere to stay.
ARTHUR: Don't be daft, gel!
EILEEN: We can't live in a barn – or a car!
    (*He bundles himself down, morosely.*)
ARTHUR: How much money have we got?
EILEEN: Most of what I had was in my other handbag. In the chest of drawers.
ARTHUR: That's clever.
EILEEN: I didn't know – did I?
ARTHUR: Always carry your money. My old dad used to say, 'A pound in your pocket is the best friend you'll ever have.' He was right, and all.
EILEEN: Well, I've got thirty bob. And fourpence.
ARTHUR: Gawd. I've only got seven and six.
EILEEN: Less than two pounds between us. We won't get to America on that.
ARTHUR: Between us and *what*, that's the question. Between me and the hangman, that's the bleed'n answer.

(She is looking out of the window.)

EILEEN: They don't hang innocent people. Not in this country.

ARTHUR: No – and they ain't bloody well going to hang me. What you looking at?

EILEEN: Perhaps if you went to the police and explained – ?

ARTHUR: *(Tense)* Is there somebody out there? Is somebody coming?

EILEEN: Yes.

ARTHUR: *(Half-scream)* Who? What?
(She turns, laughing.)

EILEEN: A cow. It's only a cow.
(He is already cowering into the hay.)

ARTHUR: You fink that's funny, do you?

EILEEN: *(Laugh)* Oh, Arthur!

ARTHUR: No. It's not funny. I don't see it.

EILEEN: We're not going to live like this, are we? Running and hiding. No laughs. No fun. Nothing.

ARTHUR: But they're *after* me, Eileen. Don't you understand?

EILEEN: I'm hungry.

ARTHUR: For Christ's sake.

EILEEN: Well, I am. And I'd like a wash, and – Where can we go? Where can we get some money?

ARTHUR: *(Frightened)* You won't leave me, will you? Eileen?

EILEEN: One of us has got to get some money.

ARTHUR: But we got to stick together!
(She goes to the glassless window again.)

EILEEN: There's a farmhouse or something across the field. Perhaps they'll sell us some breakfast – ?

ARTHUR: Too risky. We daren't!

EILEEN: Oh, don't be such a ninny.

ARTHUR: Eileen!

EILEEN: They're not after *me* – I can go where I like.

ARTHUR: You rotten cow.

EILEEN: Stop it, Arthur. You want something to eat, don't you? You can't stay in the barn for ever – can you?

ARTHUR: I've always felt this would happen.

EILEEN: What would happen?

ARTHUR: That everything would go wrong. That – that them songs weren't true.

EILEEN: What songs?

ARTHUR: It's all whistling in the dark, ennit? I mean – you
    never know what's going to hit you. And it ain't even your
    fault, not really. You can't trust nothing.

EILEEN: I thought everybody knew that anyway. It's all your luck,
    just your luck. One minute you're up, the next you're down.

ARTHUR: But if people stick by each other – eh? Eileen? That's
    what we did in Flanders. That's the only way. It didn't
    stop them shooting at us, though.

EILEEN: You stay here, Arthur. Keep out of sight.

ARTHUR: Be careful! Whatever you do!

EILEEN: I shall say our car broke down in the night. And we –
    oh, I'll think of something. Just wait here. I'll come back
    when it's safe.

ARTHUR: Will you, though? Will you?

EILEEN: Of course I will!

ARTHUR: Do you love me?
    (*She looks at him, in a manner to make him nervous.*)

EILEEN: That question –

ARTHUR: (*Anxious*) W-what about it?

EILEEN: I don't know.
    (*They look at each other, almost puzzled.*)

ARTHUR: But – *do you*?
    (*Start music: 'In the Middle of a Kiss' by Connee Boswell.*)

EILEEN: I want something to eat. That's all I know, I mean
    that's all I know *for certain*.

ARTHUR: And I want – I want everything to be *all right*.
    (EILEEN *breaks into 'song': 'In the Middle of a Kiss'.
    They stand looking at each other.*)
    (*Thickly*) You've got some straw or something in your hair.
    Stand still a minute, my lovely. (*He takes it out.*)

EILEEN: If I'm too long –

ARTHUR: Yes?

EILEEN: I should go back to the car. Then you can get away fast
    if – well, if you need to.
    (*Pause.*)

ARTHUR: And then wait? Where shall we meet?

EILEEN: Don't worry. It'll be all right.

ARTHUR: Give us a kiss.

EILEEN: (*Mock–American*) Any time, baby.
    (*They kiss, but she breaks away.*)
ARTHUR: What's the matter?
EILEEN: Your breath smells a bit, Arthur.
    (*He puts his hand to his mouth.*)
ARTHUR: That's because –
EILEEN: You need to clean your teeth.
ARTHUR: (*Depressed*) Yeh.
    (*She looks at him, smiles, presses his hand.*)
EILEEN: Cheer up, love. I'll see what I can get. Bread and milk
    and eggs, eh? You never know.
ARTHUR: And some bleed'n toothpaste.
    (*She goes to the barn door.*)
EILEEN: You can keep a look-out through the window.
ARTHUR: (*Depressed*) Yeh. I'll be fine. Just fine.
EILEEN: Ta-ta, then.
ARTHUR: Ta-ta. Take care.
    (EILEEN *smiles and goes. He shuts the barn door, and looks
    around, very down. He sighs and shrugs.*)
    (*To himself*) Bleed'n hole.
    (*Crash in the driving bounce of Lew Stone Band playing 'Pick
    Yourself Up'.*

      ARTHUR *picks up a rake and does a dance around the barn,
    swinging on rafter, kicking up hay etc., etc., and 'singing' along
    with the Bert Yarlett vocals.*

      *He collapses exhausted into the hay, and lets out a loud
    raspberry of derision.*
      Mix.)

EXT. FARMHOUSE. DAY
EILEEN *knocks on the door. She waits, looking about. There is no
answer. She goes to the window, to peer in. As she does, she meets a
face peering out. She gasps and steps back – for it is the face of a
gaunt, wild-eyed* MAN *with a tangled beard. She goes back to the
door, uncertain. It opens, or half opens.*
EILEEN: (*Frightened*) Excuse me, sir – I –
MAN: What do you want? (*A high-pitched, tense voice.*)
EILEEN: Our car has – broken down and – D-do you think you
    could sell us some food –

MAN: Food?

EILEEN: Some bread or – eggs or –

MAN: Bugger off, lady.

EILEEN: Oh. But – we are very hungry and –

    (*The* MAN *shuts the door.*)

INT. THE BARN. DAY

ARTHUR *sits morosely in the hay, his back against a thick supporting beam, the rake in his hands.*

Sound outside. He stiffens, gets up, withdraws to the back of the barn.

The door creaks open. Then:

EILEEN: Arthur . . . ? Arthur. It's only me.

    (*He steps out.*)

ARTHUR: What's wrong? What's happened?

EILEEN: There's only an old loony up at the farm.

ARTHUR: What do you mean?

EILEEN: He looked like Moses. And he told me to bugger off.

ARTHUR: I didn't think you'd come back.

EILEEN: Didn't you? Really?

ARTHUR: Not with me bad breath and all!

EILEEN: (*Laugh*) Oh Arthur!

ARTHUR: So what are we going to do? Get back to the car, eh? So long as we keep off the main road.

EILEEN: We'll have to buy petrol. And *food*. My belly is rumbling –

ARTHUR: It's still the best little belly I've ever met.

EILEEN: That's better.

ARTHUR: What is?

EILEEN: You. You've cheered yourself up.

ARTHUR: Yeh. But me breaf still smells, don't it?

EILEEN: Perhaps it'll stop them hanging you. A disability like that.

ARTHUR: Cheerful little bitch, entcha?

EILEEN: No use being anything else, love. We'll be all right, you'll see.

ARTHUR: Does it, though?

EILEEN: What?

ARTHUR: Me breath.

EILEEN: Yes. It smelt of fear.

ARTHUR: Oh. Is that all? You mean – you'll stick by me as long as I don't care about nuthink. That's nice!

EILEEN: We've only got one life, love. It doesn't seem to matter much how it ends.

ARTHUR: You're a – whatsit – a fatalist – entcha?

EILEEN: That's the word, lover boy.

ARTHUR: Take your knickers off, then.

EILEEN: (*Pleased*) What? Now?

ARTHUR: It's the only way I can keep my strength up.
 (*She starts to undo her suspenders.*)
 And I've never done it in a barn, have I?

EILEEN: We must be mad, you know. (*She takes her knickers off.*) Here? Shall I lie down here?

ARTHUR: Yeh. Then they can take me out and hang me.
 (*She lies down.*)

EILEEN: They can hang me with you.

ARTHUR: You mean that? Eh?

EILEEN: Come on. Hurry up.
 (ARTHUR *gets down beside her.*)

ARTHUR: Yes. You mean it. You-really-mean-it.
 (*The door crashes open.*)
 What the – !
 (*The bearded wild-eyed* FARMER *is standing at the barn door with a double-barrelled shot-gun pointing straight at them.*)

FARMER: Right! Got you!
 (*As* ARTHUR *tries to get up.*)
 No! Stay where you are! Stay where you are, I say or I'll let you have it!

ARTHUR: Stop pointing that thing at me!

FARMER: You filthy beasts. Doing that here.

ARTHUR: We're a married couple, we are.

FARMER: Gyppoes! No respect for your own bodies!

EILEEN: We're not gypsies. We're – Our car has broken down. We – we love each other.

FARMER: (*Without anger*) Dirty filthy lowdown scum.

ARTHUR: 'Ere! That's libel, that is! (*He goes to get up again.*)

FARMER: Stay still! Or I'll blast you to kingdom come!

ARTHUR: We can't stay down here. What the hell!

FARMER: You stay where you are you, dirty devils. Don't you move a muscle. Stay on top on top on top of each other. (*Silence. The three are held in a very peculiar tableau.* EILEEN, *head turned, is looking up at him, steadily.*)

EILEEN: (*Eventually, softly*) You want to watch. Is that it?

FARMER: Are you Jews? If you're not gypsies – then you must be Jews. That would explain (*Bark*) your behaviour.

ARTHUR: Bloody cheek.

FARMER: You're Jews, aren't you! Dirty Jews.

ARTHUR: Have a look at me willy then! I ain't no bloody Jew.

EILEEN: Shh, Arthur. Stop.

ARTHUR: What?

FARMER: Coming to my barn to do your shagging. I know who you are. I know your sort of people. You can't pull the wool over my eyes.

EILEEN: You want to watch us. Don't you?

FARMER: (*Sob*) Jews. You're Jews. I ought to shoot you now.

EILEEN: You can, you know. You can stay and watch if you want to. We don't mind – really.

ARTHUR: Eileen! What the hell – ?

EILEEN: We *are* Jews. You're quite right. You're entitled to watch us. There's nothing wrong in that.
(*The* FARMER *licks his lips, hands trembling on the shotgun.*)

FARMER: I ought to shoot you straight away. That's what I ought to do. Put you down, like a pair of dogs.

ARTHUR: Don't be daft.

FARMER: (*Sudden scream*) Get on with it! Go on! Animals!

EILEEN: Come on, Arthur.

ARTHUR: What? In front of this loony! Not bloody likely –

EILEEN: Arthur!

FARMER: I'll shoot! I'll shoot! I'll kill you both!

EILEEN: He will, love. He will.

FARMER: Jews. Come on, Jews. Let's see how you do it. Come on. Come on. Come on, Jewboy. Give it to her!
(*He levels the gun. Move slowly into bigger and bigger close-up of the* FARMER. *Then hold. His face slowly contorts, half in hatred, half in pleasure. His eyes pop. Start full intro of 'March Winds and April Showers' with Teddy Joyce and Eric Whitley and the* FARMER *finally 'sings' too.*)

The band bounces on at the end of vocal. The flame slowly dies on the FARMER'*s face. He twitches, shudders.*

   Pull out.

   ARTHUR *and* EILEEN *lie wrapped together, as still as can be. Then* EILEEN *turns her head and looks at the* FARMER, *expressionless.*)

EILEEN: We're going to get up now. Do you understand?

FARMER: (*Whisper*) Yes. Yes. You're going to get up. Yes.

   (ARTHUR *pulls his trousers round him.* EILEEN *pushes down her dress. They lurch to their feet.*)

EILEEN: Give me the gun, please.

FARMER: No. Oh, no. Can't – do – that.

EILEEN: Give it to me! You dirty old man!

   (*He bursts into tears.*)

FARMER: Please! You mustn't say that. It was all your fault – I didn't – I –

EILEEN: Give it to me. Come along now. Come on.

   (*He looks at her, blinking, then, quiveringly docile, hands over the gun. She takes it, weighs it, lifts, and aims.*)

ARTHUR: What – what are you doing!

   (*She fires. The* FARMER *is blasted backwards smack into the barn wall, his chest ripped out. It is a huge explosion.* ARTHUR *stands, gaping in total shock.* EILEEN *looks down at the body, expressionless. Then she turns, speaking quietly.*)

EILEEN: Cover him up, Arthur.

ARTHUR: (*Shocked*) W-what – ?

EILEEN: Cover him over with the hay.

ARTHUR: Bloody hell! Christ Almighty!

EILEEN: Come on, Arthur. Cover him up. Then we can go to the farmhouse.

ARTHUR: You didn't oughter have done it!

EILEEN: We'll go to the farmhouse and cook some food and wash ourselves.

ARTHUR: (*Bewildered*) Will we?

EILEEN: And we'll stay there. We'll *live* there. Until they find us.

   (*He stares at her.*)

ARTHUR: I reckon you've gone round the twist, gel.

   (*She looks at* ARTHUR, *smiles enigmatically, then levels the gun at him.*)

EILEEN: Do as I say, darling.

ARTHUR: (*Quickly*) All right, all right. Let me do me bleed'n trousers up proper.

EILEEN: Hurry up, then. I'm hungry.

(*Staring at her, he does up his buttons.*)

ARTHUR: Stop pointing that thing at me!

EILEEN: It's not loaded.

ARTHUR: (*Dubious*) No?

EILEEN: Not any more. Look.

(*As she presses the trigger,* ARTHUR *screams and jumps. She laughs, harshly.*)

ARTHUR: Gawdalmighty! You nearly – you – bloody hell, Eileen!

EILEEN: Come on. Let's cover him up. (*She picks up some hay.*)

ARTHUR: I feel sick. I'm going to be sick.

EILEEN: You can do that after. There's more than enough mess here already. (*She puts a bundle of hay over the body, then suddenly turns away, trembling with shock.*)

ARTHUR: (*Awed*) Why, though? Why? Why did you – do it?

(*She straightens, and tilts up her head, defiantly.*)

EILEEN: Because I felt like it.

(*Pause.*)

ARTHUR: (*Wearily*) Yes. That's right.

(*Fade.*)

INT. THE FARMHOUSE. DAY

ARTHUR *and* EILEEN *in the musty, dusty parlour.* EILEEN *bringing in two plates of bread and fried eggs.*

EILEEN: Sorry, Arthur. There's no bacon here. Not a scrap.

ARTHUR: (*Indignant*) No bacon? Blimey. What sort of farmhouse is this, then?

EILEEN: A very dirty farmhouse.

ARTHUR: You can say that again! I could write my name two inches deep in the dust on that mantelpiece. He must have been a filthy old geezer.

EILEEN: Never mind. I washed the plates anyway.

ARTHUR: Gawd! I'm ravenous!

(*He piles a forkful of egg into his mouth. It is too hot. Old-time music-hall routine of* ARTHUR *with scalding hot food in his mouth.*)

EILEEN: Oh, stop it.

ARTHUR: (*Gasp*) Stop bleed'n laughing!

(*Half sniggering quietly to themselves they bolt down their food.*)

EILEEN: (*Chew*) This is good.

ARTHUR: (*Chew-chew*) Very very good.

(*Take time, take time.*)

EILEEN: There are some chickens out the back, in the yard. And the cows in the field. We'll have to see to them.

ARTHUR: I had a little toy farm once. Wiv lead animals. Little black and white cow. Tiny little chickens. Cor – that takes me back!

EILEEN: Bet you never thought you'd have a farm of your own.

ARTHUR: (*Mouth open*) What?

EILEEN: Well, we might as well stay here. I don't see why not. Make ourselves nice and comfy.

ARTHUR: Don't be daft!

EILEEN: I know how to milk a cow.

ARTHUR: Stay here! With the old farmer lying dead in the barn!

EILEEN: They'll find us wherever we go.

(*He pushes his plate away with a clatter.*)

ARTHUR: No they won't!

EILEEN: (*Severely*) Arthur. (*Steadily*) Please don't be so ridiculous.

ARTHUR: Not if we get to New York they won't find us. (*Sniff*) Or Chi-ca-go.

EILEEN: Why do you say it like that?

ARTHUR: Chi-ca-go? I don't know. I like the sound of it. You can roll it in your mouth, can't you? Chi-ca-go.

EILEEN: It's not safe there, anyway.

ARTHUR: The English police can't touch you there. I ain't done nothing, in any case.

EILEEN: Yes, you have.

ARTHUR: I didn't lay a finger on that girl. May God strike me dead here and now if I did!

EILEEN: No – but you shot that poor farmer, didn't you?

ARTHUR: Wha?

EILEEN: Never mind. He asked for it.

ARTHUR: (*Splutter*) Now look here – !

EILEEN: Shall I make a cup of tea now? That would be nice, wouldn't it?

ARTHUR: (*Confused*) Tea? Yes. But –
   (*She gets up immediately.*)
EILEEN: He's got a nice old tea caddy. It's got Edward the
   Seventh on it, and little Union Jacks all round the top.
   (*She bustles out. He stares after her, mouth open.*
      Clatter-clatter from adjoining kitchen as she makes tea.
      ARTHUR *sits utterly bemused.*)
ARTHUR: (*Eventually. Shout*) Eileen!
EILEEN: (*Off*) Yes? What is it?
   (*Pause.*)
ARTHUR: (*Shout*) Never mind.
   (*Pause.*
      The old clock ticks heavily away on the parlour wall. He
      watches it, and sighs. It is coming up to 10 a.m.
   (*To himself*) What have I gone and got myself into.
   (*As if in answer, a wooden cuckoo on a spring leaps in a*
   raucous whirr out of a little wooden door in the clock: Cuckoo! –
   Cuckoo! – Cuckoo! – Cuckoo! – Cuckoo! – Cuckoo! – Cuckoo!
   – Cuckoo! – Cuckoo! – Cuckoo!)
EILEEN: (*Off*) What did you say?
   (*Close-up of* ARTHUR, *unable to decide whether to laugh or cry.*
      Wipe.)

INT. THE FARMHOUSE. NIGHT
Curtains closed, oil lamp lit. ARTHUR *and* EILEEN *at ease. He has*
a metal deed-box open on his lap, which he is rummaging through
with relish.
ARTHUR: A little gold mine this is. Look here – a little bag of
   gold sovereigns.
EILEEN: They must be worth a bit.
ARTHUR: Oh!
EILEEN: What is it?
ARTHUR: This medal – God blimey – it's a Victoria Cross.
EILEEN: Really?
ARTHUR: (*Swallow*) He must have been a very brave man. They
   don't hand those out just like that. Not the VC.
EILEEN: Poor devil.
ARTHUR: Look – here's a photo of him in his army uniform –
   (ARTHUR's *expression changes.*)

223

EILEEN: You look as though you've seen a ghost.

ARTHUR: He – Eileen – he was my old Captain. Out in Flanders.

EILEEN: Oh, Arthur.

ARTHUR: The bravest – most – decent fellow as ever I clapped me eyes on. He always used to whistle 'The Lincolnshire Poacher'. Stick his head up over the top, he would, and whistle as though he was asking for it.
(*Pause.*)

EILEEN: What are you crying for?

ARTHUR: I dunno.
(*Pause.*)

EILEEN: It's no good raking over the past. The ashes have gone cold.

ARTHUR: He copped it in the end.

EILEEN: Did he? Yes – I suppose he did.

ARTHUR: No – out there, I mean. A sniper parted his hair for him. That was the last our batallion ever saw of him. I think they put a metal plate in his bonce. Bloody terrible, ennit? The things people do.

EILEEN: Perhaps we ought to – no.

ARTHUR: Ought to what?

EILEEN: I was going to say, get him out from under the hay and bury him properly.

ARTHUR: (*Shudder*) I couldn't touch him. No thanks.
(*Pause.*)

EILEEN: He might be still alive.

ARTHUR: What?

EILEEN: Well, you never know.

ARTHUR: He's dead all right. I mean – well, he must be. Surely.
(*But his eyes swivel uneasily.*
    Start music: 'Haunting Me' by Lew Stone and Alan Kane.)

EILEEN: Best put him out of our minds.

ARTHUR: (*Without conviction*) Yeh.

EILEEN: We've got to live minute by minute.

ARTHUR: Tick tock.

EILEEN: What?

ARTHUR: Tick bloody tock.

EILEEN: That's right, Arthur. It's the only way. Forget everything.

(*They each 'sing' a verse of 'Haunting Me'.*)

ARTHUR: (*Whine*) Don't let's stay here, love. Eh? Let's take what we carry, and scarper.

EILEEN: But it's nice here. Or it will be when I can clean it up.

ARTHUR: I've never heard anything so daft in all my life!

EILEEN: All right, then. You tell me where we can go.

(*Pause.*)

ARTHUR: Chi-ca-go.

EILEEN: How?

ARTHUR: Well, we ain't going to bleed'n walk, are we?

EILEEN: Got a passport, have you, Arthur?

ARTHUR: (*Sullen*) No.

EILEEN: You see.

ARTHUR: You're getting on my nerves, you are.

EILEEN: And you're getting on mine!

ARTHUR: There's something not proper *human* about you. Pulling the trigger like that.

EILEEN: You've got no guts. That's your trouble.

ARTHUR: Bloody little slut!

EILEEN: Oh, that's nice, that is. That's very nice. Thank you.

ARTHUR: I didn't know when I was well off. That's my trouble.

EILEEN: Pimp!

ARTHUR: Whore.

EILEEN: (*Changed tone*) Oh, Arthur!

ARTHUR: (*Blink*) What?

EILEEN: We're having a lovers' quarrel. Our first.

ARTHUR: (*Pleased*) Are we? Yeh – that's right. We are. We must be getting real close to each other.

EILEEN: Like in the pictures.

ARTHUR: It is, ennit? (*He is very pleased.*)

EILEEN: The bit I like best is when the wife tells the husband that she's going to have a baby.

ARTHUR: Only he doesn't understand what she's talking about. Not straight off.

EILEEN: Then he stiffens and – and he says – Do you mean . . . ?

ARTHUR: (*Excited*) And she sort of – nods. And – and –

EILEEN: They fall into each other's arms.

ARTHUR: Yeh!

(*Silence.*)

EILEEN: Well, I'm not having a baby, so there.
(*Silence.*)
ARTHUR: Songs is the same.
EILEEN: Pardon?
ARTHUR: Songs. They're like the pictures, and that. You can
sort of learn – you know – learn how to live and that. They
just drop into your head and help you to look at things.
Know what I mean?
EILEEN: (*Dubious*) Mmmm.
ARTHUR: No, that's right, though. I hears them all the time.
EILEEN: I'd rather have the pictures. You can't beat a good film.
ARTHUR: Both together. Songs and a story. I like them both
together. Like when – (*he brightens*) – like when they can't
get anybody to put on their show in a proper theatre. And
they put it on in this barn.
EILEEN: Which barn?
ARTHUR: *Any* barn. Like that barn out there. And all the big
producers come and see it. It's a big hit. Especially when
they dance with a rake and that.
EILEEN: We put on a pretty good show in the barn, didn't we?
ARTHUR: What? Oh. (*He grins.*) Having a bit of how's-your-
father, you mean.
EILEEN: Did you mind him *watching* like that?
ARTHUR: I dunno.
EILEEN: I didn't!
(*He looks at her. She tilts her head defiantly.*)
ARTHUR: No. Nor me. Not really.
EILEEN: I would never have thought it possible.
ARTHUR: It's not right, is it? Not really.
EILEEN: I don't know what's right and what's wrong any more.
You're told one thing and you feel something else.
ARTHUR: I've heard tell that there's films where you can watch
people doing it. Men and women. Together. You know.
EILEEN: What? *Really* doing it?
ARTHUR: So I've heard.
(*Pause.*)
EILEEN: It's disgusting, really.
ARTHUR: Well, it's more like animals, ennit? They're more or
less animals, ent they?

226

(*Pause.*)

EILEEN: Do you ever think about death, Arthur?

ARTHUR: About what?

EILEEN: Death?

(*He cups his hand to his ear in pretence.*)

ARTHUR: Can't hear you, love.

EILEEN: (*Laugh*) That's all right. I didn't say anything.

ARTHUR: Wish there was a wireless here.

EILEEN: We'll just have to go to bed early.

ARTHUR: And then we can make an early start, eh?

EILEEN: What do you mean?

ARTHUR: Drive away somewhere where we can't be found.

EILEEN: You don't give up, do you?

ARTHUR: Somewhere with a wireless.

EILEEN: And a cinema.

ARTHUR: Otherwise we might as well be dead.

EILEEN: How much money have we got now?

ARTHUR: With them sovereigns, and the money in the clock –
near 'nough fifty pounds.

EILEEN: That's a lot!

ARTHUR: It's a small fortune. And we could take some of the
things here – that little ornament for one – and hock 'em.
Eh?

EILEEN: And the cutlery. And the medal.

ARTHUR: No. Not the medal.

EILEEN: Why not?

ARTHUR: No! Not the medal. That's definite! Have a bloody
heart, will you?

EILEEN: I don't see why. But all right. If you say so.

ARTHUR: I *do* say so!

EILEEN: You can grow a beard.

ARTHUR: Yeh. (*Feels his chin.*) Nobody'd recognize me then,
that's for sure.

EILEEN: So we can go back to London.

(*Pause.*)

ARTHUR: Do we have to?

EILEEN: I'm not going anywhere else.

ARTHUR: But it's not safe there. Not for me.

EILEEN: I can earn a lot of money in London.

ARTHUR: Doing what?

EILEEN: What do you think!

ARTHUR: And then I needn't go out, need I? Except at night.
To the pictures and that.

EILEEN: We could have a really good time.

ARTHUR: (*Hesitant*) I suppose so.

EILEEN: Of course we can!

ARTHUR: So that's what we'll do then – is it?

EILEEN: We've got to be brave, Arthur. Nothing is for nothing.

ARTHUR: Roll along prairie moon.

EILEEN: Swinging by in the sky.

ARTHUR: Yes! You're right, gel! I'm wiv you!

EILEEN: That's the spirit.
(*He grins at her.*)

ARTHUR: We'll make a fresh start, eh?

EILEEN: I should take that medal, though.
(*His smile dies.*)

ARTHUR: Yeh. Perhaps you're right. It should fetch a bit.

EILEEN: We've got to think of ourselves.

ARTHUR: Number one. Look after number one. That's what
I've learnt.

EILEEN: First thing we'll get is a wireless. A good one. With a
walnut cabinet.

ARTHUR: And a really good gramophone.
(*They look at each other, contemplating Eldorado.*
Fade.)

EXT. ROAD TO LONDON. DAY
ARTHUR *and* EILEEN *in the stolen car. Start bouncy music band*
intro to 'Says My Heart'. A happy, optimistic feel. Scudding by –
scudding by blue signpost: 'London 37m'.

INT./EXT. THE CAR. DAY
Exactly as Brian Lawrence vocal starts, cut to ARTHUR *in car*
'singing' 'Says My Heart', EILEEN *smiling beside him.*

EXT. THE ROAD. DAY
Jump outside the car as the band trips on exuberantly after the vocal.
Car comes round bend in road. Long shot. Music out, abruptly.

There, waiting by the roadside, is what looks like the HIKER, *complete with piano accordion.*
The car brakes and stops with a bit of a squeal.

INT./EXT. INSIDE CAR. DAY
EILEEN: What have you stopped for?
ARTHUR: (*Puzzled*) That bloke.
EILEEN: What bloke?
ARTHUR: He's – I've met him before. Plays the piano
    accordion.
EILEEN: Who? Where?
    (ARTHUR *opens the car door, vaguely bemused.*)

EXT. THE ROAD. DAY
ARTHUR *stands by the car, looking up and down. There is nobody there, and nothing in sight. He frowns.*
ARTHUR: (*To himself*) Funny.
    (*He looks about again, shrugs, gets back in car.*
    Faintly, sound of accordion: 'There is a Green Hill Far Away' which fades.
    The car won't start. A moment – then ARTHUR *gets out again, and folds open the bonnet from the side.* ARTHUR *fiddles with the car innards. A cruising police car, clearly marked, comes round the bend.* ARTHUR *looks up, his face shows horror. The police car slows and stops just beyond them.*
    ARTHUR, *stupidly, turns and runs. One of the* POLICEMEN *hurtles after him.* ARTHUR *trips and goes sprawling in the grass. The* POLICEMAN *pounces on him.*
    Fade, to sound of accordion playing 'Pennies From Heaven'.)

INT. A ROOM IN A POLICE STATION. DAY
Plain and bare. A single overhead lamp with a crudely utilitarian shade. ARTHUR *on one side of the table, a uniformed* POLICE SERGEANT *on the other.*
SERGEANT: Yes. But what did you run for? Why did you run
    away?
ARTHUR: I can't tell you that.
SERGEANT: Then it must be because you've *done* something.
    Mustn't it?

ARTHUR: Not necessarily.

SERGEANT: Come on! What do you think we are – a bunch of fools?

ARTHUR: (*Smirk*) Well, now –

SERGEANT: If you want a smack in the ribs, mate, you can have one.

ARTHUR: No offence intended. Keep your hair on.

SERGEANT: Now, then. *Why* were you running away?

(ARTHUR *looks at him. Then:*)

ARTHUR: It's a bit embarrassing.

SERGEANT: Just tell me why. Just do that, will you?

ARTHUR: Well – I was taken a bit short, you see.

SERGEANT: (*Blink*) What?

ARTHUR: I've had the trots.

SERGEANT: Getoutofit!

ARTHUR: No – honest. Me guts had been rumbling and churning all bloody morning. Why do you think I'd stopped the car? I'm not one for scenery, not meself.

SERGEANT: It's not your car, is it?

ARTHUR: Who says so?

SERGEANT: Your lady friend.

ARTHUR: No she didn't! And if she did she's a liar. But she didn't. She wouldn't.

SERGEANT: You've got no proof of ownership.

ARTHUR: I want to speak to my lawyer.

SERGEANT: (*Sneer*) *What* lawyer?

ARTHUR: You can't keep me here against my will. I ain't done nothing. Either you charge me with something, copper, or you let me go. (*He goes to get up.*)

SERGEANT: Siddown!

(*The door opens. A young* CONSTABLE *comes in, very excited. He looks at* ARTHUR.)

CONSTABLE: We got the message back, sarge. It's just come through.

(*He gives a paper to* SERGEANT.)

ARTHUR: (*Nervous*) What message?

(*Silence.* SERGEANT *reads.* CONSTABLE *stares.* ARTHUR *fidgets.*)

SERGEANT: (*Casually*) It's nothing to worry about, Arthur.

ARTHUR: What is it then? (*He stops.*) Why do you call me
   Arthur – ?
SERGEANT: Because it's your name.
ARTHUR: No. It's Reginald. Reggie for short.
   (*The* SERGEANT *looks at the* CONSTABLE. *He stands up.*)
SERGEANT: Arthur Parker. I charge you with the murder of
   Amy Farr on or about 17 May 1935.
ARTHUR: (*Gibber*) 'Ere! Hold on!
SERGEANT: I must warn you that anything you say will be taken
   down and be used in evidence against you.
ARTHUR: I'm innocent! Totally innocent!
SERGEANT: What did he say, Constable?
CONSTABLE: He said, 'It's a fair cop, guv'nor?'
ARTHUR: 'Ere! I never did! You bloody –
   (*Wham! The* SERGEANT *punches him violently in the stomach.*
   ARTHUR *doubles up, gasping in pain.*)
SERGEANT: You'll swing, you filthy bugger.
   (*He lifts* ARTHUR*'s head up, holding him by the hair.*)
ARTHUR: (*Sob*) I – didn't – do – it –
   (*The* SERGEANT *knees him in the groin.* ARTHUR *collapses
   holding his genitals.*)
SERGEANT: That's it. We ought to cut 'em off for you. What
   you did to that poor girl – blind and all!
   (ARTHUR *is gasping in agony. The* CONSTABLE *licks his lips
   nervously, his eyes swivel in panic – and then he drives his boot
   into* ARTHUR*'s ribs.* ARTHUR *screams.*)
CONSTABLE: R-rotten sod. (*But* CONSTABLE *seems close to tears.*)
SERGEANT: (*Concerned*) You don't have to kick the bugger if
   you don't want to, lad.
CONSTABLE: I'm all right, Sergeant.
SERGEANT: When I think of that poor girl, though – (*He turns
   and kicks* ARTHUR *in his stomach.*)
ARTHUR: (*Scream*) No more! No! No-o-o!
SERGEANT: Let's put him in the cells, Bob.
CONSTABLE: Right.
   (*They manhandle* ARTHUR *to his feet, and drag him out,
   crying and moaning.*
      Fade on empty room.)

EXT. THE FARMHOUSE. DAY
A uniformed POLICEMAN *knocks on the door. He waits. Knocks again. Waits. Then peers into the window.*
Fade.

INT. THE BARN. DAY
Two POLICEMEN *looking around, shifting things. One of them picks up the shotgun.*
Fade.

GRAPHICS MONTAGE
Throughout, a full minute of the Harry Roy Band version of 'Roll Along Covered Wagon': the law courts, the figure of Justice, the precincts, the lawyers, the judges, the jury box and faces, the prisoners, the police constables, the judge passing sentence, prisoner, empty dock.
Mix.

INT. THE COURTROOM. DAY
Music continuing.
JUDGE: Prisoner at the bar. How do you plead to this charge: guilty or not guilty?
    (*Move in to* ARTHUR, *who 'sings' to Ivor Moreton's rendition of 'Roll Along Covered Wagon'. The* JURY *provide the background chorus. Music ends. Silence.*)
    And how plead you to the second charge, guilty or not guilty?
ARTHUR: I didn't do it, yer honour.
    (*Mix.*)

INT. THE COURTROOM. DAY
Throughout all courtroom sequences, frequent shots, of course, of everyone connected with Arthur in the gallery or well of the court.
EILEEN *in the witness box.*
PROSECUTING BARRISTER: You are Miss Eileen Everson?
EILEEN: Yes I am. (*She looks across at* ARTHUR.)
PROSECUTOR: And you were formerly a schoolmistress.
EILEEN: Yes, I was.
PROSECUTOR: What made you give up your post, Miss Everson?

EILEEN: (*Mumble*) I was pregnant.

JUDGE: You will have to speak up.

EILEEN: I was pregnant.

PROSECUTOR: Are you able to say who was the – *would* have
been the father of the child?

(*She looks at* ARTHUR.)

EILEEN: I'd rather not say.

ARTHUR: (*Shout*) Go on, love. Tell 'em!

JUDGE: If you make one more interruption you will be taken
down to the cells. I have warned you about this before this is
the last time I shall do so. (*To* PROSECUTOR) Pray continue.

PROSECUTOR: I will repeat the question –

EILEEN: There's no need.

PROSECUTOR: Then I should like you to answer.

(*Pause.*)

JUDGE: Do you intend to answer?

EILEEN: Yes, your honour.

JUDGE: Then please do. You may answer without fear. It is not
you who is on trial.

PROSECUTOR: I put it to you, that the father of the child would
have been –

EILEEN: All right!

PROSECUTOR: Arthur Parker. Is that not so?

EILEEN: No.

PROSECUTOR: May I remind the witness that she is under oath?

EILEEN: The man who made me pregnant was Major Archibald
Paxville MP.

(*A huge gasp.* ARTHUR *hoots.*
Mix.*)

INT. THE COURTROOM. DAY

ARTHUR: I was in Gloucester, as a matter of fact. I was in the
music shop by the Cathedral.

PROSECUTOR: So you say. But who can confirm this?

ARTHUR: The manager.

PROSECUTOR: But he is dead.

ARTHUR: Is he? Oh. I'm sorry to hear that. He didn't know
much about my sort of music, but he was a nice enough
bloke. That's a shame, that is.

PROSECUTOR: Are you saying you didn't know he was dead?

ARTHUR: I didn't know. No. It's upsettin' to hear it.

PROSECUTOR: What did you do in the shop on that day?

ARTHUR: Do? What do you mean?

PROSECUTOR: You *say* you were there. What were you there *for*?

ARTHUR: To sell some sheet music.

PROSECUTOR: And did you? Or (*trap*) weren't you a very good salesman?

ARTHUR: (*Indignant*) I was very good indeed. One of the best. If not *the* best. I could always tell a hit from a dog.

JUDGE: *What is a dog?*

PROSECUTOR: The only dog I know, My Lord, is the familiar quadruped. Which barks.

ARTHUR: (*Proudly*) A dog is a song that doesn't sell, your honour. It's a term we use in the business.

JUDGE: Thank you. I suppose it is the sort of song that cats sing at night.

(*Laughter in court.*)

PROSECUTOR: (*To* ARTHUR) You didn't deal in *these* songs then, since you claim to have been such a very good salesman?

ARTHUR: (*Smirk*) I didn't give them kennel space. No.

JUDGE: I would rather you answered the question than engaged in ribaldry.

ARTHUR: Sorry. And I wish you'd do the same.

PROSECUTOR: The songs you took with you were the ones that sold? Is that what you are claiming?

ARTHUR: Yes. That's right.

PROSECUTOR: And that is what you were doing in the shop in Gloucester on May the seventeenth. The day the girl was murdered.

ARTHUR: Yes! That's what I was doing.

PROSECUTOR: Selling songs?

ARTHUR: How many times have I got to say – yes. Selling songs. That was my job, wasn't it?

PROSECUTOR: What songs?

ARTHUR: I can't remember, off hand.

PROSECUTOR: (*Scornful*) You can't remember. (*He looks at the* JURY.)

ARTHUR: (*Quickly*) 'Roll Along Prairie Moon'. I know I took an order for that. Couple of dozen. Very good song.

PROSECUTOR: Is that *all* you sold?

ARTHUR: No. 'Course not. That wouldn't keep a canary.

PROSECUTOR: What else, then?

ARTHUR: 'Yes, Yes, My Baby Said Yes, Yes'.

JUDGE: Would you repeat that?

ARTHUR: 'Yes, Yes, My Baby Said Yes, Yes'.

JUDGE: Is that a dog? Or merely the sound of a bitch on heat?
(*Laughter in court.*)

ARTHUR: I suppose you think that's funny?

JUDGE: No. I think it is very sad. But I would advise you not to
bandy words with me.

ARTHUR: Sorry. No harm meant, your honour.

PROSECUTOR: So you took an order for copies of (*drily*), 'Yes,
Yes, My Baby Said Yes, Yes'.

ARTHUR: Yes, Yes. (*Little pause.*) I mean – yes.

PROSECUTOR: You have just said that on May the seventeenth
you took orders in a music shop in Gloucester for *at least*
two song titles? Isn't that so?

ARTHUR: Yes. That's what I've said. Several times!

PROSECUTOR: I have here Exhibit F. The order book of the
shop in question. And here is something rather – strange.
17 May 1935. There are several orders. Not one of which is
for 'Roll Along Prairie Moon'. Not one of which is for
'Yes, Yes, My Baby Said Yes, Yes'. And although the
names of the salesmen are here recorded, there is no entry
on that particular day – (*looks up*) – that *very* particular day
– for Arthur Parker. How do you account for that?
(ARTHUR *badly shaken.*)

ARTHUR: He – ah – well –

PROSECUTOR: Yes? You seem a little less chirpy, don't you?

ARTHUR: He must have forgot. It's easy done, ennit?

PROSECUTOR: Or could it be that you *weren't there* on that day
at all? That you were indeed somewhere else? Only getting
to Gloucester by nightfall?

ARTHUR: (*Flustered*) No! No – I was there all right. Honest I
was. Cross me heart and hope to – (*He stops, swallows.*)

PROSECUTOR: But you did return to the scene of the murder on
May the twentieth?

ARTHUR: Not *return* there. I happened to stop there for a – well I don't know what the proper word is, I'll just call it a pee – by sheer accident.

PROSECUTOR: And that was the first time you'd ever left the road, climbed a fence, mounted a steep grassy bank to be on the spot where this girl was assaulted and murdered?

ARTHUR: The first and only time. Yes.

PROSECUTOR: So you'd never met the girl? Never talked to her?

(ARTHUR *pauses, dangerously.*)

ARTHUR: N-no. Never.

PROSECUTOR: You don't sound too sure.

ARTHUR: (*Firmly*) No. I had never met her. How could I? I hadn't been in that place before.

(*Long pause.*)

PROSECUTOR: Do you know a crockery salesman called Alfred Baker? Known as Alfie.

(ARTHUR *looks puzzled, and worried.*)

ARTHUR: I – yes. We've met up on the road from time to time. We're both commercial gentlemen, you see.

PROSECUTOR: Do you recall a conversation you had with him in a public house in Gloucester the last time the two of you met? Two (*sneer*) commercial gentlemen?

ARTHUR: I – what are you getting at? What's old Alf got to do wiv it?

PROSECUTOR: 'Old Alf', as you call him, recalls you being – how shall we say? – extremely *rapturous* about a very beautiful girl, a very beautiful *blind* girl –

ARTHUR: No, no. This is wrong. We was drunk, anyway.

PROSECUTOR: You said – and I quote – that – ah – oh, yes: (*reads*) 'You wanted to pull her knickers down.'

(*Stir in court.*)

ARTHUR: (*Shocked*) What? Alf said that?

PROSECUTOR: No, Mr Parker. *You* said it. As Mr Baker will testify. *You* said it.

(ARTHUR *in distress.*)

ARTHUR: It was – I was – he –

PROSECUTOR: Yes?

ARTHUR: It was a different girl. As I remember it.

PROSECUTOR: Ah. I see. A different girl.

ARTHUR: (*Sweating*) A different girl, entirely. 'Course it was.

PROSECUTOR: A different *blind* girl?

ARTHUR: Yes. She was – yes. A different – not the same sort of young woman at all.

PROSECUTOR: But she *was* blind?

ARTHUR: Y-yes. If I said so.

PROSECUTOR: And you did see her in Oxfordshire?

ARTHUR: Well – these counties, they all merge, don't they?

PROSECUTOR: In a field beside the A40?

(*Pause.*)

ARTHUR: Yes. Look, I know it sounds bad, but –

PROSECUTOR: I have no more questions on this occasion.

ARTHUR: But look here – ! This ain't fair. Give us a chance!

JUDGE: The prisoner will leave the witness stand and return to the dock.

(*Fade on faces of* JURY, *very certain now.*)

INT. THE COURTROOM. DAY

Summing-up time.

PROSECUTOR: Members of the jury. You have listened with commendable patience to an extremely distasteful and horrible case, in which a young and attractive and helpless girl, who was totally blind, was most brutally assaulted, raped and then strangled by a vicious and heartless assailant. The prosecution has sought to prove that the person responsible for this hideous crime is the man Arthur Parker now standing in the dock.

(*All eyes on* ARTHUR, *who, unwisely, gives an ironic little bow.*)

Let us, then, examine the facts as they have been unravelled during the past ten days in this courtroom. First, though, consider the demeanour of the accused. He has got what he and his kind no doubt call 'sauce', has he not? A great deal of sauce. We have seen that, in less amicable language, but more *accurate* language, he is a brazen liar. His neighbours, his colleagues, various shopkeepers, an estate agent, and a virtual *harem* of former mistresses, girlfriends and common prostitutes have testified under oath that at various times he has claimed to be unmarried, or a widower, or a successful songwriter, a

237

wireless producer and, upon one farcical occasion, a former centre-forward for the Arsenal Football Club. Even here he has indulged in badinage with his own counsel, several witnesses, his Honour the Judge and on at least one occasion was observed to wink ingratiatingly at you, the gentlemen of the jury. When reprimanded, he had the gall to tell us that the wink was in fact a nervous tic sustained as a result of bravery under fire in the trenches of Flanders. It was then shown to be the case that Arthur Parker was, in fact, court-martialled for cowardice, and narrowly escaped being shot as a deserter. The relationship between the *claim* and the *actual fact* on this occasion is the one consistent strand in his conduct. Thus, he claims that at the time that this appalling murder was committed he was in fact taking orders for sheet music at a shop in Gloucester. No such orders were in fact taken. No such orders were in fact received by the wholesalers. Irresistible conclusion, he was not at the shop in Gloucester. Yet he said he was, insisted he was. Why should a man seek to concoct an alibi if he had no reason to do so? Irresistible conclusion, he *did* have a reason. But what reason? To deny the connection is tantamount to asserting that an egg will not harden in boiling water. The accused has, throughout, reminded me of someone who – well, let me put it this way – (*Silence. He motions up music. Then gestures to the* JUDGE.)

JUDGE: Whistle – whistle – whistle.

(PROSECUTOR *'sings' 'Whistling in the Dark', by Ambrose and Sam Browne, to the* JURY:)

PROSECUTOR: (*'Sings'*)
'Whistling in the dark
I see the lights all over town
And I keep walking up and down
While I am whistling in the dark.
Whistling like a lark
My song goes floating on the air
I envy every loving pair
While I am whistling in – the – dark.
Who cares what I am saying

238

In my song?
Who knows that I am praying
Someone will come along?
Strolling in the park
Without a single thing to do
The night is black
And I am blue
That's why I am
Whistling in the Dark?
(*Tumultuous applause.*)

JUDGE: Silence in court! If there is any more disturbance I shall
have the public gallery cleared. This is a court of law and
not a music hall.
(*Silence.*)

PROSECUTOR: Thank you m'lud.
(*The following four speeches delivered with total solemnity.*)

JUDGE: That's all right, old mate. We're in this together. Did
you like my whistle, though?

PROSECUTOR: It was a very nice whistle, m'lud.

JUDGE: And the members of the jury? Did you understand the
whistling? Was it's purpose clear to you?

JURY: (*Together*) Yes, my lord!

JUDGE: (*To* PROSECUTOR) Proceed.

PROSECUTOR: Has not the accused been whistling in the dark in
his absurd concoctions? 'Who knows' – and mark this,
members of the jury – 'who knows that I am praying . . .
someone will come along?' Is that not the deadly spirit in
which on May the seventeenth the accused left his car by
the side of the A40 in quiet Oxfordshire, climbed a fence,
traversed a grassy knoll, and lay waiting in the grass for
'someone to come along'? Someone upon whom he could
satiate his criminal lust and murderous appetites. Someone
young, someone attractive, someone helpless? The
prosecution submits that it has proven that such was
indeed the case. Can there now be any shred of reasonable
doubt left in your minds?
(*Pause.*)
No. Surely not. Absolutely not.
(*Fade.*)

INT. THE COURTROOM. DAY

The JURY *file back into the box. They do not look at* ARTHUR.

CLERK OF COURT: Members of the jury. Have you reached your
verdict?

FOREMAN: We have.

CLERK OF COURT: And is that verdict unanimous?

FOREMAN: It is.

CLERK OF COURT: What is your verdict? Is the prisoner guilty as
charged or not guilty?

(*Pause.*)

FOREMAN: Guilty.

(*Rustle, hubbub. Silence.*)

JUDGE: Prisoner at the bar, have you anything to say before
sentence is passed?

(ARTHUR *sways.*)

    Start music: 'Maybe I'm Wrong Again' by Lew Stone and
Alan Kane.)

ARTHUR: Yes, my Lord. If you don't mind.

JUDGE: Then speak.

(ARTHUR *'sings'* 'Maybe I'm Wrong Again . . . believing in
you'.)

Have you finished?

ARTHUR: Yes, my Lord.

JUDGE: Well, there is no 'maybe' about it. You have been found
guilty by a jury of your peers of the murder of one Amy
Farr. It is now my duty to pass the only sentence that is
prescribed by law for a crime of this enormity.

(*Cut away to* EILEEN, *to* JOAN, *in court. The* JUDGE *puts on
the black cap.*)

Arthur Parker. The sentence of this court upon you is that
you be taken from this place to a lawful prison and thence
to a place of execution and that you be hanged by the neck
until you be dead, and that your body be afterwards buried
within the precincts of the prison in which you shall be
confined before your execution. And may the Lord have
mercy on your soul.

ARTHUR: Fanks very much, you rotten old bugger.

(*And he is led away.*

    Fade.)

CAPTION, EXT. – PENTONVILLE
Drawing, black and white.

INT. THE CONDEMNED CELL. DAY
Two warders - HORACE *and* ARNOLD *– are permanently on duty at this time. All three are at the little table in the cell, playing cards.*
ARTHUR *takes the last trick.*
ARNOLD: Lucky sod. Ent he, Horace?
ARTHUR: What do you mean?
HORACE: He means you keep winning.
ARTHUR: Lucky in cards. Lucky in love. I don't fink!
ARNOLD: Want another game, then?
ARTHUR: Nah. I keep seeing the ace of bleedin' spades.
HORACE: Come on. Have another. You can't win *all* the time.
ARTHUR: I can against you two. I'm fed up with cards anyway.
    There ain't enough jokers in the pack.
ARNOLD: What do you want to do, then?
ARTHUR: (*sigh*) Nothing, Arnold. Except – well, I wouldn't
    mind going for a bit of a stroll up Piccadilly way. How
    about it?
ARNOLD: Can we come, too?
ARTHUR: As long as you take your uniforms off.
    (*Silence. A moment of tension, suddenly the two warders look at
    each other.*)
HORACE: Do you want a game of draughts – ?
ARTHUR: What happens if you – ?
    (*He stops. The warders exchange glances again.*)
ARNOLD: Best not to think about it.
ARTHUR: Yeh. That's all very well, ennit? But when I swallow,
    my Adam's apple moves.
ARNOLD: What?
ARTHUR: It goes up and down, don't it?
ARNOLD: So – ?
HORACE: Everybody's does.
ARTHUR: Not like mine! Mine really goes up and down. Like a
    bleed'n lift.
ARNOLD: But what are you worried about?
ARTHUR: When that 'orrible bloody geezer puts the rope round
    me neck, and I swallow, and me Adam's apple goes up or

down and the rope slips over it – get me? – and he pulls the bleed'n lever and them doors open, I ain't going to hang proper, am I? I mean it'll bump against me chin and then it won't half hurt, won't it?

(*The other two want to laugh.*)

HORACE: They take your Adam's apple into account, Arthur.

ARTHUR: You sure?

HORACE: 'Course I am. It'd be the same if you had a whatdyacallit – a goitre. They allow for that.

ARTHUR: Just so long as it's quick. That's what counts. I mean, I don't want to *dance* in mid-air, do I?

ARNOLD: You won't do that. It's instant – honest.

ARTHUR: I like a bit of dance. Foxtrot. Quickstep. Even a tango. But on a bit of *flooring*, you understand me. Like the maple they got at the Hammersmith Palais. A real maplewood floor.

HORACE: I never been there.

ARTHUR: Oh, it's nice there. Very nice. They got little cupids and glass pillars and coloured lights and all that. Blue. Red. Yeller.

ARNOLD: Is that right?

ARTHUR: Oh – yeh! It's a real palace. Gawd, there's nothing like a good dance band, is there? Takes you right out of yourself. (*Suddenly*) What time is it?

ARNOLD: Nearly five o'clock. (*He looks at* HORACE.)

ARTHUR: That's – five, six, seven, eight – that's fifteen hours to go, then. Not long, is it?

(*Silence.*)

HORACE: Who do you reckon is the best dance band then, Arth?

ARTHUR: Say it was five minutes to eight –

HORACE: No, come on. Who? I've heard that –

ARTHUR: No, say it was five minutes to go, and you was – and you *really* wanted to go to the lav, couldn't help it, like. Would they wait?

ARNOLD: The Roy Fox band was very good.

ARTHUR: Would they, though? I reckon they ought. It'd be more dignified. In my opinion.

HORACE: You won't have no trouble like that.

ARTHUR: When I was a kid at school, and you put your hand

242

up to ask to go out to the whatsname, the teacher would
bring this bleed'n great long pointer down across your
knuckles. You had to sit there and hold it, and that was
that. Or do it in your trousers.

ARNOLD: We used to see who could pee the highest up against
the wall.

ARTHUR: That's funny. And we did!

HORACE: We did, too.

(*They all look at each other and then laugh.*)

ARTHUR: Them was the best days.

ARNOLD: Not half.

HORACE: We used to climb up this pipe – at school – and block
up the guttering.

ARTHUR: What for?

HORACE: When it rained – cor, there was one hell of a mess.

(ARNOLD *starts to laugh.*)

ARNOLD: We had this teacher – he – hoo! hoo! – he was always
talking above our heads. A right pansy, you know. He –
(*laugh*) – he was talking about India and that – and he
mentioned these fakirs –

HORACE: What?

ARNOLD: Fa-kirs. Yeh. This kid – Bill Tranter, he was – he
went home and his dad asks him what did you learn at
school today? And Billy says (*titter*) and Billy says: 'Oh, all
about them Indian fukkers.' Fakirs, you see. And his dad –
(*Starts to howl with laughter.*)
(*The other two start to laugh helplessly. And such is the
condemned cell atmosphere that it grows into near hysteria.
They howl and roll about and hold their ribs.*)
(*Between helpless laughs*) And his dad says – his dad says –
(*A rasping rap and jangle at door. The two warders
immediately fall silent.* HORACE *gets up and nods through the
judas hole. The door is opened.*

JOAN *is, so to speak, handed in by another* WARDER.

The door is shut with much jangle and bang, while JOAN *and*
ARTHUR *stare at each other.* ARNOLD *and* HORACE *look
away, discreetly.*)

JOAN: (*Eventually*) How are you, Arthur?

ARTHUR: In the – (*His voice suddenly thickens, so that he has to*

243

start again.) – In the pink.

JOAN: That's good.

(*Pause.*)

ARTHUR: Told you I'd be famous one day, didn't I?

JOAN: Oh, Arthur.

ARTHUR: If I was you I'd sell the house and go to Australia or somewhere. Get right out of it.

JOAN: I'm very sorry about – everything, Arthur.

(*Pause.*)

ARTHUR: And me, old gal. You bin a good old stick, really. I can't grumble.

JOAN: I shall never (*voice half-breaks*) forget you. No matter what.

ARTHUR: (*Moved*) That's very decent of you, all things considering.

JOAN: Where did it all go wrong, Arthur?

ARTHUR: The day I was bleed'n born.

JOAN: Are you – are you frightened?

(ARNOLD, *still wanting to laugh, swallows a guffaw.*)

ARTHUR: Who? Me? You must be joking.

JOAN: There *is* another life, Arthur.

ARTHUR: What?

JOAN: In the Beyond.

ARTHUR: As long as it's not harps. I can't stand a harp. Give me a good trombone and a couple of clarinets. That'll do.

JOAN: Everybody will be at peace one day. That's what you must think of. There'll be no more pain or suffering.

ARTHUR: No more how's-your-father either.

JOAN: (*Frown*) What?

ARTHUR: A bit of the other. There'll be none of that. I've had all I'm going to get now.

JOAN: Try to be dignified, Arthur. Haven't you hurt me enough?

ARTHUR: Sorry. No – I am.

(*Pause.*)

JOAN: Goodbye, darling. Goodbye, my poor dear love. God bless you.

ARTHUR: (*Choked*) Give us – give us a kiss, then.

(*They kiss.*

244

ARNOLD *gets up and taps on door. Signal exchanged. Door opens with loud jangle again.*

  HORACE *puts his hand gently on* JOAN's *arm. The kiss ends.*)
Blimey! Why didn't you tell me you could kiss like that!
(*She half-laughs through a sheen of tears.*)

JOAN: Toodle-oo, old fruit.

ARTHUR: Ta-ta, old pip!
(*A look, and she is 'handed on' to outside warder. Door jangles and bangs shut.*
  Silence.)
(*Thickly*) Yeh. Them was the days all right. When we was bits of kids.
(*Start music: 'I Like To Go Back in the Evening' – Jack Jackson band, with vocal trio.*)

HORACE: I could pee the highest.
(*Pause.*)

ARNOLD: Not as high as me, I'll bet.
(*Pause.*)

ARTHUR: A great big golden arc.
(*Pause.*
  ARTHUR, ARNOLD *and* HORACE *all 'sing' 'I'd Like To Go Back . . .'*
  Mix exactly on the word 'sweetheart' in the last line of the song:)

EXT. HAMMERSMITH BRIDGE. NIGHT
Music (non-vocal) carrying over.
EILEEN *standing on bridge, staring down at the river, pale, expressionless. Hold, until music ends, on dancing, dark water. Mix.*

INT. THE CONDEMNED CELL. DAY (MORNING)
We 'go in' through opening door with the EXECUTIONER, *his* ASSISTANT, *the* DOCTOR, *the* GOVERNOR.
ARTHUR *is standing, with the same two* WARDERS, *and the* CHAPLAIN.

CHAPLAIN: I am the resurrection and the life, saith the Lord.

GOVERNOR: Good morning, Parker. May I introduce to you Mr Peterstow.

EXECUTIONER (*Peterstow*): (*With Northern accent, extending his hand*) How do, lad.

(ARTHUR *swallows, grins in sickly fashion, and grasps the proffered hand. As he does, the* EXECUTIONER *quickly pinions his arm behind his back, pulls the other hand after it, and straps the wrists together with a short leather strap.*)

ARTHUR: That's not very nice, is it?

EXECUTIONER: Be brave, lad. There's a good 'un.

(*Swiftly, little procession marches out of door, down short corridor to:*)

INT. THE SCAFFOLD. DAY

ARTHUR *supported, is wobbling now. He buckles at knees, and is pulled upright.*

ARTHUR: Hang on a bit – I got an itchy conk.

(*But marched swiftly on to the trap below the rope, where ankle strap is waiting. His ankles are strapped.*)

I said, hang on will you? Or scratch me nose for me bloody hell.

(*The* EXECUTIONER *puts the noose over* ARTHUR*'s head.*

Start music: 'In the Dark', by Roy Fox band; singer, Denny Dennis.

The EXECUTIONER *tightens the knot and 'sings' along with Denny Dennis.*

He takes a folded white hood out of his pocket and slips it swiftly over ARTHUR*'s head.*

Hold up the music.

The EXECUTIONER *steps aside, pulls the lever. A bang! as doors open and rope cracks tight.* ARTHUR *dangles.*

Screen goes blank.)

GRAPHICS

A little white ball bounces along each word written up in big white letters on a black screen as Denny Dennis continues singing 'In the Dark'.

As the little white ball bounces off the last word, the letters fade, leaving only the little white ball. The little white ball turns slowly into the moon, shining down on Hammersmith Bridge, gilded by moonlight in a drawing – or, rather, an elaborate and romantic painting.

Move in on painting to EILEEN *on bridge. During movement dissolve to:*

EXT. HAMMERSMITH BRIDGE. DAY
Close in on EILEEN. *St Paul's in distance strikes eight o'clock – execution time. She puts her hands on the rail, ready to jump.*
EILEEN: (*counting strike of clock*) One – two – three – four – five – six – seven – eight. Goodbye, Arthur. (*She tenses to leap.*)
ARTHUR: Hang on!
(*She turns, mouth open.*)
EILEEN: Ar-thur! What – what are you doing here?
ARTHUR: I'm like a bad penny, enn I?
EILEEN: (*Confused*) What?
ARTHUR: I keep turning up, don't I? A Penny from Heaven.
(*She gurgles in her throat.*)
EILEEN: Oh my darling! My love!
ARTHUR: (*Smirk*) Couldn't go all through that wivaht a bleed'n 'appy endin' now, could we?
(*They both turn, smiling, and face the camera.*)
ARTHUR/EILEEN: The song is ended, but the melody lingers on.
(*Music: 'Pennies from Heaven', with words.*
    Pull back and back, ARTHUR *and* EILEEN *waving at us from the bridge. Back and back until they are tiny figures.*
    Freeze picture, music continuing. Set it in a mock songsheet cover.
    Fade out.)

247